AF335037

Mississippi's Old Capitol:
Biography of a Building

Engraving by T. C. Story from a map of Mississippi by LaTourrette, 1845.

Mississippi's Old Capitol: Biography of a Building

John Ray Skates

Mississippi Department of Archives and History
Jackson, Mississippi

Acknowledgments

This history was produced to celebrate the 150th anniversary of the completion of the Old Capitol and to honor those who have been instrumental in its survival. I would like to also acknowledge with appreciation the work of those who made this book possible: the Board of Trustees, Mississippi Department of Archives and History; Dr. Ray Skates, researcher and writer; the American Association for State and Local History, which provided grant funds for the research and writing; other members of the publications committee, Elbert R. Hilliard, Chrissy Wilson, H. T. Holmes, and Ken P'Pool; the library staff for their help with research; copy editor Carol Cox; designer Cavett Taff; financial officer Joe Rutledge; and production supervisor Barney McKee.

Patti Carr Black
Director, State Historical Museum
Old Capitol Restoration

*This book is gratefully
dedicated
to Charlotte Capers*

Contents

Acknowledgments

I wish to thank the many people who provided interviews or other historical information used in the preparation of this book. Former Director of Archives and History Charlotte Capers, former Governor J. P. Coleman, and former Governor and archives board member William F. Winter provided essential details on the restoration of the building and the creation of the State Historical Museum. Joe and John Ware, partners in the architectural firm of Overstreet, Ware and Ware at the time of the restoration, furnished critical information on the building. Former employees of that firm, Mr. Ed Lewis, Mr. Cecil Pearson, and Mr. Charles Hudspeth also furnished much helpful information; also, Mrs. Renna Johnston Clark, interior designer, described the interior design of the restoration. Mrs. Kate Don Adams of Natchez furnished information on the career of interior designer Earl Hart Miller. Mr. Clarence Waddle, former construction superintendent for the Robert Crouch Construction Company, gave insight into construction problems in the restoration. Mrs. Johnnie Wagner, Mr. Paul Rankin, and Mr. Dick Andrews of the Mississippi Health Department, who all served with that department before 1959 when it was housed in the Old Capitol, explained the layout of the building and grounds before the restoration. Ron and Mimi Miller of Natchez helped locate some of Mississippi's early seats of government.

I thank also the staffs of the Library and Museum Divisions of the Mississippi Department of Archives and History, who were gracious, tolerant, and helpful beyond the call of duty. I owe thanks especially to the Archives and History Editorial Review Board—Elbert Hilliard, Patti Black, Ken P'pool, Hank Holmes, Chrissy Wilson, and Cavett Taff—who spent many hours reading and reviewing the manuscript. Without their thorough and always constructive criticism, this book would have suffered many errors and infelicities. Finally, I am grateful to Elbert Hilliard, Patti Black, and the Board of Trustees of the Department of Archives and History for trusting me to write the story of Mississippi's most beloved building.

J.R.S.
University of Southern Mississippi

Foreword
by William F. Winter

It is a well-noted fact that most people identify themselves and their communities with their historic buildings. Boston has its Faneuil Hall and Old North Church. Philadelphia has Independence Hall; New Orleans, the Cabildo; San Antonio, the Alamo.

While perhaps not ranking as high in national significance or recognition, Mississippi's 150-year-old Old Capitol is our state's equivalent of those other noted and honored landmarks. It is without question the state's most historic structure.

Neglected, abused, and almost relegated to the wrecker's ball at various times in its existence, the copper-domed edifice at the head of Capitol Street, like the state it once served as the seat of government, has witnessed a stormy and eventful past.

That it has survived is a testimonial not so much to its own durability as to the tenacity and persistence of its defenders. Spared from the torch by General Sherman in 1863, it almost fell victim to a latter day Mississippi Legislature. Only the leadership of a visionary and history-minded Governor, J. P. Coleman, ensured the preservation of this national landmark.

My own personal affection for this magnificent old building stems from the experiences of my early childhood when I visited its then worn and battered offices in the company of my legislator father. It was he who first related to me some of the historic events which had taken place there. The voices of Andrew Jackson, Henry Clay and Jefferson Davis still seemed to echo out of the Old Capitol's storied past.

In the intervening years, however as the building gave up its last tenants in the early 1950's its earlier glories seemed to be forgotten. It sat desolate and forlorn, untended and unwanted. Some of my colleagues in the legislature suggested that this choice site could be better served with a new and modern building.

Mississippi's little band of citizen historians thought otherwise. Encouraged by the Department of Archives and History, the Mississippi Historical Society, the Daughters of the American Revolution and a small but determined group of supporters in the Legislature, Governor Coleman in 1956 threw his full influence behind the efforts at restoration.

The success of that undertaking is now, of course, evidenced by more than just the preservation of this magnificent building. Its dedication as Mississippi's State Historical Museum may well prove to be the old building's noblest use. For what more valued purpose could it possibly serve than to be the visual interpreter of the history of our state?

During more than a century and a half in which Jackson has emerged from a raw frontier village to a major metropolis and Mississippi has grown from a trackless wilderness to the dynamically modern state that we know today, the Old Capitol has stood through war, flood, pestilence, and depression, now serving to remind us of the generational ties that bind us together and the shared experiences that make us one people. It is our Interdependence Hall.

Mississippi's Old Capitol:
Biography of a Building

"View of the Fort of the Natchez," c. 1796

Before the Old Capitol

In 1798, ninety-nine years after the first Europeans established a toehold on the mosquito-infested and malaria-ridden shores of Biloxi Bay, the Natchez District finally came under American rule. By then the United States had existed for only two decades, and the new nation's claim to the trans-Appalachian west dated back only fifteen years.

The new Mississippi Territory was far removed—culturally, politically, and geographically—from the older and more developed states of the eastern seaboard that had fought and won the revolution against imperial Britain. In fact, the Mississipi Territory in 1798 was a sparsely populated hinterland that, during the incessant eighteenth-century dynastic and imperial wars among European kingdoms, had been progressively swapped, conquered, ceded, and sold among the powers of Europe. Seats of government had been many. As a part of French Louisiana, the future territory had been ruled first from Biloxi Bay,[1] then Mobile, and finally New Orleans. From 1763 to 1781, Britain held the Natchez District as part of the newly formed colony of West Florida. Royal governors appointed by King George III ruled the colony from Pensacola. Spain conquered West Florida during the American Revolution, and Spanish governors at Natchez reported to the governor-general of Spanish Louisiana at New Orleans.

When the Mississippi Territory was formed in 1798, the new United States dependency encompassed much of present-day Alabama and Mississippi. However, this vast area held fewer than 5,000 newly created American citizens. Natchez, on the far western edge of the new territory, numbering perhaps 1,500, was the only town of any consequence.

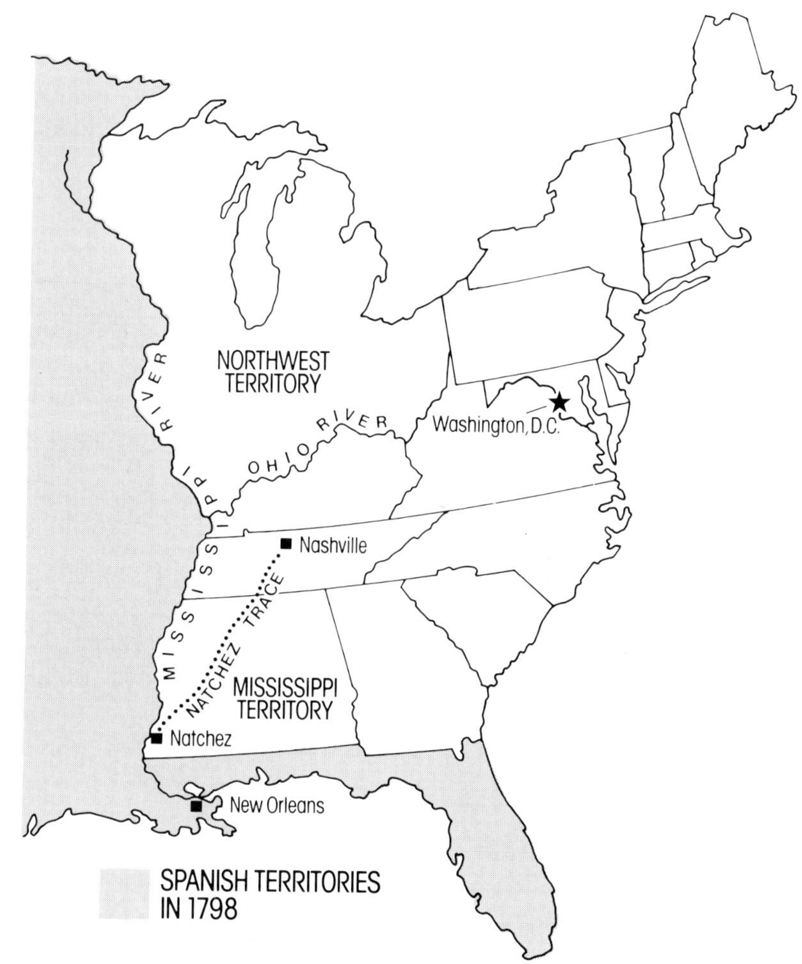

Before Jackson

The new territory was isolated from the older states by hundreds of miles of Indian-inhabited wilderness. No road connected the settlements around Natchez with Georgia or the Carolinas. The famed Natchez Trace, stretching northward to the Tennessee settlements, was hardly more than a 400-mile-long path. Travel downriver on the Tennessee and Ohio into the Mississippi to Natchez required weeks. The fastest and safest route to the Atlantic states involved traveling to Spanish New Orleans and then going by ship to Charleston or Wilmington or New York. On such a far-flung frontier almost no thought was given to a permanent seat of government.

When territorial Governor Winthrop Sargent arrived at Natchez in August 1798, he faced daunting duties: the establishment of United States authority in an area where loyalty to the new national government was uncertain and the creation of local and territorial government. He would have to accomplish these duties in a society rent by nationalistic and partisan divisions and surrounded by potential Spanish and Indian enemies.

Sargent lacked even a proper building to house himself and his government. The Spanish governors had ruled from the "Government House" on the bluff at Natchez. When the Spanish evacuated in 1798, this structure, along with the fort on the bluffs, had been turned over to the United States. Sargent found these buildings occupied by troops of the United States Army. The new governor protested to General James Wilkinson, commanding general of the U.S. Army in the west, that as governor he was "the proper guardian of all the public property not absolutely appertaining to the fortresses," and he requested that the buildings be turned over to him.[2]

Apparently Wilkinson refused, for in April 1799, seven months after taking office, Sargent renewed his request that Wilkinson order the garrison at Natchez to relinquish the buildings. Sargent cited an agreement on the matter between their respective superiors, the secretaries of state and war. Wilkinson disputed that such an agreement had been made and again refused to turn over the buildings. Sargent reported to Secretary of State Timothy Pickering that when he attempted to use one of the vacant buildings, he was turned away by guards, the commander saying that orders came only from the secretary of war. The dispute dragged on throughout 1799 without resolution. Meanwhile, Sargent continued to send his letters from "Near Natchez" or from "The Grove," a plantation south of Natchez.[3]

Apparently this civil-military dispute was eventually resolved, for when W.C.C. Claiborne succeeded Sargent as territorial governor in 1801, the General Assembly was meeting at the "Government House" in Natchez—the Spanish seat of government that had been turned over to the United States when Spain gave up Natchez to the Americans in 1798.

As the oldest and largest town in the territory, Natchez quite naturally became the territorial capital. Yet even under the Spanish, backcountry resentment had arisen against the merchants and bureaucrats of Natchez. Under Sargent, that antipathy became a revolution, and one of the aims was to remove the capital of the territory from "aristocratic" Natchez to the friendlier "republican" surroundings of the backcountry. In the first two years of Sargent's administration, a political schism widened between the Federalist followers of Sargent and the more democratic planters of the countryside. Upon his arrival, the stiff and aloof governor had cast his lot with the Natchez merchants and conservative planters. With the election of Thomas Jefferson to the presidency in 1800, Sargent's opponents, led by the friends and relatives of Thomas Green of Pickering County, had a friend in the White House. W.C.C. Claiborne, a

Natchez Trace

twenty-six- year-old Jefferson protege, replaced Sargent in the governor's chair. The planter-republicans who had already dominated the General Assembly under Sargent now had a kindred spirit as governor.

In 1802 the legislature wasted no time in sealing the victory. The members renamed Pickering County for Thomas Jefferson, and they voted to remove the capital from the unfriendly environs of Natchez to the more amicable surroundings of the countryside. It was certainly not uncommon for frontiersmen to demand that capitals be located in places more accessible to the backcountry. In Georgia, Savannah had been abandoned for Milledgeville, and later Atlanta; in South Carolina, Charleston lost out to backcountry Columbia; in Virginia, Williamsburg gave way to Richmond. Indeed, the backcountrymen were not finished in Mississippi, for two decades later Jackson was founded for reasons similar to those that had led to the removal of the capital from Natchez.

People who favored the move from Natchez justified their position by condemning the "unhealthfulness" of the town and the poor quality of its water. Actually, the republican farmers and planters of the outlying districts harbored feelings of jealousy, resentment, and suspicion toward the wealthier and more conservative town dwellers. One Natchez opponent of the move ascribed the backcountry resentment towards Natchez to the quality of its taverns. They were, he charged, "too genteel for the visitors, because in most of them the patrons were subjected to the annoyance of table cloths and clean sheets." Some rustics, he continued, felt "awkward and irksome everywhere but in the woods, and . . . take no delight in a tavern unless they can have a row or a wrestling match."[4]

The real reason for removing the seat of government from Natchez was partisan acrimony. The enemies of Governor Sargent, led by Thomas Green and Cato West of Jefferson County, were in complete political ascendancy as a result of the election of Thomas Jefferson to the presidency and his appointment of Claiborne to replace Sargent. They looked upon Natchez as the home ground of their enemies—the "aristocrats." The tiny hamlet of Washington, they felt, would be "sufficiently peaceful for the most rustic member of the legislature."[5]

Washington lay on the Natchez Trace six

miles east of Natchez, and as late as 1797 the land upon which the new capital was to be located had been encompassed by a plantation. It was un-prepossessing and unpromising. Economically, the village lived under the shadow of nearby Natchez. The town had fewer than thirty houses, one store, and three taverns, all along a single street.[6]

Nonetheless, in February 1802, the legislators decreed that the next session of the General Assembly "shall meet and be convened at the town of Washington there to hold their next ensuing session." This law precipitated a governmental exodus from Natchez. Governor Claiborne moved his residence to the new seat of government, and Washington replaced Natchez as the Adams county seat. Congress established the territorial court and the land office there and built Fort Dearborn on St.Catherine's Creek to house a garrison of U.S. Army troops. When the legislators chartered Jefferson College in 1802, they made certain that it was located at Washington.[7]

Washington continued to serve as the capital of the territory until Mississippi was admitted as a state in 1817. The town grew and prospered from its governmental role. By 1815 a thousand people lived there, and three hotels housed visitors. Government officials and officers from Fort Dearborn gave the town a cosmopolitan flavor and a lively social life. But Washington lagged economically. Certainly, little money was invested in government buildings, for the General Assembly met in rented rooms above Charles Defrance's Tavern. Between

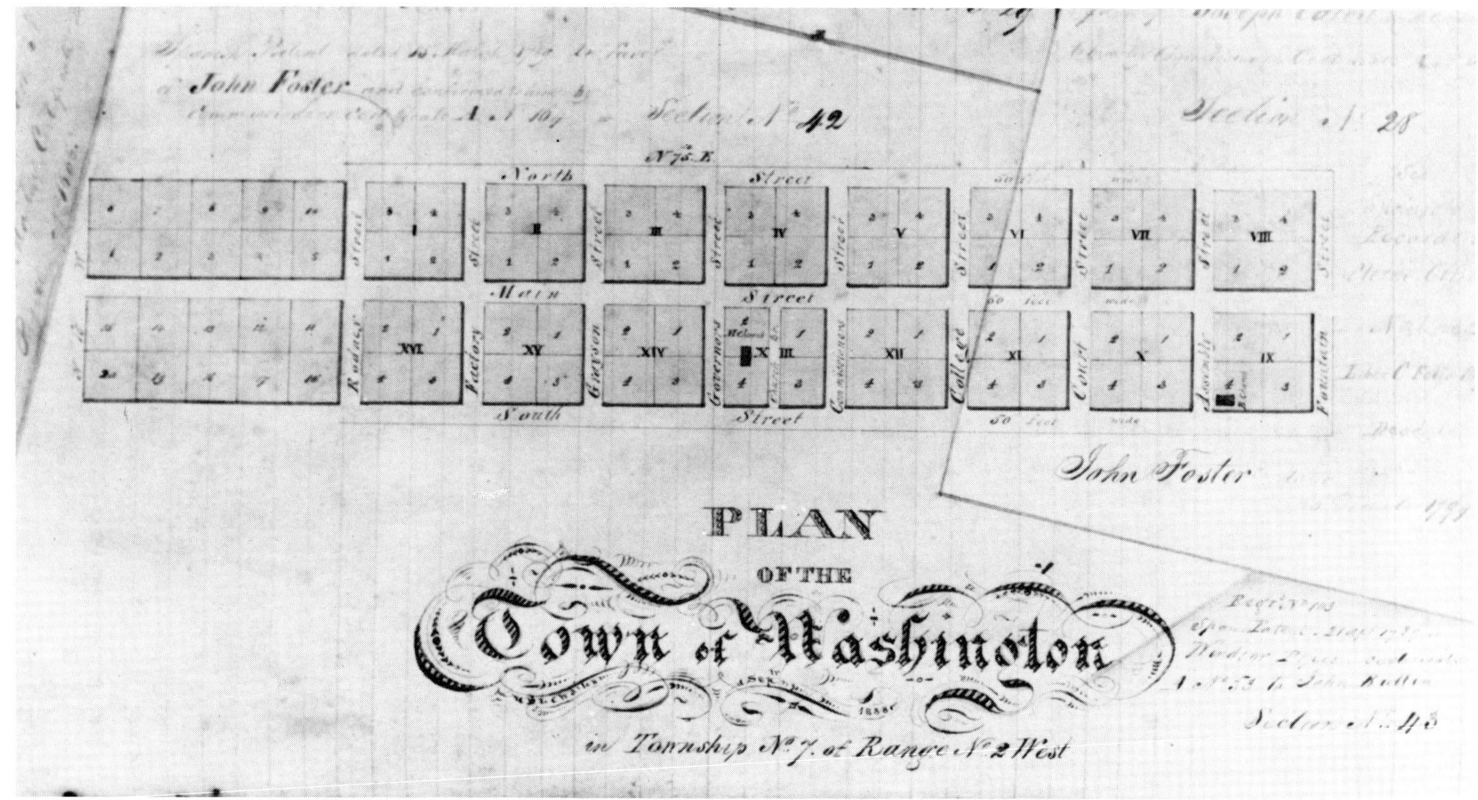

"Plan of Washington [Mississippi]"

6

sessions the landlord reserved a large room for storing the furniture and records of the assembly. Rent for the session of 1816–1817 was $150.[8]

By 1817, when Mississippi was admitted as the Union's twentieth state, partisan divisions and town-countryside enmity had largely dissipated in the river counties around Natchez. The inhabitants of this older region settled their differences in order to face a common threat. The backwoods settlements east of the Pearl River had grown mightily, and inhabitants there threatened to wrest political control of the new state from the older river counties.

The constitution for the new state of Mississippi was drafted at Washington in the Methodist Church on the grounds of Jefferson College. Ironically, the Constitution of 1817 marked Washington's eclipse as the capital. The constitutional convention was the last major government event to occur there. The delegates to the convention could not agree on a permanent state capital. The backwoods delegates from the eastern counties were as fearful of the river county "aristocrats" as their Jeffersonian predecessors earlier had been suspicious of Natchez. The delegates left the decision for the future. The constitution set the first session of the legislature at Natchez. Thereafter, the seat of government would be decided by the legislature. The first session convened at Washington on October 6, but because of spreading yellow fever, the legislators quickly adjourned on October 9. They reconvened at Natchez, probably in Texada, a building that still stands. The legislature continued to meet there through the 1820 session.

A backwoods boom began in the new state in 1820—a boom that was to dominate the next four decades and change the social, economic, and political character of Mississippi. In 1820, the Choctaw Indians, under intense pressure from land-hungry settlers, agreed to cede a huge tract of their lands in central Mississippi to the federal government. The treaty was negotiated and signed at Doak's Stand, a now remote site in northeastern Madison County. The United States representatives were frontier hero and future president Andrew Jackson and his friend General Thomas Hinds of Jefferson County. Hinds had served as Jackson's cavalry commander at the Battle of New Orleans. The cession was named Hinds County.

The new cession almost doubled the amount of land available for settlement. Public land offices did a booming business selling the new lands at the official government price of $1.25 per acre. As settlers flocked to fill up the lands, Hinds County was subdivided into a number of new counties— Simpson, Copiah, Rankin, Madison, Bolivar, Yazoo, Washington, and Holmes. The Cession of Doak's Stand marked a critical turning point in early Mississippi history: thereafter, the backwoods were in political and economic ascendancy while Natchez and the older river counties fell into relative decline. Inevitably, new demands arose among the settlers to move the seat of government. Natchez, they charged, was too far from the new centers of settlement, and the old inhabitants were unsympathetic to frontier problems. The new settlers demanded a more central capital that would be more amenable to frontier values.

In February 1821, the legislature decreed that "the next and each ensuing session of the Legislature of this state shall be held at the town of Columbia, until otherwise ordered by law." State officers—the auditor, the treasurer, the attorney general—were to move to Columbia with the legislature.[9]

Obviously, the move to Columbia was considered temporary. The federal government had already offered two sections of land in the new cession so that the state could found a new capital. Five days after mandating the move to Columbia, the legislators appointed a three-member commission "to locate two sections of land in the country lately ceded to the United States by the Choctaw

Indians . . . for . . . a seat of government for this state." The lawmakers specified that the site must be "within twenty miles of the true centre of the state." The commissioners, Thomas Hinds, William Lattimore, and James Patton, were ordered to make a report to the next session of the legislature showing the advantages of their choice and recommending "the best points for the erection of a state house."[10]

Jackson

In selecting a wilderness site in the state's interior, the Mississippi legislators were simply following a pattern established by the older states from which many of them had emigrated. During the last years of the eighteenth century, North Carolina, South Carolina, and Georgia had all appointed commissioners to select sites for new capitals. North Carolina established Raleigh, South Carolina created Columbia, and Georgia, destined to change its capital several times before settling on Atlanta, planned capitals first at Louisville, then at Milledgeville.[11]

Thomas Hinds was the state's leading military figure. After his experiences with Andrew Jackson in the war against the Creek Indians and against the British at the Battle of New Orleans, he was appointed brigadier general and, later, major general of the Mississippi Militia. He had run for governor in 1819, but he was defeated by George Poindexter. Apparently, Hinds had a natural capacity for leadership, for he was respected by both his men and his superiors.

Both William Lattimore, a native of Norfolk, Virginia, and his brother David were, by education, physicians. The brothers came to Natchez soon after the formation of the territorial government. They were staunch republican supporters of President Jefferson and Governor Claiborne, and both were drawn to politics. David was appointed

The territorial legislature rented space in Charles de France's tavern in Washington from 1808 through 1811. Since then it has been known as Assembly Hall.

to the territorial council; William served four terms as the territory's delegate to Congress. He was serving in Washington in 1817, where he helped arrange the compromise over the division of the territory that led to Mississippi's admission to the Union. He returned home to serve as a delegate to the first constitutional convention.

James Patton, the lieutenant governor who had been elected with Poindexter in 1819, was an ex-South Carolinian who had settled in the most politically influential town east of the Pearl, Winchester in Wayne County. Patton had become a locally renowned military leader in the war against the Creek Indians. Patton was apparently chosen for the commission because of his skills in surveying and mapmaking. But Patton did not serve, and he was soon replaced by Peter Vandorn, a Princeton graduate who had come to Natchez when it was still a Spanish province and who had settled at Port Gibson. Like Patton, Vandorn was also experienced at surveying and mapping. He also had served as clerk of the house of representatives. His appointment did not come in time for him to accompany Hinds and Lattimore on their search.

Following statehood in 1817, the legislature met in Natchez, renting space in Texada, built in the early 1800s for residential and commercial use.

Vandorn's son, Confederate General Earl Van-Dorn, achieved fame in the Civil War.[12]

Hinds and Lattimore met at the Choctaw Agency (west of what is now Ridgeland) and began their search. Major Thomas Freeman, the state surveyor, had calculated that the geographic center of the state lay near Doak's Stand. The two commissioners had already agreed on a number of criteria for an appropriate site: high ground, good water, healthful air, and fertile soil. The site should also be accessible by navigable stream and by road.

The Pearl and the Big Black rivers were the only navigable streams in the area. After some investigation, Hinds and Lattimore decided that no place on the Big Black was suitable, and they turned their attention to sites on the Pearl. Within the limits set by the legislature, only one site appeared promising—a pleasant place called Yellow Bluff—but it had to be ruled out because of frequent flooding.[13]

Ten miles south of the Choctaw Agency, Le Fleur's Bluff rose about twenty feet above the flood plain of the Pearl River. The place had been named

for French trader Louis Le Fleur, father of the more famous Greenwood LeFlore, who was born there in 1800. Le Fleur's wife (and Greenwood Leflore's mother), Rebecca Cravat, was one-fourth Choctaw. Louis Le Fleur had operated a trading post on the bluffs until 1812 when he moved further north on the Natchez Trace to a place that would later be called French Camp.

The commissioners were impressed. They noted a spring at the bluff and a stream nearby. Well water, they suggested, could be found "within thirty feet of the surface." While nobody then recognized the connection between mosquitoes and the summer "sickly season," people did understand that low-lying, swampy areas were unhealthful. Thus, they sought high ground with "good air" that gave protection from the "noxious exhalations of swampy lands." On this score, the commissioners equivocated about Le Fleur's Bluff. They feared that if the town were built on the bluffs and the bottomlands below it were cleared, the place would not be healthful. On the other hand, they said, if the nearby bottomlands were left uncleared to form a barrier to the bad air from the lowlands, the site would be as healthful as any other in the state. They found fertile soil and timber ample enough to support a large population. The commissioners argued that even though Le Fleur's Bluff lay thirty-five miles away from the center of the state, relatively easy navigation down the Pearl to Monticello and Columbia and the possibility of building roads to connect the Tombigbee (Columbus) settlements with the western towns made this location a desirable one.

The commissioners closed their report to the legislature by noting that while the site was outside the limits set by that body, "Every mile which the Commissioners found it necessary to recede from the center, brings the proposed Seat of Government nearer to almost every settlement in the state." Furthermore, they argued, nobody could cry favoritism, for "the location will be made on

Winthrop Sargent, Mississippi's first territorial governor, was appointed by President John Adams.

the vacant lands of the United States, to which no citizen of our state has a claim, and in the vicinity of which no settlement has yet been formed . . . . None can complain of a partial choice."[14]

Meeting at the Stovall Springs Hotel in Columbia, the legislature accepted Hinds's and Lattimore's recommendation of the Le Fleur's Bluff location. But the lawmakers refused to dismiss the commissioners. They substituted Peter A. Vandorn of Port Gibson for James Patton and ordered the three commissioners to lay off a town "known by the name of Jackson, in honor of Major General Andrew Jackson." The three were given wide au-

thority—to hire surveyors "and as many other persons as may be necessary to lay off the town"; to choose the sites for government buildings; to sell lots; and to appoint a "superintendent of buildings" who, under the supervision of the commissioners, was charged with building "a commodious house on an economical plan for the reception of the general assembly at the next session."[15]

In June 1822, the legislature met in special session at Columbia. By then, Hinds, Lattimore, and Vandorn had completed their town plan and presented it to the lawmakers. The town was laid out checkerboard fashion on the high ground immediately west of the Pearl River. The legislators had specified that the commissioners should reserve sites for a county court house and an "academy or college." No mention was made in law of a site for the state house.[16]

In laying off the town plan for Jackson, Hinds, Lattimore, and Vandorn used an old idea originated by Thomas Jefferson. Jefferson had told his idea to William C.C. Claiborne, who was interested in a plan for expanding the city of New Orleans. Claiborne, who had known all three commissioners when he was governor of the Mississippi Territory, passed the idea along to them. The plan retained a grid system, long popular as a plan for American cities. Jefferson's unique contribution had been to leave alternate blocks in the grid undeveloped, so that, like a checkerboard, developed squares faced undeveloped woodlands on all four sides. The commissioners put this original feature into their plan for Jackson. The undeveloped squares were sold off in the 1830s to generate money to build the Old Capitol. The commissioners also left the woodlands between Le Fleur's Bluff and the Pearl River as a town "Commons." These woods were intended to provide a healthful buffer zone to inhibit the spread of "bad air" from the swamps.[17]

Peter Vandorn's plan reserved a "Capitol

Green" at the eastern end of Capitol Street. This centerpiece of the town was flanked on the north by "College Green" and on the south by "Court Green." Even at that early date the "commodious house" must have been considered temporary, for the act ordering the commissioners to lay out the town ambiguously referred to "temporary buildings," and Vandorn's plan called for the state house to be built on the northeast corner of President and Capitol Streets, a block west of Capitol Green. On June 30, 1822, the legislature accepted Vandorn's plan for Jackson. Already they had ordered that state offices be moved to the new site and that subsequent sessions of the legislature be held there. In the first legislative session held at Jackson, the lawmakers further protected the vacant greens by requiring "one year's previous notice . . . in regular session of the General Assembly" before the lands could be disposed of.[18]

The commissioners who had laid out Jackson chose Abram Defrance, first sergeant-at-arms for the senate and brother of Charles Defrance (in whose tavern the territorial legislature had met), and Bennet Hines to construct a two-story brick state house of 2,400 square feet. The building was intended for the use of the legislature only. State officers were housed elsewhere, principally in nearby buildings on Capitol Street. Mississippi's first state house was ready for the legislators who assembled at Jackson two days before Christmas 1822.[19]

The eight senators and twenty-two representatives who assembled in the new building spent the first day organizing their respective houses and choosing officers. The next day, Christmas Eve, they heard Governor Walter Leake's message. The occasion, he noted, was significant, for it was the first time the legislature had met in a building owned by the state of Mississippi. Leake reminded the legislators that while the building might be far from luxurious, "This town was but a short time since entirely in the woods, in the midst of a

W. C. C. Claiborne, appointed Mississippi's second governor by President Thomas Jefferson, was, like his mentor, an anti-Federalist. In a heavy-handed political play, he moved the capital of the Territory from Natchez to Washington, Mississippi.

wilderness" only recently inhabited by "untutored savages."[20]

Nevertheless, the parsimonious, cautious, and legalistic frontier legislators wanted to make certain that no money had been wasted and no laws violated. They immediately conducted an investigation into the construction of the building. They found that the brickwork was up to specifications; woodwork, however, was "a very material departure from the contract." Yet they must have been pleased, for they excused the lapse by considering that the building had cost only $3,000, that it had been constructed in a very short time, and that Jackson's isolation had made it difficult to obtain proper materials. That the legislators were pleased may be a commentary on the itinerant nature of their previous meetings. Fifteen years after moving into their first state house, they appropriated money to pay for new benches.[21]

In December 1822, when the legislators and state officers arrived, Jackson was hardly a town at all. It existed mostly on paper and in the hopes of the politicians who moved there. A few cabins clustered along muddy roadways from Tombigbee Street on the south to Amite Street on the north. Settlement hardly extended past Congress Street to the west, and "West" Street marked the western limits of town. Despite Jackson's location on the Pearl River and the town's nearness to the Natchez Trace, Jacksonians found themselves isolated from the faster-growing settlements around Vicksburg to the west and Columbus on the Tombigbee to the northeast.

The first Jacksonians were government officials. A post office was established in October 1822, but round trips by mail carriers would be made only every two weeks between Jackson and St. Francisville, Louisiana, between Jackson and Shieldsboro (Bay St. Louis), and between Jackson and Port Gibson. By 1827, mail carriers could cover the distance to Columbus in forty-three hours, to old Greenville in Jefferson County in twenty-one hours, to Yazoo Courthouse in nine hours, and to Columbia in fifty-six hours. Lieutenant Governor David Dickson, who was also a practicing physician, took on the additional role of postmaster.[22]

In their 1821 act establishing the town, the legislators had subsidized settlement by allowing preference on ten lots (later increased to fifteen) to "responsible" persons who promised to build "neat log or frame houses thereon, not less than thirty feet in length." Nonetheless, when the lawmakers arrived in December 1822 for their first meeting in Jackson, they found accommodations and amenities scarce. Jackson had no hotels, and it is thought that a single tavern had opened for business.[23]

By 1825, Jackson had taken on some comforts—taverns and hotels—and attracted professional people and businesses that gave the town a settled life slightly removed from its frontier origins. Undoubtedly hoping to attract the business of legislators returning in 1823 for their

The diorama of The Treaty of Doak's Stand in the Old Capitol Museum features Choctaw and American leaders, Pushmataha, Mashulatubbee, Andrew Jackson, and Thomas Hinds.

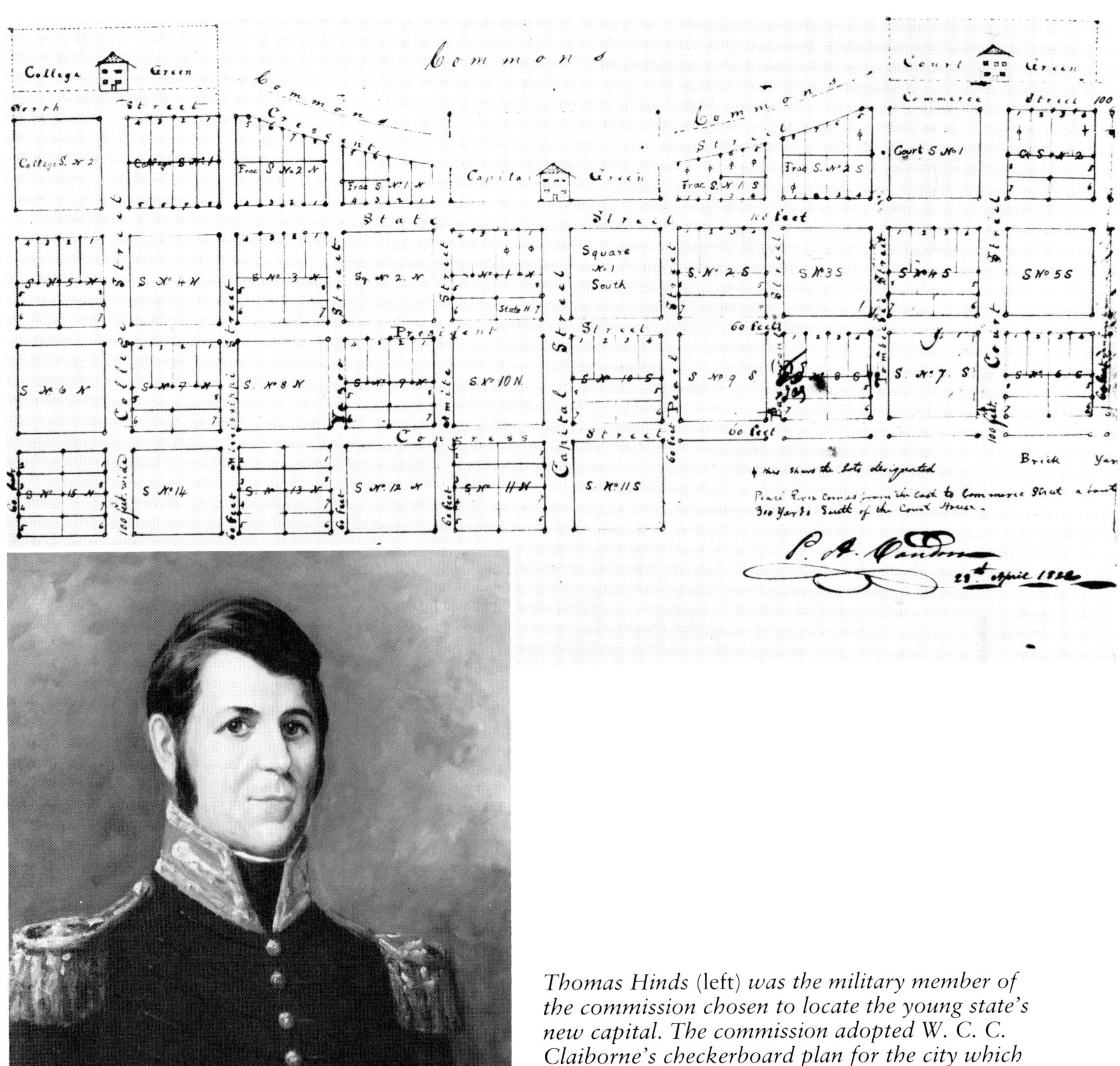

Thomas Hinds (left) was the military member of the commission chosen to locate the young state's new capital. The commission adopted W. C. C. Claiborne's checkerboard plan for the city which he had received from Thomas Jefferson seventeen years earlier.

"Natchez, on the Hill, from the Old Fort," 1831

Moving the Capital

In his travels in 1846, Sir Charles Lyell of London heard an ironic story about why Mississippi's government was moved from Natchez to Jackson. He related the story to his dinner companions at a hotel in Jackson.

"Natchez was the metropolis of the state, and the chief town of Adams County, which was so wealthy as to pay a third of all the taxes in Mississippi. It was a city to which the richest and best-informed citizens resorted, representing both the landed and moneyed interests of the state. It was, moreover, a center of communication, because it commanded the navigation of the great river. That the Houses of Legislature should meet here, was so natural and convenient, so fitted to promote good government, that the Democratic party could not be expected to put up, for many years, with an arrangement of affairs so reasonable and advantageous. They accordingly decided, by a majority, that some change must be made, and gave orders to a surveyor to discover the exact geographical center of the state. He found it in a wilderness, about fifty miles in a straight line east of Natchez, and pointed out an old cypress tree, in the middle of a swamp, accessible only by a canoe, as the spot they were in search of. This was welcome news, all might now be placed on a footing of equality, the spot being equally inaccessible and inconvenient for all. When the architect, however, came to build the capitol, he took the liberty, instead of erecting the edifice on piles in the center of the swamp, to place it on an adjoining rising ground, from which they had cleared away the native wood, a serious abandonment of principle, as it was several hundred yards from the true geographical center."

—A Second Visit to the United States of North America
(New York, Harper & Brothers, 1849)

second session in Jackson, the Eagle Tavern and the Jackson Hotel opened that year. Government business also attracted two printers. Peter Isler received the contract to print house and senate journals; George B. Crutcher was chosen to print the laws. Isler moved his newspaper, the *State Register*, from Columbia to Jackson, and Crutcher began the *Pearl River Gazette*. Attorneys, of course, came to the new seat of government in large numbers. During the first two years of Jackson's existence at least six lawyers opened offices there. Physicians and merchants set up businesses, and in 1824 some of Jackson's leading citizens advertised to attract a schoolteacher. A Kentuckian soon opened a school at a "high and healthy" site six miles north of town. Churches hardly existed on the American frontier; typically, no churches were founded during Jackson's early years. Occasionally itinerant preachers held forth in the state house.[24]

After 1825, Jackson's modest growth evaporated, and by 1830 the town almost ceased to exist. Only the annual meetings of the legislature gave the place activity. In 1827, Congress moved the land office to Clinton; in 1829, the legislature moved the county seat to Raymond. Jackson's role as state capital suddenly became very tenuous. In 1828 and 1829, bills providing for moving the capital to Clinton were passed in the senate only to fail in the house by the narrowest of margins. Unlike Jackson, Clinton was on the Natchez Trace; it also had a better road to rapidly growing Vicksburg. Two academies had already been established at Clinton, giving the town a more refined

Vicksburg, c. 1861

A City Springing Up in the Forest

The earliest known description of Jackson was recorded in the diary of an unknown printer and school teacher on May 31, 1823:

"... [I] got to Jackson about sun ½ an hour high, stopt at Winn's Tavern, went to the state house which is a large brick edifice about 60 by 35, having the appearance of a dwelling house, 1 year back there was but one cabin in the place, and not one tree amiss, now there is about 10 frame as many hewn log & one brick house, and the mechanics are very busy on all sides, they informed me that there would be another brick house put up this season & several frames. here we may truly say that there is a city springing up in the midst of the forest and as it were by enchantment, and if government patronizes it, it may become one of considerable magnitude, there are at present 3 taverns & 2 stores, & 2 printing offices, one of which publishes a weekly newspaper called the pearl river gazett, it is edited by Mr. Isler a tolerably smart man . . . the town . . . [is situated on] pearl river . . . it is a very crooked river, and navigable for steam boats 6 months in the year and for smaller craft all the year."

—William D. McCain
The Story of Jackson, v. 1, p. 21

The first state house, Jackson

air than rustic Jackson. In 1830, a similar bill passed the house only to fail in the senate. A major inducement by Clintonites was their promise to build a $50,000 state house for the government. Legislative sentiment clearly favored moving the capital. Jackson retained the designation only by default; each powerful legislator coveted the prize for his own community. Thus, Clinton lost out.[25]

Jacksonians could rely upon neither trade nor transportation to help the town flourish. Transportation and trade depended on rivers. Because of its age and location, Natchez still claimed supremacy in that realm. Yet the same opening of the interior lands that had spawned Jackson allowed future economic growth to focus on a new town with an even more strategic location than Natchez. Lying on the Mississippi River between the mouths of the Yazoo and Big Black, Vicksburg became a river port for the interior. For the remainder of the century, Jackson would be eclipsed by this thriving neighbor forty miles to the west.

Jackson's future as the state capital was secured by the Constitutional Convention of 1832. The convention delegates mandated that until 1850 all sessions of the legislature would be held in Jackson; if, during the first session thereafter, the legislators failed to move the seat of government from Jackson, it was to remain there permanently. Moreover, the High Court of Errors and Appeals (the Supreme Court), which since statehood had continued to meet at Natchez, was ordered to move to Jackson. Finally, in 1830, the great Choctaw cession of Dancing Rabbit Creek gave renewed vigor to the backwoods, and, thus, to Jackson as the capital. With stability assured, at least until 1850, the exodus of government offices was reversed and business began to prosper.[26]

By 1833, Vicksburg was rising as the state's center of trade and was rapidly gaining on Natchez, her older rival, as the state's premier city. Jackson's future, while still tenuous, was certain enough to convince legislators that a new, grander, and more permanent state house was needed. They wanted a capitol built quickly and economically; it would take far longer and cost far more than any of them realized.

NOTES

[1] The original settlement, sometimes called "Old Biloxi," was on the eastern side of the bay at present-day Ocean Springs. In 1702 the settlement was abandoned in favor of a new fort at Mobile Bay. In 1720 the French returned and established "New Biloxi" on the present site of Biloxi.

[2] Dunbar Rowland, ed., *Mississippi Territorial Archives*, vol. 1 (Nashville: Press of Brandon Printing Company, 1905), 129–130.

[3] *Ibid.*, 138–142, 180–81.

[4] William B. Hamilton, *American Beginnings in the Old Southwest: The Mississippi Phase*, Ph.D. Dissertation (Duke University, 1938), 578–579.

[5] Charles S. Sydnor, *A Gentleman of the Old Natchez Region: Benjamin L.C. Wailes* (Durham: Duke University Press, 1938), 25–29.

[6] *Ibid.*, 29–30.

[7] *Territorial Laws*, 257–258; Sydnor, *Wailes*, 28.

[8] Sydnor, *Wailes*, 43. The building that housed Defrance's Tavern is still standing.

[9] *Laws of Mississippi*, 1821, 106.

[10] *Ibid.*, 97.

[11] Michael W. Fazio, "The Chequer Board Plan of Jackson, Mississippi: A Chapter in the Origin and Disposal of the American Public Domain" (unpublished manuscript, Cornell University, 1980), 1. A copy of this paper is in the MDAH.

[12] *Ibid.*

[13] William D. McCain, *The Story of Jackson: A History of the Capital of Mississippi, 1821–1951* (Jackson: J.F. Hyer Publishing Company, 1953), 4–5. The Commissioners provided no information on the location of Yellow Bluff, nor did a search of early nineteenth-century maps reveal any information on this site.

[14] Hinds's and Lattimore's full report is printed in Dunbar Rowland, *History of Mississippi: Heart of the South* (S.J. Clarke Publishing Company: Chicago-Jackson, 1925), 516–528.

[15] *Laws of Mississippi*, November 28, 1821.

[16] *Ibid.*

[17] Fazio, "The Chequer Board Plan of Jackson," 9–10.

[18] *Laws*, November 28, 1821, June 29, 30, 1822, January 1, 1823.

[19] McCain, *Story of Jackson*, 13.

[20] *Senate Journal*, 1822, p. 13.

[21] *The Official and Statistical Register of Mississippi, 1904* (Nashville: Press of the Brandon Printing Company, 1904), 582.

[22] McCain, *Story of Jackson*, 17.

[23] *Laws*, November 21, 1821; McCain, *Story of Jackson*, 14–15.

[24] *Ibid.*, 14–18.

[25] *Ibid.*, 22–27.

[26] *Ibid.*, 32–33.

ILLUSTRATION NOTES

p. 2 Engraving: Georges Henri Victor Collot, *A Journey in North America* (Paris, 1826), 3 vols.

p. 3 Line drawing by Bill Wilson, 1990.

p. 5 Photograph. Works Progress Administration, MDAH.

p. 6 Ink drawing with color wash. MDAH.

p. 8 Photograph. Historic Preservation Division, MDAH.

p. 9 Photograph. Historic Natchez Foundation.

p. 10 Oil by Gilbert Stuart. Department of State, Washington, D.C.

p. 11 Engraving by J. B. Longacre from a miniature by A. Duval.

p. 12 Diorama, MSHM.

p. 13 Oil by N. H. Busey, 1925. Hall of Fame, MSHM.

p. 13 Ink drawing. MSHM.

p. 14 Etching by James Tooley, 1835. Historic Natchez Foundation.

p. 15 Engraving, 1861. Historic New Orleans Collection.

p. 16 Oil by Cornelius Hankins, 1905. MSHM.

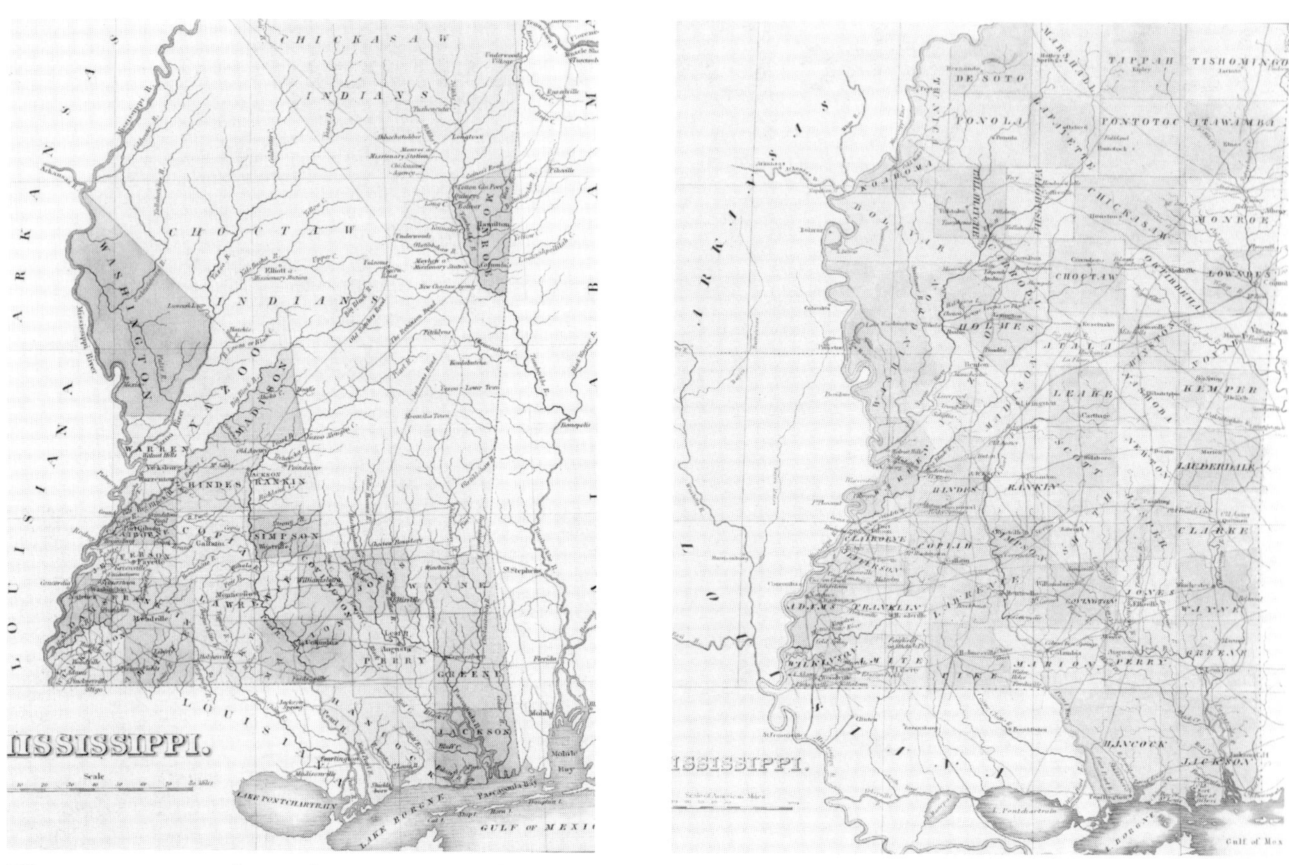

These two maps show the increase in the number of Mississippi counties from twenty-six in 1831 (left) to fifty-six in 1840. This growth paralleled the growth in population from 136,000 to 375,000.

Building the Old Capitol

In 1833 Mississippi was on the verge of rapid and unparalleled growth. The new state constitution conferred more democracy than any other constitution in the Union; emigrants from the older states came in great numbers to take up cheap, newly ceded Indian lands; the state's economy was blossoming; and a surplus was on hand in the state treasury. Impatience and optimism combined to produce a sense of quick opportunity and inevitable progress. Some of Mississippi's promise and faith in the future could be embodied in a set of imposing public buildings—structures that would mark the state's transition from a turbulent and rambunctious frontier to a settled and prosperous society.

Practical considerations also made it possible for political leaders to consider building grander and more permanent public structures. Until 1832 Jackson's future as Mississippi's capital was doubtful. But the 1832 constitution ensured Jackson's place as the state capital at least until 1850. Legislators and state officers were dissatisfied with the cramped and uncomfortable accommodations that had housed state government since 1822; they wanted new quarters in a state house that would befit Mississippi's bright future.

False Start

Soon after New Year 1833, Governor Abram Scott advised the members of the legislature on his plans for financing the public buildings. Jackson's future as the state capital was certain, the governor said. The town's unsold lots had become "an object of great importance." He suggested using funds from the sale of lots to help defray "expenditures for public buildings which may hereafter be ordered." Governor Scott's idea to finance the new state house with money obtained from the sale of

Abram Scott

Nashville, Tennessee
July 6 1833.

Sir,
    The late Governor Scott was kind enough to offer me the appointment of Architect to superintend the erection of a State house in Mississippi. I feel grateful for this evidence of confidence, but owing to a declining state of health I feel myself obliged to say, that I cannot undertake the duties of the appointment which had been tendered to me.

    I have the honor to be

    Most Respectfully
    Your Obt. Servt.
    D. Morrison

His Excellency
Charles Lynch,
Jackson.
Mississippi.

David Morrison to Governor Lynch, July 6, 1833

town lots was not a new one. Other southern states had obtained funds through similar sales.[1]

Six weeks later the legislators laid on the governor's desk for approval "An Act to provide for the erection of a State House and other public buildings in the town of Jackson, and for other purposes." The act went further than the governor had suggested. The legislators appropriated $95,000 directly from state funds "for the erection of a state house and suitable offices for the secretary of state, state treasurer, auditor of public accounts, and attorney-general, therein." They also appropriated an additional $10,000 to build a "suitable house for the governor." Lots would be laid off and sold to pay for the buildings, but should the sale of town lots fail to produce sufficient money for the appropriation, the lawmakers gave authority to the governor to draw on state bonds "which sum so drawn, shall be reimbursed . . . by a direct tax to be levied in equal sums, in the years 1840, 1841, and 1842" if regular state revenues proved insufficient to repay the debt. The usually parsimonious lawmakers were acting with uncharacteristic generosity.[2]

The governor was empowered to appoint a state architect to plan and supervise construction of the buildings. But the lawmakers themselves made some specifications—that "the materials of which the buildings are made shall be of the most lasting and durable character" with stone foundations, brick walls, and cypress timbers; that the state house should be big enough to hold both houses of the legislature, the High Court of Errors and Appeals, and the principal state officers. Although the legislators appropriated $95,000, the architect was instructed to limit the contracts for the state house to $75,000; the remaining $20,000 would go into a contingency fund. The governor was empowered to suspend the architect's work at any time he deemed it "a serious detriment to the state." Governor Scott approved the act on February 26, 1833.[3]

Governor Scott preferred to appoint a Mississippian to the position of state architect, but he soon found that search fruitless. On May 20, 1833, Scott wrote to David Morrison, a Nashville architect who had recently remodeled Andrew Jackson's Hermitage and designed Rachel Jackson's tomb. Morrison was recommended by Governor Carroll of Tennessee, and Scott offered him the job. Governor Scott was feeling the press of time, for he asked Morrison to "come down *without delay*" if he accepted the offer or "to notify me *forthwith* in the event of your refusal." Evidently, Morrison wanted the job, but he wrote Scott that he could not come to Jackson before November. He complained of bad health, and he advised the Mississippi governor that a commitment to build a Tennessee hospital for the insane also would delay his arrival in Mississippi for several months. At this critical point in the negotiations, Governor Scott suddenly sickened with cholera and died.[4]

The recently adopted Constitution of 1832 provided for no lieutenant governor, and the president of the senate, Charles Lynch, a studious and quiet man from Monticello, assumed the duties of governor. Ten days after Scott's death, Governor Lynch, mincing no words, renewed the negotiations with Morrison. "It is desirable that the commencement and completion of this work should be attended with as little delay as possible." If Morrison accepted, Lynch emphasized, there must be no delay for any other business. Morrison should "repair to this place immediately." Faced with the immediate necessity of moving to Jackson, Morrison declined the job.[5]

Lynch had sent his letter to Morrison in Nashville by an aide named P.B. Harrison, probably of Jefferson County. Upon Morrison's refusal, Harrison contacted John Lawrence, who had already been recommended by Governor Carroll for the carpentry work. Three days after Morrison refused the job, Lawrence wrote Governor Lynch that Harrison had shown him the legislative act authorizing the construction of a state house and had offered him the job of state architect. Lawrence indicated that he wanted to accept, but that the required $50,000 bond was "more rigid than out [ought] to be required of [an] architeck." He would, Lawrence continued, "except [accept?] for the salary offered to still become the architeck if you will due [do] away with the bond." Governor Carroll, Lawrence promised, could testify to his honesty and professional abilities and would "rite you to that a fect."[6]

Other would-be candidates were suggested to Governor Lynch. One of them, Hugh Roland of Kentucky, mounted a full campaign for the job. Roland wrote in early August that he had recently learned of the legislation in Mississippi authorizing a new state house. Although he had "no personal acquaintance" in Mississippi, Roland promised that he could furnish "such references as will be perfectly satisfactory." At the moment, Roland added, he was busy constructing a large hotel in Louisville, Kentucky. He would complete that project in October, and he could then come directly to Jackson.[7]

In September Lynch was bombarded with letters of recommendation supporting Roland's application. Governor Carroll of Tennessee and Governor John Breathitt of Kentucky both wrote letters of support, and the owners of the hotel that Roland was building in Louisville praised his work. Apparently, Lynch failed to respond, for on October 14, 1833, Roland again wrote to Governor Lynch inquiring about the status of his application. By then Lawrence had already been chosen.[8]

Governor John Gayle of Alabama recommended his own state architect for the job. William Nichols was then working in Alabama, the second southern state in which he had attained a great reputation for designing solid and beautiful buildings. Now Nichols sought to bring his talents to Mississippi, and he applied to Governor Lynch. Accurately, though perhaps immodestly, he described himself as knowing more about building state capitols than any other man in the country; and, having worked for years in both North Carolina and Alabama, he was especially experienced in "building in the southern country." He would, Nichols assured Lynch, produce "an edifice not surpassed for elegance, convenience, nobility, and economy of expenditure." Lynch failed even to respond to Nichols. On October 12 when Nichols wrote asking for the status of his application, John Lawrence was already in Jackson drafting his plans to present to the upcoming session of the legislature.[9]

John Lawrence, the new state architect, arrived in Jackson from Nashville in October 1833 after a trip on horseback of more than two weeks. The next month he presented his plan for a Gothic Revival state house to the newly convened legislators. The plan must have pleased them for they ordered Lawrence to begin letting contracts for the ground floor on the condition that the contracts conformed "to the proposed plan exhibited to the members of the legislature, which plan is hereby declared to be adopted."[10]

Simultaneously, the lawmakers sought to raise money quickly to fund the $95,000 appropriation that they had approved in February. First, they made the entire sum available for immediate use by releasing the $20,000 earlier ordered to be held in a contingency fund. They also authorized the governor to raise $70,000 in cash by discounting at state banks the notes given in payment for Jackson town lots. The money was to be used solely for the state house.[11]

Lawrence had been hired by Governor Charles Lynch, but only a month after the architect's arrival, Lynch relinquished the governorship to Hiram Runnels. Runnels had been elected in May 1833 in a special election held following the adoption of the Constitution of 1832.

Laying the Cornerstone, 1834

Masonic lodges traditionally officiated at the laying of cornerstones for public buildings. The Grand Lodge of Mississippi, led by John Quitman, and two local Masonic orders conducted the ceremony for the laying of the Old Capitol's cornerstone. For the ceremony Quitman probably wore this jewel given him by his Natchez lodge in 1826.

Order of the Procession

At the laying of the Corner Stone of the State Capitol, in Jackson, Mississippi, on Friday, the 28th instant.

Citizens two and two,
Tyler, with drawn sword,
Two Stewards with white rods,
Entered Apprentices,
Fellow Crafts,
Master Masons,
Secretary and Treasurer,
Senior and Junior Wardens,
Mark Masters,
Post Masters,
Royal Arch Masons
Select Masters
Knights Templars,
Master.
Pearl Lodge, with all visiting brethren,
not members of the Grand Lodge,
or of some organized visiting
Lodge
Music.
Tyler, with drawn sword,
Two Stewards, with white rods,
Master Masons,
Secretary and Treasurer,
Senior and Junior Wardens,
Mark Masters,
Post Masters,
Royal Arch Masons,
Select Masters,
Knights Templars,
Master.
Clinton Lodge, No. 16, Commencing
with Masters.
Three Past Masters, with vessels containing
corn, wine, and oil.
Principal Architect.
Five Orders borne by Past Masters.
Three Lights, borne by Past Masters.

One Steward)   (One Steward,
with white)   HOLY BIBLE   (with white
rod.)   (rod.

Grand Chaplain,
Clergy and Orator,
Officers of the Grand Lodge.
Principal Builders and State Architect,
Governor of the State and Suit,
Two Deacons, with black rods.

Mississippian, Nov. 21, 1834.

The procession, the left and right columns marked *Marched on horseback*.

Despite the legislature's later generosity, money problems plagued Runnels and Lawrence throughout 1834 and 1835, and lack of funding delayed the beginning of construction into the second half of 1834. On November 21, 1834, the *Mississippian* announced that the cornerstone for the new state house would be laid on the twenty-eighth. The Masonic order would conduct the ceremonies, and the celebrations would include an evening ball at the Planters' Hotel near Capitol Green on the south side of Pearl Street.[12]

Although the state treasury held $75,000 in notes from the sale of Jackson lots, Governor Runnels could not convince the banks to accept them. The Planters' Bank pled that they could take only "such notes as are negotiable or payable at other banks." The bank officers claimed that they were thus prohibited from accepting notes made to the state treasury. The bank agreed, however, to make a six-month note for $10,000 personally to Governor Runnels and to take the Jackson lot notes as security. So that work on the building could proceed and "to enable the architect to comply with his authorized contracts," Runnels agreed.[13]

Yet on the day the Masons were laying the cornerstone for the building, Governor Runnels was forced to issue a proclamation suspending further work. Banks still refused to accept the notes from the Jackson town lots, and, Runnels warned, the only remedy was "early legislative action." This action was not to be forthcoming.[14]

In January 1835 the legislature convened in the midst of a bitter personal feud between Mississippi Senator George Poindexter and President Andrew Jackson. Poindexter, who was running for reelection, had become the leader of the anti-Jackson forces in Mississippi. In this special session, the pro-Jackson house of representatives chose to seat delegates from the newly created counties of the Chickasaw cession. But the anti-Jackson senate refused to seat them, maintaining

The North Carolina State House as renovated by William Nichols, c. 1820. This landscape was painted shortly after Nichols completed his work.

that the delegates should not take their seats until the next regular session of the legislature convened in November. The Whig-controlled senate refused to recognize the legality of the house of representatives. After ten days of complete stalemate and paralysis, the legislature adjourned without passing a single bill.[15]

Throughout 1835 Runnels continued to borrow from the banks to fund construction of the state house. During 1835 he personally borrowed $18,922 and secured the loans with $20,000 in Jackson lot notes. Of these personal loans, State Auditor John Mallory reported that $18,352 had been spent during the year.[16]

Criticism surfaced both in the press and among public officials about the slow progress on the state house and about Lawrence's plans. Since his arrival in Mississippi, Lawrence had been advertising in the newspapers for private clients, creating the impression that he was not giving his full efforts to his job as state architect. The editor

The Alabama State Capitol at Tuscaloosa, built by William Nichols in 1827–31, shows the raised basement form that the English-born Nichols favored.

of the *Mississippian* pronounced Lawrence not to be an architect "in the true sense of the word," and judged Lawrence's construction "unstable and unworkmanlike."[17]

On October 9, 1835, Governor Runnels fired John Lawrence and suspended further work on the state house. By then Lawrence had laid the foundation and completed the walls for the ground floor. One month later, only days before leaving office, Governor Runnels hired William Nichols.[18]

William Nichols

When William Nichols became Mississippi's state architect in 1835, he was fifty-three years old and had been practicing his profession for more than three decades. He had already served as state architect in North Carolina and Alabama, and,

although he never held the title, in effect Nichols was state architect in Louisiana for two years before coming to Mississippi. His stay in Louisiana was brief, but his career in North Carolina spanned twenty-seven years, from 1800 to 1827, and he worked in Alabama from 1827 to 1833. In both North Carolina and Alabama, Nichols spent much of his time on public buildings, but his official duties did not preclude extensive private commissions for the design of houses, fraternal lodges, private schools, and commercial buildings. When he arrived in Mississippi, Nichols was perhaps the foremost architect working in the American South. Although three-quarters of his buildings have perished as a result of demolition, fire, or war, those that remain furnish memorials to "one of the longest, most productive and least recognized careers in the history of American architecture."[19]

Nichols was born (c.1780) and reared in Bath, an English city of great architectural distinction. Nichols's family apparently was established in the building trades, and almost certainly the young Nichols was trained as a builder by his kinsmen. Samuel Nichols, a carpenter and builder of some note, lived in Bath at the time. In the eighteenth century, young men commonly apprenticed with established masters to learn a profession. How and when William Nichols progressed from craftsman to architect is unknown. Possibly, Nichols came to the United States as a skilled carpenter, and, taking advantage of the scarcity of trained builders and architects in the new world, became a self-taught architect.[20]

Nichols immigrated to North Carolina in 1800 when he was about twenty years old. He lived and worked in various towns in that state for the next quarter of a century. In North Carolina Nichols developed into a professional architect skilled in the increasingly popular Greek Revival school, a style that was to be his mainstay for the rest of his career. Occasionally, Nichols delved into

Thomas J. Wharton's Description of Jackson in 1837

The present State House was in course of erection when I came—was at the first windows. . . .

It was in the month of October, 1837, I left my native city, Nashville, Tennessee, having previously provided myself with a license to practice law there. Jackson, Mississippi, was my objective point. . . .

The whole distance, 400 miles was traversed on horseback.

My imagination was enlivened, at starting, by the picture it had drawn of what was to be my future home—and for which I had bid adieu to every earthly object nearest and dearest to the head and heart. It is said, that "distance leads enchantment to the view,"—but with me, as time and distance diminished, and I drew nearer and nearer the termination of my journey, my imagination became more intense, assuring me "if there was an Elysium on earth," it was Jackson, Mississippi—the metropolis of the great cotton growing, slaveholding aristocracy of this proud commonwealth. As althings earthly have an end, so had my long fatiguing journey, and on the evening of the—day of October, 1837, about the hour of 4 p.m., I crossed Pearl river and, in a few minutes dismounted at the Mansion House, southeast corner State and Pascagoula streets. Gilbert & Dawson, proprietors. A party of gentlemen, seated on the portico, were absorbed in a game of chess or backgammon. Another party were running horse races on State street. After supper, curiosity led me to take a stroll up State street to the Eagle Hotel, then occupying the site of Judge Campbell's residence—northeast corner of State and Amite streets. There was an underground, dark and cavernous saloon—fitly located as all such "air holes of hell" may be supposed to be. It was crowded with a gay and festive party, making night hideous with their bacchanalian revels.

Instead of the flourishing young city my imagination had promised I should see, the population did not exceed, I would suppose, 900. The buildings were scattered at long distances, over the corporate limits of the town—were of the plainest materials, and wholly devoid of architectural taste or design, and even then, wore the appearance of decay, though the town was in its infancy. Many of the squares, now [1895] covered with handsome buildings, and luxurious home of wealth and refinement, were thickset forests, not a house upon them, nor a primeval forest tree detached from the soil. The State House, then occupied by the legislature when in session, was a small two story structure with two rooms—the one above for the Senate—that below was the Hall of Representatives. It stood where the Harding building is now—opposite the CLARION-LEDGER office.

I did not think that at present rates it would cost more than $1,500. None of the State officers occupied it.

There was a plank walk three or four feet wide, and elevated above the ground, extending from the back door of the Hall of Representatives to the side door of a saloon or "dram shop," which stood on the corner below and directly in front of the present residence of C. C. Campbell, Esq. Over that plank walk a stream—a human stream—was continually pouring, day and night, during the session of the Legislature. From the present State House to the northern terminus of State street there were only four houses, viz: the Eagle Hotel, the one now occupied by M. D. Patton, attorney-general (built of lumber sawed in Lawrence county and hauled here in wagons), and now occupied by Thos. Atkinson. On all West street, from its intersection with State street, to its northern terminus—on both sides—only two buildings stood—one on the Catholic Church grounds—then occupied by C. C. Mayson, Secretary of State, and one now occupied by D. P. Porter, Sr. On Capitol street, from the creek to the depot, on both sides, lay a heavy forest. Two cabins stood at the corner of Capitol and Mill streets. They were owned and occupied by two Irishmen, Mike and John Blake. Thickset woods and hunting grounds occupied all other parts of those now important streets. Where the postoffice now stands, stood the residence of Judge Phillips, State Treasurer, and which building continued there until it gave place to the postoffice. Such is a brief and imperfect sketch of the first view presented my eyes on my arrival at the Capital of Mississippi.

—Daily Clarion Ledger
Dec. 14, 1895

Gothic Revival, as in his design for the Mississippi penitentiary, but it was his Greek Revival buildings that made Nichols's reputation and still form the greatest part of his architectural legacy.[21]

Information on Nichols's early years in North Carolina is scarce, and when he began to practice as an architect is uncertain. Yet it is clear that before 1806 Nichols was in New Bern, North Carolina's second oldest town and colonial capital, working either as a builder or as an architect, and he may have been involved in "the creation of the distinguished architecture of that town." He almost certainly designed the New Bern Academy, a beautiful brick building with a Doric portico.[22]

In 1806 Nichols, now married to Mary Rew of New Bern, moved his new wife eighty miles north to Edenton, a low-country town like New Bern near the coast. He worked there and in surrounding Chowan County for the next twelve years. His first wife died there, and in 1815 Nichols married Sarah Simmons. In Edenton, he became an American citizen. The War of 1812 had created a feeling of intense patriotism and anti-British sentiment, and apparently Nichols wanted to ensure his status as a bona fide American. His architectural practice in Edenton consisted mainly of law offices and plantation houses.[23]

From 1817 to 1823 Nichols reached the zenith of his career in North Carolina. He worked in Fayetteville, then North Carolina's premier city, designing bank offices and houses for the town's leading citizens. In 1819 Nichols was appointed state architect, and while he continued an extensive private practice, Nichols transformed the old North Carolina state house at Raleigh into an imposing Greek Revival structure that previewed his design for the Mississippi state house more than a decade later. At the same time he designed and supervised the construction of several University of North Carolina buildings at Chapel Hill.[24]

Early nineteenth-century North Carolina, hampered by a lack of ports, inadequate transpor-

Charles Lynch

tation, and primitive agriculture, failed to keep economic pace with its neighbors. In the 1820s and 1830s North Carolinians by the tens of thousands abandoned their increasingly worn lands in the old state and headed west. To them the "West" meant Alabama and Mississippi, new states that were booming with cheap, fertile, and abundant lands. North Alabama and Mississippi resembled the North Carolina Piedmont; in Alabama's and Mississippi's river bottoms and prairies, North Carolina emigrants could see a reflection of the low country. In climate, topography, and vegetation, North Carolinians found the newer states of the Old Southwest familiar. Large numbers of North Carolinians migrated to Alabama and Mississippi in the 1820s. William Nichols was one of them.

Nichols came to Alabama in 1827 as state architect to design and construct buildings in a new state booming with the promise of flush times. Alabama had become the Union's twenty-second state in 1819. In 1826, one year before

Nichols's arrival, the Alabama legislature established the state capital at Tuscaloosa, a hamlet in west-central Alabama on the bluffs over the Black Warrior River. The new capital nestled inside the arc formed by the Black Belt, one of the most fertile plantation regions of the Old South. The area was an architectural blank. No state buildings had been put up; the University of Alabama, to be located in Tuscaloosa, had to be planned and built; rich Black Belt planters in the surrounding countryside needed grand houses to befit their rising wealth and status.

As state architect, Nichols had the greatest opportunity of his career—not just the chance to build a state house but to lay out a university, design the buildings, and construct them. Nichols spent four years working in and around Tuscaloosa, and they were the most productive years of his life. He designed the state house, the university and its buildings, the state bank, town hall, Methodist and Episcopal churches, and numerous houses. Nichols's plan for the University of Alabama featured a complex of buildings around a central park. His biographer calls the design "one of the outstanding, albeit unrecognized, architectural projects of early nineteenth-century America."[25]

The Alabama state house, built at Tuscaloosa between 1827 and 1831, was reminiscent of Nichols's design for its North Carolina counterpart. Ironically, the latter burned in 1831, the same year that his new Alabama capitol was completed. The state house at Tuscaloosa was obviously another step in Nichols's progression toward the Mississippi state house, Nichols's supreme achievement in capitol-building. The central rotunda, the grand front portico without steps, the circle of columns in the senate chamber, were all present in Nichols's design for the Alabama building. These features would be refined and repeated later in the Mississippi state house.[26]

After Nichols completed the Alabama capitol

in 1831, he was appointed state engineer. He spent the next year surveying the route for a canal near Muscle Shoals and the year following that surveying the route for a railroad connecting the Coosa River with the Tennessee. But Nichols wanted to return to architecture. In 1833 he asked his friend Governor John Gayle of Alabama to recommend him for the job of state architect in Mississippi. Nichols actively sought the position and thought of himself as the leading candidate. When Mississippi's governor passed him over in favor of John Lawrence, Nichols was sorely disappointed. In December 1833 Nichols and his wife packed up and moved to Louisiana, where he had accepted a job as assistant state engineer. The title indicated engineering, but the duties were architectural.[27]

In Louisiana Nichols worked on the state penitentiary at Baton Rouge, which was already under construction when he arrived. In his second year there, however, Nichols found himself designing yet another state house. New Orleans was then the capital of Louisiana, and the old Charity Hospital (1815) was selected to house the state government. Nichols drew the plan for remodeling the building and transforming it into a state capitol. The building proved temporary, for in 1848 the capital was moved to Baton Rouge. The building was later demolished.[28]

Nichols's stay in New Orleans later proved profitable. There he met the largest community of builders and architects in the South. He used the dome on the New Orleans Merchants Exchange, designed by New Orleans architect James Dakin, as a model for the dome over the Mississippi capitol, and he later called upon New Orleans craftsmen to do much of the delicate ornamental work on the Mississippi state house.[29]

When Nichols came to Mississippi in the fall of 1835 as the new state architect, his first job was destruction, not construction; he had to tear down John Lawrence's false start. State officials had become disillusioned with Lawrence's Gothic Revival

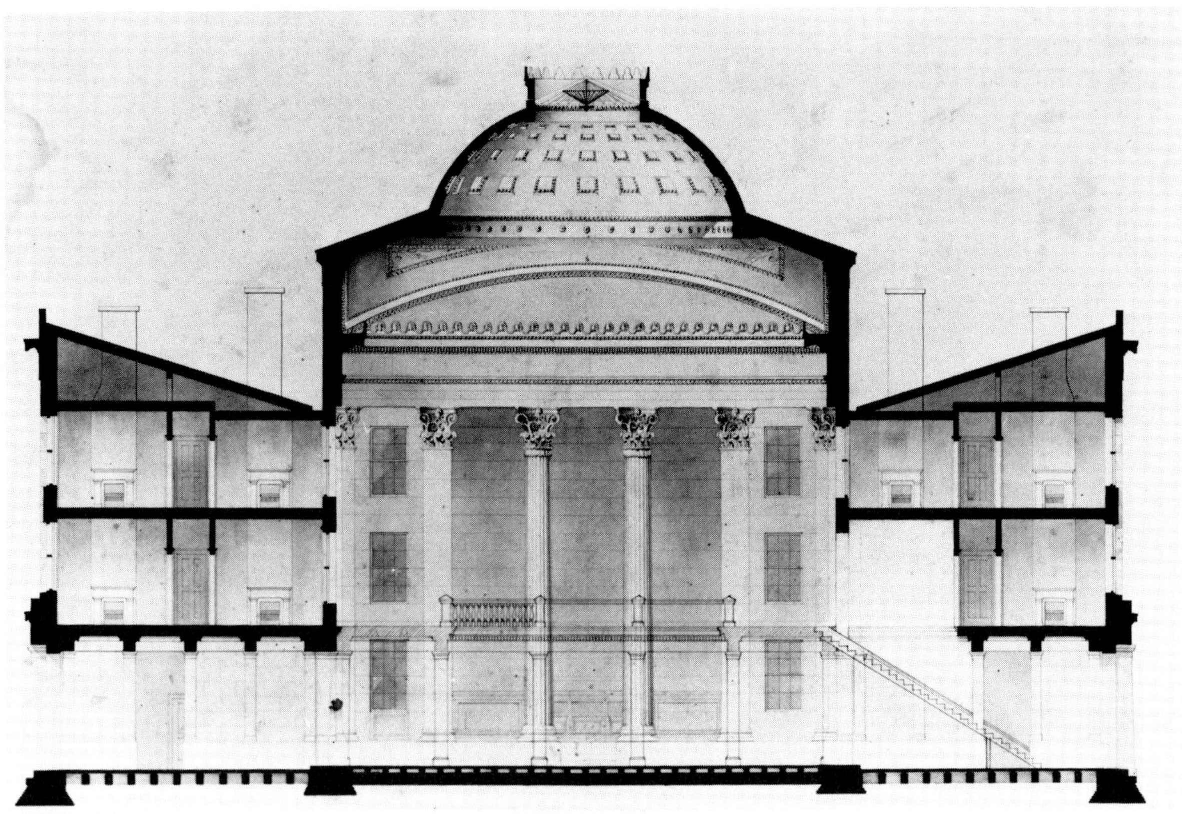

While living in New Orleans, Nichols studied this dome by James Dakin in the Merchants' Exchange. He repeated its pattern of ornamentation in the rotunda of the Old Capitol.

design. Runnels, who had fired Lawrence, had left office on November 20, 1835. When the legislature convened in January 1836, Charles Lynch, the man who had hired Lawrence in 1833, was again governor. The two legislative houses immediately chose a joint committee to investigate the work on the state house and to recommend how to speed the construction of all the public buildings as well as how to administer the projects more effectively.

The committee report was ready by February 10. The committee members not only condemned Lawrence's plan, they questioned his qualifications as an architect. Lawrence was not guilty of dishon-esty nor of "practicing false pretences upon the state," the committee reported. Nonetheless, the committee concluded that Lawrence was not "conscious of his own want of capacity" and "greatly mistakes and overrates his own qualifications."[30]

The committee members evaluated Lawrence's design as deficient in every respect—"against all architectural proportions of order, and the various compartments so bunglingly arranged, as to exhibit neither skill, convenience, nor comfort." The house and senate chambers they found uncomfortable and "in violation of all taste, and of a most undignified appearance." Also, the outward design of the building was "equally deficient in taste, as the inner apartments are in utility." The building, they charged, would look more like a church than a capitol. The entire design was "badly selected from mixed orders" and "composed of disproportioned , ungraceful parts." In short, they concluded, Lawrence did not "possess capacity or skill enough" to construct a state capitol, and "his incompetency as an architect" justified Governor Runnels's decision to fire him. "The interests of the state," the report argued, required "a total and abrupt abandonment" of the building.[31]

Nichols submitted a Greek Revival design that was in stark contrast to Lawrence's Gothic plan. The committee judged the new plan superior to Lawrence's "beyond all comparison," since it combined "simplicity, beauty, and strength with the most perfect harmony and convenience."

Greek Revival architecture had become the standard form in the South when William Nichols submitted his plans for the state house to the Mississippi legislature in 1836. For a variety of reasons—cultural, nationalistic, and practical— even more than other Americans, southerners between 1820 and 1850 embraced classical Greek and Roman forms for their grandest public and commercial buildings, their homes, and their churches.[32]

Eighteenth-century colonial architectural forms on the Atlantic seaboard had followed English patterns, and in the lower Mississippi Valley Spanish and French models had been used. But a spirit of intense nationalism pervaded America after the War of 1812, and European models, especially English ones, fell into disrepute. The new nation saw itself as a rising empire like Rome and a democracy like Athens. Educated people studied the classics and followed Greek and Latin literary forms. Their writings were packed with classical allusions. Although Greek Revival buildings were erected all over the United States, the form became most popular in the lower South, especially in Alabama, Mississippi and Louisiana.

In a young, bumptious and transitory frontier society, classical forms represented reason restraint, order, and permanence for which the citizens strived.

Practicality added to the popularity of Greek Revival in the lower South. Many southern Greek Revival houses were encircled by colonnaded galleries that shaded the windows from the hot sun and provided covered outside space. Large windows, sometimes reaching from ceiling to floor, invited breezes to circulate through the house. All of the elements combined to produce structures of stunning grandeur and beauty.

A number of authors published builders' handbooks in the early nineteenth century, and these helped to carry Greek Revival into the rural South. The oldest and most popular of these

Charles Manship, attracted to Jackson because of the work available in the building trades, not only found employment in the construction of the Old Capitol, but also a wife, Adaline Daley, daughter of the carpentry contractor.

design books was James Stuart's and Nicholas Revett's *Antiquities of Athens*. Stuart and Revett had gone to Greece in 1751 and had spent three years measuring and drawing the classical ruins. The resulting information, published in London from 1761 to 1816, filled four volumes.

In the nineteenth century their work was abridged to handbook form. The book contained carefully drawn plates of buildings with precise details of columns, capitals, and floor plans, all marked with exact measurements. William Nichols used these drawings as guides when he designed the capitals for the columns in the Old Capitol.[33]

The Old Capitol was expected to be the architectural embodiment of the new state constitution. Notwithstanding the anomaly of slavery, Mississippi in the 1830s, like all frontiers, was a democratic society, and President Andrew Jackson, a frontiersman of humble beginnings and few pretensions, personified that faith in rule by the common man. The Constitution of 1832 was constructed to solidify such Jacksonian principles as legislative supremacy over the executive and judicial branches, the election of all public officials, including judges, and universal suffrage for white males. Jacksonian Democrats believed fundamentally that the people ruled—that all public officials were accountable to the people and that the best way to ensure that accountability was through frequent popular elections. The Mississippi Constitution of 1832 was perhaps the best statement ever made of Jacksonian ideals.

Jacksonians were suspicious of a strong executive branch and advocated legislative supremacy. The legislative chambers dominated the upper two floors of both wings of the building, far eclipsing in elegance and size the modest governor's office on the ground floor. The people could watch their government at work from large, open galleries in each house of the legislature. The purity and simplicity of Greek Revival architecture also suited democracy. What better style to emulate than that of classical Greece, the original seat of democratic ideals?

Nichols's conception of the Mississippi capitol evolved from his previous designs for the North Carolina and Alabama state houses. The centerpiece was a central rotunda topped by a large dome. Wings extended north and south from the rotunda. The building rose to three stories—a ground, or "basement" floor, and two upper floors. In the end of the north wing, rising from the second floor to the roof, was the house chamber. The rostrum and speaker's chair were positioned against the north wall. Seats for the representatives were arranged in rows facing the rostrum. Across the rear of the chamber ten large columns rose from floor to ceiling. On the level of the third floor, a visitor's gallery supported by the columns extended along the circular rear wall of the chamber. In the end of the south wing was the senate chamber. Like the house chamber, it rose from the second floor to the roof. On the second-floor level, the senators would be seated within a circle of Corinthian columns, a feature Nichols had also used in his Alabama capitol at Tuscaloosa. The columns supported a circular gallery from which visitors could watch the proceedings in the senate below. The shallow-domed ceiling contained a central, circular skylight.

A great portico was centered on the front of the building facing west down Capitol Street. The Ionic columns of the portico sat atop rectangular entryways leading into the ground floor. Inside, twin circular staircases led to the upper floors. Smaller, recessed doors provided entry into the ground floor at each end of the building. Behind the rotunda, a semi-circular bay broke the severity of the long back wall. The rooms of the bay would house the chancery court on the first floor, the High Court of Errors and Appeals on the second, and the state library on the third.

The ground floor was built of stone, but the outer walls of the upper stories were constructed of brick. The brick was covered with stucco to match the appearance of the stone on the ground floor. Greek Revival buildings in the South were commonly covered with stucco and scored with lines to imitate the appearance of classical stone construction. In October 1838, Caleb A. Parker contracted "to plaster the upper stories of the front and two ends . . . where the brick work is visible . . . so as to make a good imitation . . . of the rock of the basement story." The entire structure was enclosed by a stone and iron fence designed by Nichols.[34]

The committee members turned their attention to "the many abuses connected with the progress of the present building," principally to the "entangled contracts and liabilities" growing out of Lawrence's unilateral discretion and unsupervised work. They recommended the appointment of a board of commissioners to oversee the construction of all public buildings. The board, not the architect alone, would issue and settle contracts, make payments, keep a ledger of accounts, and investigate problems and abuses. The committee was "not unmindful . . . of a proper regard for economy"; the members believed that the cost of Nichols's state house would be no greater than the amount necessary to finish Lawrence's plan. Finally, the committee recommended that the legislature speedily appropriate enough money to continue work on the capitol. The committee members assured their colleagues that the seat of government would remain at Jackson and that the style of the capitol should fulfill the promise of the capital city.[35]

Within two weeks of the joint committee report approving Nichols's plan, Governor Lynch signed a bill embodying all of the committee's recommendations. William Nichols was appointed state architect with a salary of $2,000 per year. Richard Davidson, Perry Cohea, and Henry K.

Moss, all of Jackson, were designated a "board of commissioners of public buildings." Nichols was to inform them of his needs for materials and workmen; the board would then issue the contracts and approve payments. The commissioners, who were to meet at least once a month and more frequently if "occasion shall require," were allowed five dollars each per day that they were "necessarily employed in discharging their duties under this act." The legislators appropriated to the state house another $65,000 of the proceeds from the sale of Jackson town lots.[36]

Almost simultaneously, the legislators ordered another major construction project—the building of a state penitentiary. Both the state house and the "governor's home" had been authorized in 1833. Nothing, however, had been done toward constructing the latter. Now the board of commissioners would have three major construction efforts proceeding simultaneously. No mention was made in the act of the responsibilities of the state architect.[37]

Nichols inquired. He knew from the 1833 act that he was responsible for designing and constructing the governor's house and the state house. Was he now to have the penitentiary added to his responsibilities? Nichols asked Governor Lynch. The governor replied that in his and the commissioners' opinions "the act . . . appointing you Architect of the State requires you to give your attention to *all* the public buildings including the penitentiary." But, the governor continued, Nichols's annual salary of $2,000 was not adequate to cover the additional duties. The commissioners agreed to increase Nichols's salary to $3,000.[38]

The commissioners wasted no time in getting down to work. The bill creating the board and appointing the three commissioners was approved on February 27; the board's first meeting was held four days later on March 3. Moss was elected president, and S.P. Baley was selected as the clerk. The commissioners charged Davidson and Nichols with inspecting Lawrence's work and reporting to the board.[39]

The commissioners met again the next day to hear Davidson's and Nichols's report. The two inspectors had found that the brickwork on the "basement story" was "entirely at variance with the terms and the conditions of the contract." They discovered that "whole courses were laid entirely with batts or brick ends," that the brick was "half-burned," and that in many places the mortar was "too poor and weak to adhere to the brick." Davidson and Nichols agreed that Lawrence's foundation and walls were so weak and unsound that they would not support the weight of a large building. On the same day that Davidson and Nichols rendered their report, the commissioners ordered the building contractors, John Robb and Alexander Baird, to pull down Lawrence's construction. In an 1840 report, after Nichols's new state house was completed, the legislators were still harsh in their criticism of Lawrence's efforts. "Not only the rubish [sic] had to be removed from the site of the present building," stated the report, "but a worse rubish [sic] in the character of incompetent workmen and supernumerary contractors had to be set aside." Two years of work under Lawrence had produced nothing of value, and the commissioners intended to begin anew.[40]

Construction, 1836–1841

Nichols's new work on the Old Capitol began during a time of prosperity, but state government was soon beset by financial crisis. One of the most serious economic depressions in the history of the nation occurred from 1837 through 1842. The country experienced rampant bank failures, the drying up of money and credit, and widespread default on loans. Mississippi's freewheeling frontier economy, short of hard money and riding a speculative boom in federal land sales, was especially hard hit. It is remarkable that the construction of three major public buildings—the Governor's Mansion, the penitentiary, and the state house—was continued. It is miraculous that the buildings were completed during the virtual bankruptcy of the state treasury.[41]

The crisis arose from a number of ill-considered fiscal policies and from bitter political squabbling—some national and some the state's own doing. The sale by the federal government at very cheap rates of millions of acres of lands from the Choctaw cession of 1830 and the Chickasaw cession of 1832 created a speculative land bubble. Land speculation became a mania, and the speculators demanded abundant and easy credit to finance the boom. Backcountry legislators from twenty-six new counties that had been created from the recently ceded Indian lands eagerly voted charters to new banks. The banks could print bank notes. These notes could be borrowed to buy land; the land in turn could be used as collateral to borrow more freshly printed bank notes. Little hard money circulated in Mississippi, and the banks lacked adequate reserves of specie to back their notes.

In 1837 the crisis came. Federal land offices had accepted the increasingly inflated bank notes in payment for lands. In July 1836 the United States Treasury had suddenly announced that henceforward the government would require hard money in payment for public lands. This "Specie Circular" pricked the speculative bubble, and land prices began to fall.

An added blow to Mississippi's economy came with the effects of the Distribution Act of 1836. A giant surplus had built up in the United States Treasury from the sale of public lands. Many Mississippi banks depended on federal deposits of these funds for adequate reserves. The Distribution Act required that these federal funds be distributed to the states based on their represen-

An 1823 print shows bricks being hauled and stacked to make temporary kilns to produce brick, a process probably used at the site of the Old Capitol.

tation in the Congress. As a result, federal funds were drained from Mississippi banks. Banks were forced to foreclose loans made in times of easy money; speculators went broke in droves as both money and credit dried up.

In 1838 the state legislature tried to re-establish sound banking by chartering the Union Bank and pledging the state's credit to help capitalize it. The state of Mississippi sold $5,000,000 in bonds and invested the funds in Union Bank stock. In 1840 the Union Bank followed its predecessors into bankruptcy, and the depression persisted into 1842. No doubt the hard times would have lasted even longer had the state legislature not chosen to repudiate the Union Bank bond debt in 1842.

The fiscal crisis was accompanied by unusually bitter political acrimony. The followers of Andrew Jackson, including virtually all of the legislators from the twenty-six new counties of the Choctaw and Chickasaw cessions, were challenged in the mid-1830s by an increasingly vocal group of anti-Jacksonians, who came mostly from the counties along the Mississippi River. These "Whigs"

challenged the growing dominance of the back-woods counties and objected to the freewheeling fiscal policies endorsed by the backcountrymen. Partisan squabbling over representation for the new counties paralyzed the 1835 and 1837 sessions of the legislature.

Throughout this era of fiscal embarrassment and political turmoil, work on the state house progressed, and after the faltering start in 1834 and 1835, the legislators were generally unstinting in their appropriations to buy materials and to pay the contractors and workmen. On one occasion in 1838, however, contractors refused to accept payment in "the very depreciated paper which is tendered them . . . in behalf of the State Treasury," especially the notes of the Mississippi and Alabama Railroad Company "with which . . . the Treasury is filled."[42]

Once the decision had been made to demolish Lawrence's building and to begin afresh, the Board of Commissioners of Public Buildings faced the necessity of ascertaining the status of Lawrence's contracts. Nichols was ordered to measure the bricks that had been delivered by the brick contractor, Edwin Moody, and to determine how much the state owed Moody. The commissioners asked Lawrence to furnish the original proposals submitted by the contractors, his original plan for the state house, and his account books. The contractors were asked to appear before the board to make any claims for money owed to them. Meantime, Nichols and board member George Finucane, of Jackson (Davidson had resigned in March and left the state), were charged with investigating "what work has actually been done on the capitol" and what contractors had performed it.[43]

As Nichols worked on the state house from 1836 to 1841, he also had to plan and direct two other major projects. A house for the governor had been authorized in 1833 along with the state house, but priority went to the latter. The financial chaos of 1837 further delayed the beginning of a house for the governor, and not until 1838 did Nichols draw up plans for that building, now called the mansion. Construction began in 1839, and the house was finished in 1842. The penitentiary, authorized in 1836, also received priority over the mansion. The large castle- like Gothic Revival penitentiary was sited on a low hill north of the Governor's Mansion. Construction of the penitentiary and the capitol went on simultaneously, and Nichols was forced to divide his time between two major projects. By the time he began work on the mansion in 1839, the state house was complete except for interior finishing and decorating work. Luckily for Nichols, the three construction sites were within sight of one another.[44]

The southern frontier was always short of skilled workmen, or "mechanics" as they were called in the Old South. Then, as now, workmen tended to congregate in the cities where the work and the money was. In the hamlets and the small towns, clusters of professionals—mostly physicians and attorneys—congregated to serve the outlying areas. In the countryside, the farmers and planters provided their own skills or did without. So short were "mechanics" even in towns like Natchez and Vicksburg that skilled slaves were highly prized and were often "hired out" by their owners, since

they could produce more income this way than by working in the fields. The shortage attracted untrained and unskilled itinerants who were in search of quick money. The work done by these self-styled craftsmen was often unreliable and inferior. William Nichols must have been familiar with these frontier workmen, for he had worked in the South for more than three decades.

The written record provides little insight into William Nichols's character. Yet from his recorded actions in dealing with contractors who were working on the Mississippi state house, a picture of Nichols emerges—a careful and thorough planner, he was meticulous, precise, demanding in his supervision of contractors, stubborn in his insistence that no corners be cut in fulfilling his plans, and confident in his aesthetic correctness. In short, Nichols was a thorough professional often forced to work with less than professional contractors, suppliers, and workmen—in relationships that were bound to produce conflicts.

On March 31, 1836, the Board of Commissioners of Public Buildings awarded the contract for the stonework and brickwork on the ground story of the state house to John Robb and Alexander Baird. The partners had held the contract under Lawrence, and the two had already estab-

To Brick Layers.

Several Brick Layers can get
immediate employment and liberal wages, to work on the
Capitol of Mississippi, now erecting
in the town of Jackson. None but good
workmen need apply.
  Edwin Moody.

  Mississippian,
  May 15, 1835

lished a division of labor—Robb would supervise construction while Baird ran the quarry. This arrangement would soon destroy their partnership and produce some delay in completing the first story.

Nichols's specifications were clear and precise. Robb and Baird were to furnish all of the stone, mortar, scaffolding, and workmen. Both ends of the ground floor and the front facing Capitol Street were to be constructed of "ashlar," square blocks of stone that had been cut so precisely that they fit together almost without mortar. This stone face was to be backed with brick, the brick and stone to be firmly joined with "headers or through stones." The stone was to be laid in straight courses of twelve inches to the level of the portico floor. Nichols also wrote detailed specifications for the stone-columned entries on the north and south ends of the building, along with directions for the base and arcade under the portico, the steps, fireplaces, and chimneys. For this work Robb and Baird were to be paid $22,366.50, and the work was to be finished by July 4, 1836.[45]

The stone for the Old Capitol was quarried locally. Lawrence had acquired a quarry site southwest of Jackson near Mississippi Springs, a small antebellum resort east of Raymond. A quarry was established there, and the blocks of stone were carried by wagon to Jackson. Unfortunately, the local limestone proved inferior—it was soft and broke easily. Nichols used it nonetheless.[46]

On August 9, 1836, Nichols asked the commissioners to investigate charges against him that were being circulated by two of Lawrence's contractors who had not been continued under Nichols. E.S. Farrish, who had held the carpentry contract, refused to accept a new contract under Nichols. The commissioners then offered the contract to Daly and McKee of St. Tammany Parish, Louisiana. Lawrence's brick supplier, Edwin Moody, also lost his contract with the advent of Nichols.

Nichols advised the board that Farrish and Moody were spreading false charges that he was in secret partnership with carpentry contractors Daly and McKee and also with Robb and Baird, the contractors for stonework and brickwork. The charges no doubt seemed plausible since these contractors had worked with Nichols in other states. Nichols requested the investigation "for the interest of the state and my own reputation." The board, Nichols said, should call the complainants and ask them to explain their charges under oath.[47]

Two weeks later, in an attempt to investigate the complaints, the commissioners called Nichols, Farrish, and Moody. Farrish failed to appear, but Moody came and brought Thomas Emmons, a "witness" who, Moody assured the commissioners, had knowledge of Nichols's secret partnership with Robb. The commissioners questioned Emmons, who promptly denied any knowledge of such a secret partnership. Moody then asked that Andrew Gormandy be called. Gormandy, too, denied knowledge of any wrongdoing by Nichols. When Moody was called, he refused to testify. The commissioners wasted no time in declaring Nichols guiltless and the rumors against him "false and malicious."[48]

On September 5, the same day the commissioners ratified their faith in Nichols, a crisis erupted regarding the stonework and brickwork for the ground floor. Robb and Baird dissolved their partnership, and Baird, who was in charge of quarrying and finishing the stone, refused to do any more work. The commissioners promptly voided the contract. Baird accused his partner Robb of drawing $8,200 while "I have never received the first cent." If Robb could prove that the money was spent on the state house "and bring our accounts together and have a fair settlement," Baird promised, "I will then take up my mallett again and go to work."[49]

Nichols went to the stone quarry near Mississippi Springs to investigate. He found that Baird had been diverting stone quarried for the state house to other purposes. Nichols reported that "the ground around the quarry is covered with headstones and footstones . . . [and] large square tombs." He charged Baird with pilfering the best stone from the state's quarry while sending the inferior stone to be used in the state house. This diversion, Nichols said, would delay the completion of the ground story. The stone- and brickwork should already have been finished so that carpenters could begin "shutting in" the structure before winter. Robb agreed to finish the work as sole contractor. The commissioners accepted.[50]

Finding suitable brick suppliers was a constant problem for Nichols throughout the construction of the Old Capitol. Edwin Moody, the brick contractor under Lawrence, was ordered at the commissioners' first meeting to continue his deliveries at the rate of 5,000 bricks per day until he had supplied 200,000. Not only did Moody refuse to comply, but he began removing brick that he had already delivered to the construction site. When it became obvious that Moody had no intention of fulfilling his contract, the board contracted with James B. Joplin and William S. Orr to supply 100,000 bricks immediately. On May 2, 1836, former governor Hiram Runnels was also awarded a contract to supply 1,500,000 bricks at eight dollars per thousand.[51]

The commissioners apparently foresaw the difficulties in obtaining a steady supply of good brick. Unreliable deliveries and poor quality forced the board to send Nichols on a trip to New Orleans to look at a brickmaking machine; Nichols reported that the machine was impractical. By mid-August the poor performance of Joplin and Orr produced a confrontation. Nichols's complaints about Joplin and Orr illuminate his difficulty in finding reliable, skilled craftsmen in the small backwoods town of Jackson. The brick, he charged, "for want of skill . . . had been badly

The Choragic Monument of Lysicrates in Athens provided the model for the columns and capitals in the Senate chamber.

burned." Some brick, Nichols continued, "had been over burned and warped," while the greatest part he found "less than half burned." Upon Nichols's complaints, "Joplin would get angry and cease to deliver for a day or two, and then without giving notice . . . with a host of waggons [*sic*] pour in his indifferent ware before I was apprised of it." The contractors then agreed to give Nichols notice so that he could inspect each load, but after he rejected some loads, "further notice was not given, but the bricks were brought and laid down without inspection, and this the contractors called a delivery. Bad bricks were thus mixed with good." Nichols told the commissioners that his oath "to protect the interest of the state" made it impossible to certify that Joplin and Orr had fulfilled their contract. The state, he said, had "suffered injury" by their poor performance. "For this infraction to be passed over lightly," he warned, would make it impossible "to exact a faithful compliance with any other contractor." Nonetheless, on the same day that Nichols submitted his very critical report, the commissioners allowed payment in full to Joplin and Orr for the delivery of 96,131 bricks.[52]

Later, after former governor Runnels also proved to be an unsatisfactory brick supplier, the brick contract was awarded to Landy Lindsay, who agreed to supply three million bricks for nine dollars per thousand. Twice Nichols reported to the board that Lindsay was furnishing inferior brick. Nevertheless, the commissioners continued to pay Lindsay on schedule. In reply to Nichols's second complaint, Lindsay argued that his brick-making machine had broken down and he was having to make bricks by hand at greater cost. The commissioners ordered Lindsay to remove 3,000 inferior bricks, but they continued his contract and allowed him an additional dollar per thousand to compensate for increased labor costs. A pattern seemed to be emerging—Nichols attempting to hold contractors to strict account; the commissioners overlooking their shoddy work.[53]

Elements of Greek Revival Architecture

There are several versions of the **anthemion,** a stylized honeysuckle or palmette, in the Old Capitol; this one is in the ceiling of the ground floor corridor.

Multi-lobed and gilded **acanthus leaves** ornament the column capitals in the High Court of Errors and Appeals.

Found in the Old Capitol

The Greek **Ionic Order** is expressed in the massive columns in the house chamber and is repeated in the more massive columns of the portico.

Battered and shouldered door surrounds are found on all major interior doorways on the ground floor and, as illustrated here, on the second floor.

Columns set in antis, round columns placed between square columns or piers, are used at the south entrance.

Acroterions are ornaments placed on the end or center of pediments. Here an anthemion is placed as an acroterion over a second floor doorway.

By July 1837, however, the commissioners despaired of Lindsay's ever being able to fulfill his contract and began negotiating with other sources for brick. By August, Lindsay's brickyard was finally beginning to operate efficiently. He had recruited workers in Cincinnati, and the difficulties with brick suppliers began to recede. In December 1837 the board noted that bricks were being dumped from the wagons into piles and large numbers were being broken. They ordered the wagoneers to stack the bricks neatly by hand "instead of tumbling them out"—a minor irritation compared to earlier problems.[54]

Bricklaying was also a problem. On February 28, 1837, the commissioners accepted Robert McDonald's bid to lay the brick for the second and third stories. In June the commissioners accused McDonald of delaying progress on the building by refusing to hire enough workers, and they ordered him to increase his work force. In December McDonald suddenly died, and his widow attempted for a few weeks to fulfill the contract. In January 1838, Mrs. McDonald asked to be relieved, and the commissioners signed a new contract with John and William Gibbons.[55]

The carpentry contract for "shutting in" the state house went to Robert McKee and David Daly.

No doubt these contractors, who came from the New Orleans area, were acquainted with Nichols from his days in that state. The timing of their appearance in Jackson to seek the contract would indicate that Nichols contacted them on his trip to New Orleans to investigate the brickmaking machine. "Shutting in" the building included laying floor joists and floors, framing the roof, installing tongue-and- groove ceilings, framing windows, staircases, and fireplaces. The work of McKee and Daly must have been satisfactory, for no complaints appear in the records.[56]

A contract with New Orleans artisan Ezra Williams to carve all of the capitals for the columns was approved on March 4, 1837. In his specifications to Williams, Nichols specified that the twelve Corinthian capitals to be used in the senate chamber be copied from the plates of the monument of Lysicrates in Stuart's *Antiquities of Athens*. The capitals for the eight pilasters in the rotunda were to be modeled on the same source. The fourteen capitals in the house chamber, he ordered modeled on those of the Erechtheus and those in the high court of errors and appeals on those of the Temple of the Winds. The capitals for the chancery courtroom should resemble, he said, those of the Roman Pantheon.[57]

Hand-carved fragment of a wooden ornament removed from the Old Capitol dome during the 1959 restoration.

Many of the workmen, especially skilled craftsmen, had to be recruited from outside Mississippi. Nichols enticed some workmen and contractors like McKee and Daley and Robert McDonald, the bricklaying contractor, to come up from New Orleans. Ezra Williams was also from New Orleans, but he apparently did the carvings in his workshop there and shipped them to Jack-

son. At least one agent journeyed upriver to Cincinnati in search of skilled workers. Brick contractor Landy Lindsay's partner, Thomas Harris, was from that city, and he made a trip there in the summer of 1837 to hire workmen for their brickyard. In September 1837 the commissioners agreed to pay for advertising that had appeared in the Cincinnati *Mirror*. These efforts attracted,

"Our State House"

A day or two since, at our request, Capt. Nichols, state architect, politely conducted us through the interior of the new state-house, and explained the manner in which it is to be arranged. The more we see of the building, the more we are pleased. The interior will rival in splendor and utility any state-house in the United States, whilst the exterior presents a beautiful outline of architectural symmetry which reflects the highest honor upon its projectors, as well as upon the people of the state who through their representatives, made such munificent appropriations for its erection. We have heard it said that the edifice is too large and too costly for the state. Not at all. Let it be remembered by such cavillers that this is not an edifice designated for a day. It is to stand for a great length of time. Perhaps in the lapse of time, long after we shall have departed from this world, those who occupy our stations in society, may point to the moss covered walls of this same building, and venerate it for its antiquity. Ours is a rich state, and she should have a house for her Legislature built upon a plan corresponding with that wealth. Nor is praise alone due the architect, the different contractors and the workmen have done well. They have labored day and night, with cheerfulness to get the house ready for the Legislature next January; and all seem determined that it shall be ready. We allude to this subject frequently, we do so, because we feel really gratified and pleased.

—*Southern Sun,* Jackson, Miss.
December 15, 1838

among others, a twenty-five-year-old Cincinnati stonecutter named Cornelius Skates to Jackson. He stayed and became a stone contractor on both the state house and the penitentiary.[58]

The names of the bricklayers, plasterers, water haulers, wagoneers, carpenters, painters, roofers, and laborers are lost. That some of them were slaves rented by contractors is proved by numerous payments recorded by the commissioners of public buildings and by the common practice among slaveowners of renting out their slaves.[59]

Considering the many delays and frustrations, the difficulties in finding contractors and workmen, and the fiscal problems that afflicted the state, progress on the state house went forward with relative speed. In the first year of work under Nichols, from mid-1836 to mid-1837, the foundation was laid and the ground floor constructed. During the second year, from mid-1837 to mid-1838, the two upper stories were added. Martin H. Devereaux of New Orleans began laying on the copper roof in April 1838. Thus, two years after beginning, Nichols had succeeded in closing in the building. The major task remaining was to finish the interior. Carpenters were busily at work on that by the summer of 1838.

Despite the progress, the legislators had come to Jackson in 1838 frustrated and critical because the state house was not yet ready to receive them. They aimed their ire at the Board of Commissioners of Public Buildings, who, the legislators believed, had been too lax and overly indulgent with the oftentimes lackadaisical performance of contractors. The legislators abolished the board and substituted ex-governor Charles Lynch as a single commissioner of public buildings. He was given all the powers that the board had previously held, but strong language was put into the act to ensure that the new commissioner would hold contractors to strict account.[60]

Nichols received a vote of confidence in the new legislation. Heretofore, he had been obliged to look to the commissioners to enforce his supervision of contractors. The lawmakers now gave Nichols the power to "superintend constantly" the construction of public buildings and to "give . . . directions to the mechanics." The legislators appropriated an additional $120,000 to complete the state house.[61]

By early February 1838 Lynch's and Nichols's attentions were increasingly occupied by the penitentiary. Many of the contractors had completed their work on the state house and received contracts on the penitentiary. Nichols, who had spent almost all of his time during 1836 and 1837 on the capitol, could afford now to devote some time to the other building.

The contracts and payments during the latter half of 1838 reveal the progress on the state house. In July, Charles Lynch's son, William H. Lynch, was given a $400 advance to travel to Philadelphia and New York to buy furniture. The staircases were also finished by July, and by August Martin Devereaux had covered the roof with copper. In September laths were delivered, and workers began plastering the interior. By December Ezra Williams had finished his capitals for the interior columns; they had been shipped to Vicksburg by steamboat, hauled by wagon to Jackson, and installed.

In mid-December 1838 Nichols conducted A.R. Johnston, the editor of the *Southern Sun*, on a tour of the state house. The newsman was pleased. The interior, he said, "will rival in splendor and utility any state house in the United States," and the exterior presented "a beautiful outline of architectural symmetry." Critics of the building's size and cost, he wrote, should remember that the building was not only for the living, but for posterity. Future generations, he predicted, would "point to the moss covered walls of this same building, and venerate it for its antiquity." Mississippi, he reminded his readers, was "a rich state, and the state house should reflect that wealth."[62]

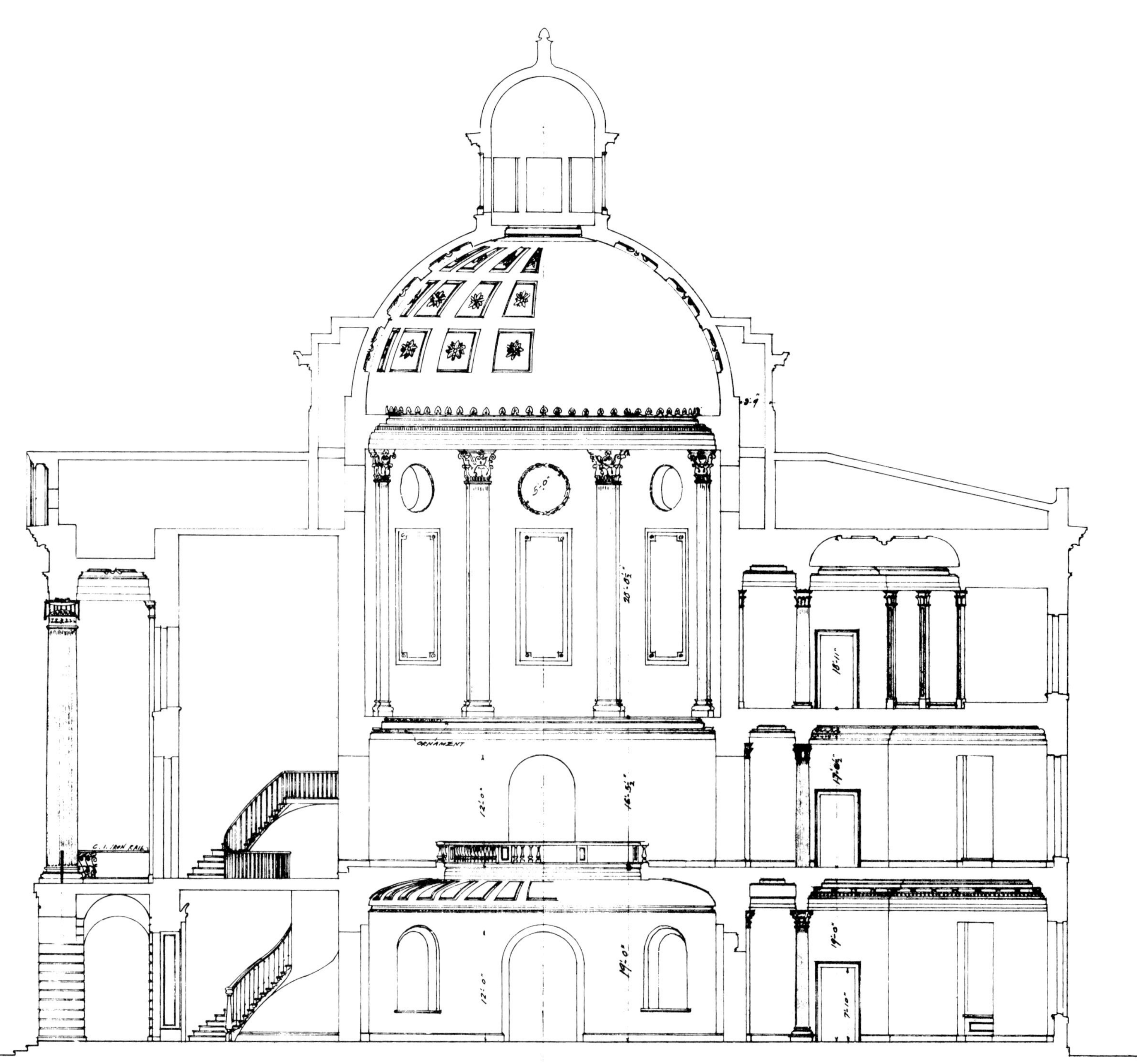

A cross-section of the Old Capitol, drawn by E. L. Malvaney in 1916, shows the portico on the left, the vestibule with its spiral stairs, the rotunda and its dome and on the right, from the top, the original State Library, the High Court of Errors and Appeals and the Chancery Court. Except for the railing on the portico and the arches in the loggia below it, this view is true to Nichols's design.

The legislators gathered in the new state house for their 1839 session on January 7. They met amidst workmen who were busily laying carpet, hanging chandeliers, building cabinets, and plastering. The furniture, which had been ordered from the North, was shipped by steamboat to Vicksburg and by rail from Vicksburg to Amsterdam on the Big Black. There the rails ended, and the furniture was hauled to Jackson by wagon. One load of chairs brought a wagoneer forty-five dollars. As late as October 1839 some plastering continued. Except for small details, work was finished by February 1840. A chandelier arrived in June 1840, and the final expenditure for building the state house was made on October 13, 1840, to Skates and Rogers for flagging the rotunda. Nichols had already turned his full attention to the

Senate desk and chair ordered by Nichols for the Alabama capitol. The design is based on those used in the U.S. Senate and is believed to be the same style ordered for the Old Capitol.

Governor's Mansion, and Commissioner Charles Lynch was confronting fiscal problems.

In 1839 Lynch was forced to give a personal note of $25,000 to get money to finish the Old Capitol. Because of the state's continuing fiscal crisis, Mississippi notes could be cashed only "at a ruinous discount." At least one contractor, Martin Devereaux, probably suffered "considerable loss from the non- payment of the check he received in payment of his work."[63]

The final cost of construction for the Old Capitol is impossible to determine; total expenditures may be calculated in a number of ways. However the costs are figured, they far exceeded the original estimates in 1833. Appropriations for the state house from 1833 to 1840 totaled $342,000; the amount that came from the sale of Jackson town lots cannot be found. No doubt the major portion of costs were paid from general appropriations. The account books of the commissioners from 1836 through 1841 show expenditures of $363,000. In addition, from 1833 to 1835, Lawrence had spent about $25,000. Some expenditures continued into 1844, but it is unclear whether these should be attributed to construction or to repair. Likewise, after 1841 some dissatisfied contractors brought suits against the state. Whether these suits should be included in the costs for the state house is uncertain. Unrefined calculations point to a cost of about $400,000 for the Old Capitol—a huge sum of money for that time.[64]

However high the cost was, the legislators had finally got what they had set out to build in 1833, and their 1840 report praised the building mightily: "noble . . . in its outline, correct in its proportions, beautiful in its finish . . . and in ornament simple and elegant." Nichols, too, received high praise. The state architect "had studied his profession with attention and success," said the legislators. They praised his "selections from ancient models" and his taste in applying them.

The state's first penitentiary was constructed in Jackson under Nichols's supervision.

"This edifice," the lawmakers concluded, was "destined to become a record of the good taste and judgment of the times and a monument to the munificence of the Legislature."[65]

NOTES

[1] Message, Governor Scott to the General Assembly, January 8, 1833, RG 27, Governors Correspondence, Vol. 16, MDAH.

[2] *Laws of Mississippi*, 1833, 468–473.

[3] *Ibid.*, 470.

[4] Letter, Scott to Morrison, May 20, 1833, RG 27, Governors Correspondence, vol. 16; McCain, *Story of Jackson*, 35.

[5] Letter Lynch to Morrison, June 22, 1833, RG 27, Governors Correspondence, vol. 18; McCain, *Story of Jackson*, 35.

[6] Letter, Governor Carroll to Governor Scott, April 1, 1833; letter, Lawrence to Lynch, July 10, 1833, RG 27, Governors Correspondence, vol. 18, MDAH.

[7] Letter, Roland to Hiram Runnels, August 4, 1833, RG 27, Governors Correspondence, Vol. 19, MDAH. Runnels had been elected to the governorship in May 1833, but he did not take office until November. Thus, both he and Lynch received correspondence concerning the position of state architect.

[8] Letters, Roland to Runnels, September 9, 1833; Breathitt to Lynch, September 11, 1833; Carroll to Lynch, September 13, 1833; Krats, Anderson, and Bell to Lynch, September 14, 1833; Tannehill to Lynch, September 14, 1833; Vick to Lynch, September 16, 1833; Roland to Lynch, October 14, 1833; all in RG 27, Governors Correspondence, vol. 18, MDAH.

[9] Letter, Nichols to Lynch, October 12, 1833, Governors Correspondence, vol. 18.

[10] Letter, Governor Carroll to Governor Lynch, September 13, 1833, RG 27, Governors Correspondence, vol. 18, MDAH; *Laws of Mississippi*, 1833, 521.

[11] *Ibid.*, 520. The practice of discounting notes was widespread in the early nineteenth century. In return for accepting the risk of collecting the debt, banks would advance cash on such notes at a discount from face value.

[12] *Mississippian*, November 21, 1834.

[13] *House Journal*, 1835, 41.

[14] *Mississippian*, November 28, 1834.

[15] Miles, *Jacksonian Democracy*, 100–101.

[16] *Mississippian*, 1835 Auditor's Report, January 18, 1836.

[17] David G. Sansing and Carroll Waller, *A History of the Mississippi Governor's Mansion* (Jackson: University Press of Mississippi, 1977), 8; *Mississippian*, January 10, 1834, February 19, 1836.

[18] McCain, *Story of Jackson*, 35; Sansing and Waller, *Governor's Mansion*, 8–9.

[19] C. Ford Petross and Robert O. Mellown, *William Nichols, Architect* (Tuscaloosa: The University of Alabama Art Gallery, 1979), 31.

[20] *Ibid.*, 3,6.

[21] *Ibid.*, 2.

[22] *Ibid.*, 10.

[23] *Ibid.*, 10.

[24] *Ibid.*, 11–14.

[25] *Ibid.*, 15–18.

[26] *Ibid.*, 18, 40. The Alabama capitol at Tuscaloosa was abandoned by state government in 1847 when the seat of

William Nichols after the Old Capitol

William Nichols, 62 years old in 1842, suddenly faced unemployment. He had just finished the Governor's Mansion *(right)* and the state penitentiary when the 1842 legislature abolished his job. For a few years he owned and operated a hotel in west Jackson near the railroad depot, and he also undertook private commissions as an architect. Certainly he remained in Jackson, for he designed and built the First Presbyterian Church on North State Street between 1843 and 1846.

In 1845 Nichols again found public employment. The Board of Trustees of the newly chartered University of Mississippi hired him to design the university campus and buildings. Nichols, who earlier had planned the University of Alabama, was experienced in campus design. From 1846 to 1848, Nichols designed and built the first buildings at the University of Mississippi. The Lyceum *(below)* he built still stands at the head of his original circular campus.

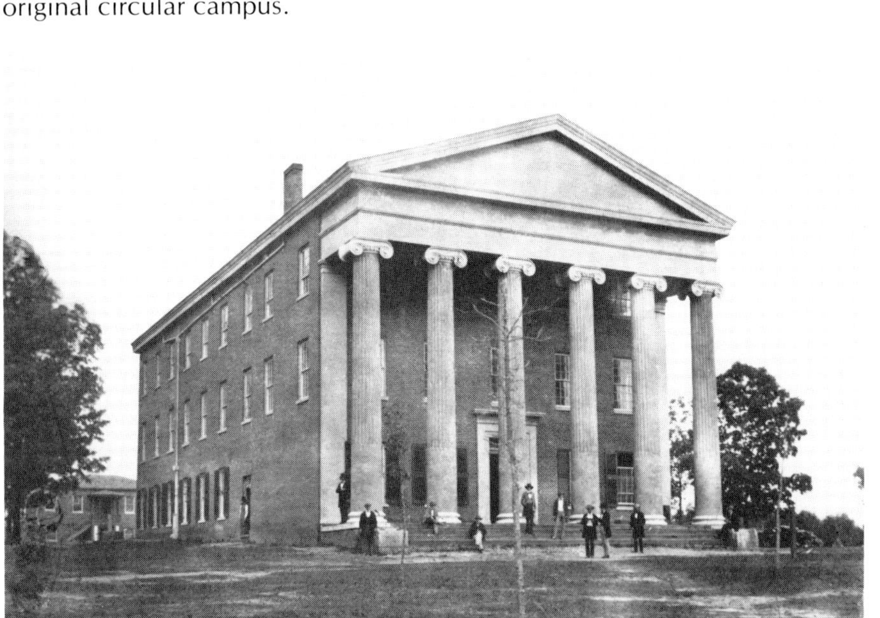

After completing his work at the university, Nichols designed and built a courthouse in Yazoo City. Yazoo County was by 1850 a rapidly growing area that threatened Jackson's hold on the state capital. Nichols's Yazoo courthouse did not survive the Civil War, but contemporary descriptions pictured it as one of Nichols's most beautiful buildings—sixty feet square with parthenon-like porticos on each side.

Nichols next went to Lexington in Holmes County to undertake two commissions. His design for the Lexington Female Academy resembled the Lyceum at the University. He also designed "Terry-Stone," a house for Colonel J. M. Dyer that was an early "Italianate" building in Mississippi.

Nichols was well into his old age when he went to Holmes County. He died at Lexington and was buried there in Odd Fellows Cemetery. The tombstone identifies him simply as

William Nichols, Archt.
A Native of Bath England
Died
Dec. 12, 1853
Aged 73 Years

government was moved to Montgomery. The building was destroyed by fire in 1923.

[27] *Ibid.*, 22–23, 26; letter, Nichols to Lynch, October 12, 1833, RG 27, Governors Correspondence, vol. 18, MDAH.

[28] Peatross and Mellown, *William Nichols*, 26.

[29] *Ibid.*

[30] *Senate Journal*, 1836, 217.

[31] *Ibid.*, 214–215.

[32] A standard work on this subject is Talbot Hamlin's *Greek Revival Architecture in America* (New York: Oxford University Press, 1944).

[33] Proceedings, March 29, 1837.

[34] Petross and Mellown, *William Nichols*, 3, 42; Proceedings, October 28, 1838.

[35] *Senate Journal*, 1836, 216, 217–18.

[36] *Laws of Mississippi*, 1836.

[37] *Ibid.*

[38] Letter, Lynch to Nichols, March 22, 1836, RG 27, Governors Correspondence, vol. 22, MDAH.

[39] Proceedings of the Board of Commissioners of Public Buildings of the State of Mississippi, 1836–1841, March 3, 1836, RG 43, vol. 14, Building Commission, MDAH.

[40] *Ibid.*, March 4, 1836; Report from the Committee on Publick Buildings, 1840, RG 43, vol. 14, Building Commission, MDAH.

[41] For full treatments of the era of "Flush Times" and the ensuing depression, see Edwin A. Miles, *Jacksonian Democracy in Mississippi* (Chapel Hill: University of North Carolina Press, 1960) and John E. Gonzales, "Flush Times, Depression, War, and Compromise," in Richard A. McLemore (ed.), *A History of Mississippi* (Hattiesburg: University and College Press of Mississippi, 1973).

[42] Jackson *Mississippian*, September 7, 1838.

[43] Proceedings, March 15, 1836.

[44] The penitentiary was on the site of the "New Capitol." Sansing and Waller, *Governor's Mansion*, 9; Petross and Mellown, *William Nichols*, 45.

[45] Proceedings, March 30, 1836.

[46] David N. Young, "A History of Public Buildings in Jackson, Mississippi, 1822–1860" (M. A. Thesis, Mississippi College, 1954), 20; Benjamin L. C. Wailes, *Report on the Agriculture and Geography of Mississippi* (E. Barksdale, State Printer, 1854), 216, 258.

[47] Proceedings, August 9, 1836.

[48] *Ibid.*, August 25, September 5, 1836.

[49] *Ibid.*, September 5, 1836.

[50] *Ibid.*, September 5, 26, 1836. The location of the quarry was mentioned in the letter books of nineteenth-century geologist B. L. C. Wailes. See article by Gordon Cotton in the Vicksburg *Evening Post*, April 27, 1980.

[51] Proceedings, March 17, May 2, 1836.

[52] *Ibid.*, August 22, 1836.

[53] *Ibid.*, January 3, 5, May 8, June 3, July 5, 1837.

[54] *Ibid.*, September 25, December 18, 1837.

[55] *Ibid.*, February 28, June 12, 1837, January 9, 15, 1838. Later, William Gibbons became an architect. Among his buildings were the Jackson City Hall and the Mississippi Lunatic Asylum on the site now occupied by the University Medical Center.

[56] *Ibid.*, June 22, 1836.

[57] *Ibid.*, March 4, 1837.

[58] *Ibid.*, September 11, 25, 1837, December 14, 1838, July 29, 1839.

[59] *Ibid.*, June 3, 1837, December 7, 1838.

[60] *Laws of Mississippi*, 1838, 137.

[61] *Ibid.*, 141–142.

[62] Jackson, Mississippi, *Southern Sun*, December 15, 1838.

[63] *House Journal*, 1840, 146.

[64] McCain, *Story of Jackson*, 41–42; William D. McCain, "The Cost of Building Mississippi's Second State House," Old Capitol Subject File, MDAH.

[65] Report from the Committee on Publick Buildings, 1840.

ILLUSTRATION NOTES

p. 18   Alexander Findlay, cartographer, 1831. Young and Dellecker, engravers. MDAH.

p. 18   Jeremiah Greenleaf, cartographer, 1840. MDAH.

p. 19   Oil, ca. 1832. Artist unknown. Hall of Governors, MDAH.

p. 20   Official archives, Office of the Governor, MDAH.

p. 23   MSHM collections. Engraved on reverse: "Harmony Lodge No. 1 To John A. Quitman as a mark of Esteem, Natchez, 1826."

p. 23   Engraving. Charles Scott, *The Analogy of Ancient Craft Masonry to Natural and Revealed Religion* (Philadelphia, Grigg, Elliot and Co., 1849).

p. 24   Oil by Jacob Marling, 1820 (detail). North Carolina Division of Archives and History.

p. 25   Photograph. University of Alabama Library.

p. 27   Oil. Artist unknown. Hall of Governors, MDAH.

p. 29   Line drawing. Historic New Orleans Collection.

p. 30   Photograph. MSHM.

p. 34   Line drawing by W. H. Pyne. Charles Peterson, *Building Early America* (Philadelphia, 1976).

p. 37   Line drawings. *Cyclopedia of Architecture, Carpentry and Building* (Chicago: American Technical Society, 1908), 10 vols. Figure 75; Plate XLVIII.

p. 37   Photographs. MSHM.

p. 38, 39   Photographs. MSHM.

p. 40   MSHM collections.

p. 41   Photograph. MDAH.

p. 43   Measured drawing, 1916, by H. N. Austin and H. J. Kramer, draftsmen. E. L. Malvaney, Architect. Official Records, MDAH.

p. 44   Photograph by Robert Mellown. University of Alabama.

p. 45   Photograph by A. D. Galloway. Collection of Charles Galloway, Jr.

p. 46   Photographs. MDAH.

p. 46   Photograph (Lyceum). John Davis Williams Library, University of Mississippi.

A Public Forum
1839–1865

Jackson and Mississippi flourished during the two decades before the Civil War, and the state capitol was the centerpiece and the symbol of the town's and the state's progress. Despite some structural problems (most caused by a chronically leaky roof) and some degradation in its appearance, Nichols's building witnessed during its first quarter century a number of historic events. The building was inaugurated by the passage of a progressive law in 1839 granting property rights to married women and a visit in 1840 by Andrew Jackson, the town's aging political father. A decade later the building witnessed the beginnings of the debate over secession, a controversy which raged for ten years before destroying the Union and bringing on a four-year war that brought conquering soldiers into the halls of the Old Capitol. During the war years the capitol deteriorated considerably, and in 1865 the increasingly shabby building became the scene of Mississippi's final defeat and occupation—the displacement of the state government that it had been built to house.

The Building, 1839–1860

The legislature first convened in the new building on Monday, January 7, 1839. In the evening, after the lawmakers adjourned for the day, the building was "brilliantly illuminated." One onlooker observed that the members must have felt "overjoyed at their escape from the old and delapidated building" that had housed them since 1822. State officers apparently delayed moving in until late 1839 or early 1840; instead, they remained in their offices a block down Capitol Street near the old state house.[1]

As the legislators held their first meetings in the new state house, they determined that the little building a block away down Capitol Street had served its purpose. In February 1839 they allowed Pearl Lodge Number 23, Ancient York Masons, to use the upper floor as a lodge. The next year the commissioner of public buildings spent forty-seven dollars on repairs to the old building.[2]

The 1840 legislature also ordered the commissioner to consult with the state architect about completing repairs on the old state house and on the nearby state offices "to the end that the same may be placed in a suitable situation to rent out to the best advantage." One room in the old office of the secretary of state was reserved as an office for William Nichols. The old state house housed the Jackson *Mississippian* until 1863. The fate of the old building is uncertain.[3]

Simultaneously, the legislators ordered that the grounds around the new building be cleaned. They ordered the commissioner to "remove all the houses and cabbins [*sic*] . . . not necessary for the use of the state."[4]

In 1840 the legislators found some rooms in the new building occupied by people who were not "officers of government." Evidently, some citizens had taken up residence there. The lawmakers ordered the commissioner of public buildings to remove all non-government officials from "all the apartments within the Capitol." Apparently too, some state officers had taken up residence in their

Capitol Street, looking east toward the Old Capitol from the vicinity of Farish and Roach Streets.

offices, for the legislators also forbade occupying "any room in the capitol at night or as a bedroom." In 1846 the lawmakers relented somewhat and allowed the state treasurer and the auditor "to lodge of sleep in their respective offices."[5]

In 1842 the legislature allocated space in the building. Generally, the lawmakers reserved the ground floor for the major officers of state government—governor, secretary of state, attorney general, treasurer, auditor, and adjutant general. The bay behind the rotunda and the office adjacent to it on the north were reserved for the chancery court and the chancellor. The clerks of chancery and of the High Court of Errors and Appeals were also housed on the ground floor.[6]

With the exception of the bay behind the rotunda, which was reserved for the chamber of the High Court of Errors and Appeals, the second floor was exclusively reserved for the legislature. The wing on the south housed the senate chamber, senate committee rooms, and the office of the senate clerk. In the northern wing was the house

chamber, house committee rooms, and offices for the house clerks.[7]

On the third floor were the galleries over the house and senate chambers, more committee rooms, the state agricultural society, and high court offices. The state library occupied the bay behind the rotunda on the third floor.[8]

Only a single realignment of offices occurred during the next twenty years. In 1856 the state chancery court was abolished by constitutional amendment, thus freeing the ground floor bay and the chancellor's office for other uses. The legislature in 1858 ordered the state library to occupy the ground floor ellipse and the two adjacent offices. The office on the south of the ellipse was assigned to the recently chartered Mississippi Historical Society. The old state library on the third floor was given over to storage for surplus stationery, journals, laws, and other publications.[9]

Upon completion of the new state house and the imminent completion of the Governor's Mansion and the penitentiary, the legislators in 1841 abolished the position of commissioner of public buildings and transferred those duties to the state treasurer. The legislators created an entirely new office— keeper of the capitol—to oversee and administer the new state house. The keeper was to have charge of all keys, furniture, stationery, and other state property in the capitol. He was to open the building promptly at 8 a.m. and close it at 10 p.m. He was assigned an office on the ground floor adjacent to the front door, and, alone among state officers, he was allowed to live in his office. An 1844 salary reduction act combined the duties of librarian and keeper of the capitol.[10]

In 1841 the same bill that abolished the office of commissioner of public buildings and established the position of keeper of the capitol cut in half William Nichols's salary as state architect. The next year the office was abolished. After designing and building the Old Capitol, the Governor's Mansion, and the penitentiary, William Nichols was without a job. Over the next eleven years before his death in 1853, Nichols designed churches, courthouses, and private houses. He also designed the first buildings for the University of Mississippi, among them the famous Lyceum.

The metal-covered roof and dome of the new state house leaked almost from the first. Problems began to appear only three years after completion of the building. The zinc-covered roof on the Governor's Mansion leaked so badly that the water threatened to ruin the interior. In 1844, after reports by architects William Gibbons and William Nichols, the legislature appropriated $2,240 to repair the mansion and $435 to repair the capitol. Nichols was hired to supervise the work. Compared to the repairs at the mansion, work on the capitol was minor; the cupola and the copper covering on the dome required some mending. In addition, both buildings were fitted with "Franklin rods" to protect the structures during electrical storms.[11]

In 1850, during Governor John A. Quitman's administration, the woodwork on the building received new paint. Windows were cleaned, broken glass replaced, and loose panes reputtied. All exposed woodwork received "two good coats of pure white lead in well boiled oil." The outer surfaces of all doors, which were natural grained, received two coats of oil and varnish. For this work painter James Wilson received $223.75.[12]

In the 1850s modern conveniences began to be added to the building. During the late eighteenth century in France and England, scientists had discovered that flammable gas could be pro-

The State Library quickly outgrew the one room it was allotted in 1842 and was given two additional rooms on the ground floor. While the emphasis of the collection was legal works such as these, it also contained material on travel, medicine, biography, and church history.

duced by heating coal or wood in tightly covered furnaces. By the early nineteenth century, central gas plants in London were producing gas commercially and piping it to light street lamps and public buildings. A gas plant was built in Jackson in 1857 at the corner of Congress and Pearl. In 1860, after reorganization, the plant became the "Jackson Gas Light Company." The city of Jackson contracted with the company to install street lamps on downtown streets and pipe gas to them. For an additional ten dollars per month, the company agreed to furnish a lamplighter.[13]

The legislators wasted no time in bringing the marvel of gas lighting to the state house. In 1857, the same year that the gas plant opened, the lawmakers appropriated $3,500 "for placing gas fixtures in the Capitol and Executive Mansion."[14]

Payment vouchers, however, indicate that the installation was not completed until 1860. On August 1 of that year, the treasurer paid the Jackson Gas Light Company $668.85. Apparently, pipes and fixtures had been installed earlier in the house and senate chambers and in the governor's and treasurer's offices. The workmen drew water from the gas pipes and repaired leaks in the house chamber. Then they ran pipe and installed chandeliers and wall fixtures in all the other offices and committee rooms. Large four- and five-light chandeliers were hung in the offices of the auditor, secretary of state, and adjutant general and in the large committee rooms, the library, and the high court chamber. These were supplemented by one- and two-light wall brackets. Smaller, three-light chandeliers were hung in the small committee rooms.[15]

Although the exact date cannot be found, sometime before the Civil War the capitol was fitted with a "water closet." In 1862 the legislators paid thirty dollars "for hire of boy to attend to water closet during last session of legislature."[16]

Married Women's Property Rights

The 1839 legislators, the first to convene in the new state house, were reform-minded. They passed the "Gallon Law" to curtail drinking in saloons; the law forbade the sale of liquor in quantities of less than a gallon. They eliminated from the penal code corporal punishments such as flogging and branding. They eliminated imprisonment for debt and tried to curtail gambling and dueling.

The 1839 legislature also became the first lawmaking body in the United States to confer property rights upon married women. Heretofore, English common law held that after marriage a woman's property became her husband's. A married woman could own no property in her own right, and even property that had been willed to her or that she had earned before her marriage became her husband's. Consequently, her property could be seized and sold to pay her husband's debts.[17]

The issue was first raised in the state by a landmark High Court of Errors and Appeals decision in 1837. Betsy Love and John Allen, members of the Chickasaw tribe, were married "under the tribal customs of the Chickasaws." According to those customs, the husband acquired no right to the property possessed by his wife at the time of the marriage. In 1829 the state of Mississippi extended the jurisdiction and laws of Mississippi over all Indians, but the law expressly recognized the validity of marriages "entered into by virtue of any custom or usage of the Indians as if the same had been solemnized by the laws of this state."[18]

Betsy Love owned a slave, Toney, at the time of her marriage to John Allen. Later, Allen defaulted on a debt to John Fisher, and Fisher sought to seize the slave as the property of John Allen. The case came before the High Court on Fisher's ap-

Tilghman Tucker

peal of an adverse judgment in the circuit court of Monroe County. The High Court had to decide if "under the laws of this state, Allen, by his marriage with Betsy Love, acquired such interest in her property, as to subject it to the claims of his creditors."[19]

In their opinions, Judges Cotesworth P. Smith and William L. Sharkey both recognized that Chickasaw customs conferred on the husband no rights to the property that his wife brought to the marriage. Furthermore, they concluded, "The slave Toney, who had been levied upon to satisfy Fisher's claim against Allen, was proved to be the separate property of Betsy Love . . . and from what has been stated of the rights which arise to the husband under the laws and customs of the Chickasaws, it is obvious that no title to this slave vested in Allen, which could subject him to the claims of Allen's creditors."[20]

The High Court opinion was rendered in 1837. Two years later the Mississippi legislature took up the issue. As with most reform issues, the motives of the individual legislators were murky and mixed. A genuine wish to reform an unjust practice combined with expediency, and perhaps even personal advantage, to make possible the passage of "An Act for the Protection and Preservation of the Rights and Property of Married Women." One powerful legislator, it was alleged, wished to marry a wealthy widow, but he was heavily in debt and wanted to protect her property from his creditors. Senator Thomas Hadley of Jackson, who introduced the bill, was rumored to be in financial difficulty and may have wished to protect his wife's property from his creditors. Another story attributes passage of the act to the influence of Hadley's wife, who operated a boarding house near the capitol. Many legislators took their meals with Mrs. Hadley, and, the story goes, she put any lawmakers who opposed the bill on short rations.[21]

But, in fact, most legislators may have supported the passage of the married women's property act for prosaic political motives. The economic depression that had begun in 1837 had worsened by 1839 to become a full-blown economic disaster. Debt default was rampant among men who had only recently held paper fortunes built on land speculation and the free-money policies of most banks. Protecting the property of married women may have been good reform, but it was also a good means of debt relief and, therefore, good politics. Creditors saw immediately the threat posed by the act. During the debate in the legislature, one senator predicted that within "six months all the married women will have all the

Chief Greenwood Leflore Addresses the Senate

He [Greenwood Leflore] came rapidly into prominence as a statesman and was recognized as a leader in the political life of the state. He was elected to the lower house of the legislature twice in 1831, and again in 1835, then to the upper house in 1842.

While he was in the Senate some of his young colleagues often interspersed their speeches with Latin phrases. So many of them were doing this that it had become irksome to sit through these discourses. At last one made his whole speech in Latin, a thing never done before. Greenwood Leflore, being the next speaker, arose slowly, and deliberately looking around him began to talk in his native tongue. The Assembly thought this was a good joke on the Latin scholars. After Colonel Leflore had talked a while they thought he would sit down, or go on with his speech in English, but much to their surprise he continued in Choctaw. They tried to silence him, but he went on and on, until he had spoken for an hour. When he thought he had taught a sufficient lesson to these learned men he concluded his speech. Before resuming his seat he said, "My friends, which speech was better understood, the gentleman's which was in Latin, or my speech, which was given in Choctaw?" This ended the elaborate discourses in dead languages.

—Florence Rebecca Ray
Chieftain Greenwood Leflore and the Choctaw Indians of the Mississippi Valley

property and it will thus be exempt from their husband's creditors." On the other hand, debtors certainly recognized that the act could help save at least some of their holdings from the auctioneer's hammer.[22]

The bill passed the senate by a vote of nineteen to nine. A few days later the bill passed the house. The act explicitly allowed married women to own real and personal property in their own names. The concerns of creditors, who feared that husbands could escape their debts merely by signing over their property to their wives, were satisfied by a special provision excluding from the act property that came to the wife from her husband after marriage.[23]

Andrew Jackson's Visit

In 1840 former president Andrew Jackson was seventy-three years old. He lived with his family and slaves at the Hermitage near Nashville, where he spent his days minding the plantation and offering advice to his chosen successor, President Martin Van Buren. Revered by his constituents as the greatest man of the age, Jackson was wracked by ailments, both physical and financial, which threatened constantly to overwhelm him. He was destined to live another six years, but in 1840 his days seemed short.

Despite his many problems, late in 1839 General Jackson accepted an invitation from the city of New Orleans to attend ceremonies commemorating the twenty-fifth anniversary of his victory over the British at the Battle of New Orleans. Many suspected that it might be his last journey, and General Jackson's progress to and from New Orleans was to become a triumphal tour.

When it became known that Jackson would travel down the Mississippi River to New Orleans, a movement arose among Jacksonians to invite the former president to visit his namesake city. On November 26, 1839, a committee of citizens issued him an invitation to "visit the City of Jackson as the guest of the State of Mississippi." Jackson accepted. In addition to his sentimental ties to the state and his appreciation for the staunch support that Mississippians had always given him, Jackson had a pressing personal motive for wanting to visit the city. His son, Andrew, Jr., had recently bought a Coahoma County plantation near Sherard from former Mississippi governor Hiram Runnels, and Jackson wanted to convince Runnels to extend the terms of payment for his financially beleaguered son.[24]

Jackson's acceptance excited the city; the visit would be the greatest event in the history of the young town. When the legislators convened in early January 1840, they formed a joint committee

This portrait of Andrew Jackson was executed in New Orleans a few weeks before the elder statesman's visit to the Old Capitol in the city named for him. The Old Capitol is the only building left of the Jackson that Andrew Jackson saw.

to organize their part in the grand occasion and to cooperate with the committee of Jackson citizens. State architect William Nichols, who was supervising the plastering of the new state house, struggled to decorate the unfinished building with greenery for the grand event. The editor of the *Mississippian* called upon "the ladies of Jackson" to "lend the architect a helping hand."[25]

The state house was to be "illuminated" for the occasion and decorated with evergreen wreaths. A band and various militia companies would furnish music and pomp. The legislature appropriated $600 to charter stagecoaches to transport Jackson and the other dignitaries into town, and they paid $329.75 to the Eagle Hotel for the visitors' room and board.

General Jackson was scheduled to arrive on January 17, and on the night of January 8 the joint legislative committee met in the senate chamber with the citizens committee to plan the arrangements. General Jackson would be conducted from Vicksburg by both committees. Militia companies would meet the procession on the western outskirts of Jackson and lead the general to the steps of the capitol. There, Governor A.G. McNutt

A Suggestion

We understand that Captain Nichols, the State architect, is arranging suitable apartments in the State capitol, for the reception of the illustrious Jackson, in January instant. This is as it should be— the house of the people should be the home of their guest. Will not the ladies of Jackson, the fair, for whom the soldier and patriot toiled, lend the architect a helping hand in decorating the apartments?— we know he will most thankfully receive their assistance.

The Mississippian
Jan. 3, 1840

would meet Jackson and escort him to the Eagle Hotel directly across Amite Street from the capitol. The next day a procession would accompany Jackson from the hotel to the capitol. In true Jacksonian fashion, the procession would be led by the legislative committee. Fifth in line, just behind the band, would come Governor McNutt and his staff. Jackson would be met at the door of the state house by Speaker of the House Jesse Speight.[27]

As the people of the city busily planned their grand reception, General Jackson proceeded downriver. He stopped in Memphis to conduct some personal business, and he paused forty- five miles below Helena to inspect his son's Coahoma County plantation. A delegation of Vicksburg dignitaries and a company of militia met him there to conduct him downriver. Jackson arrived in Vicksburg about three o'clock in the afternoon on January 5. The New Orleans celebration was scheduled for January 8. Time was so short that Jackson remained aboard his steamboat *Clarksville* to receive the city's welcome. About seven that evening his boat pulled away from the wharf and headed for New Orleans.[28]

Jackson's participation in the New Orleans festivities so exhausted the old general that he was unable to visit Chalmette, the site of his great victory a quarter-century before. After resting briefly, Jackson reboarded his steamboat and started back upriver to keep his appointment with the people of Mississippi. He and his party made an overnight stay at Natchez before proceeding on to Vicksburg.[29]

Jackson's steamboat pulled into the wharf at Vicksburg on Thursday evening, January 16. He went directly to the house of his friend, Dr. William Gwin, where he was welcomed by the committee of Jackson citizens and the joint legislative committee. The next morning, Friday, January 17, Jackson and his attendants, an escort of militia, and the committee of citizens and legislators "left in the [rail] cars for the capital." They arrived at Raymond, the end of the rail line, at noon. After an official welcome there, the group departed in a long convoy of private carriages and elegant stagecoaches for the four-hour ride to Jackson. The procession arrived on the western edge of town at about five o'clock in the evening. At that point Jackson was saluted with a cannonade. Major General H.W. Dunlap of the Mississippi militia took charge of all militia companies and escorted General Jackson up Capitol Street to the state house. The building was be-

The oldest known photograph of the Old Capitol probably dates from the mid 1840s. The Spengler's Corner building, one-story in this photograph, had a second floor ballroom added in 1847.

decked with decorations, and people thronged the windows, the portico, and even the dome as Governor McNutt welcomed the general to Mississippi. After a short visit to the governor's office, Jackson was escorted across Amite Street to his rooms in the Eagle Hotel.[30]

On Friday evening a "Grand Military and Civic Ball" was held in the city theater. At nine o'clock Jackson and his "suite" visited the ball where he was introduced to the citizenry. The next morning, Saturday, a procession led General Jackson to the state house where he was met on the portico by Speaker of the House Jesse Speight whose welcoming remarks resembled a formal oration. Because his voice was too frail to reach the crowd, Jackson asked his nephew and personal secretary, Major Andrew Jackson Donelson, to read his reply. This ceremony was originally planned for the house of representatives chamber, but only minutes before Jackson's arrival, the house and the senate agreed to change the site to the portico. Whether the change was made to please the large crowd outside or to save the old visitor from climbing the stairs to the second-floor chamber was not recorded.[31]

After the ceremony, Jackson returned to the Eagle Hotel before going to ex-governor Hiram Runnels's house for dinner, and, no doubt, for a conversation about Andrew, Jr.'s, debt to the ex-governor. At the meeting Runnels extended payment on the note for a year. In the evening Jackson attended a "levee" (reception) at the home of Governor McNutt. However, exhaustion overtook the old general, and he remained for little more than an hour before retreating to the Eagle Hotel. The next morning, Sunday, January 19, Jackson returned to Vicksburg to board his steamboat for Nashville.[32]

Henry Clay's Visit

Henry Clay came to Jackson in 1843 seeking to become the presidential nominee of the Whig Party in 1844. His greatest ambition was the presidency, which he had sought without success since 1824. His ideas—support for a national bank, a protective tariff, reservations about slavery, and a national program of internal improvements—gave him some support among the wealthy classes of Vicksburg and Natchez, but made him anathema to most Mississippians who were followers of Clay's mortal political and personal enemy, Andrew Jackson.

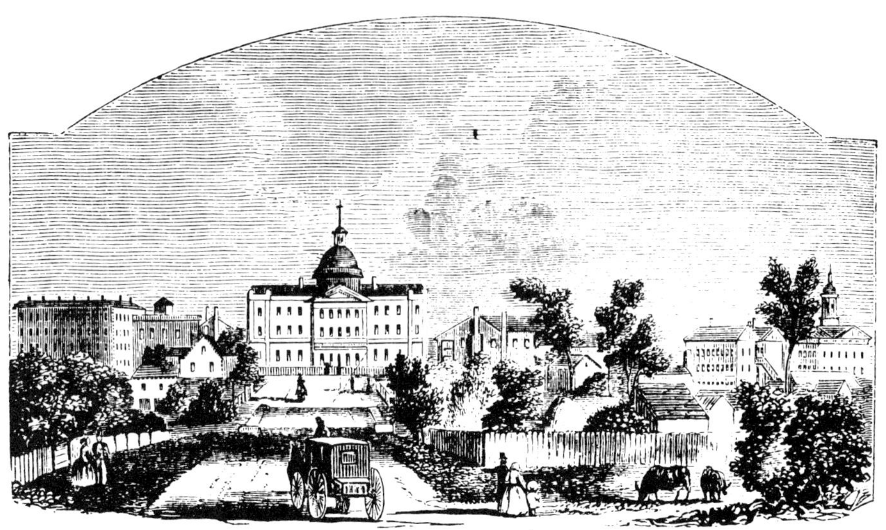

"View of Jackson (Central Part). The view shows the front of the State House. The Governor's House is seen a little to the left, also the Bowman House. The City Hall and Mrs. Dickson's house are on the right."

"As I First Saw It.
Something About the Capital City in 1855."

I came to Jackson in April, 1855. I was then a lad of 21 . . .

There was then no railroad south of Jackson, and so I came up from New Orleans on the grand old steamer "Natchez . . ."

Jackson was then an exceedingly quiet city, and it is not yet as lively as I hope it will be. It had a white population of 2,700 and a black or slave population of 950, and there were eight free negroes and mulattoes in the city. Its realty was estimated at $784,000, and its property and poll-tax was $8,200. . .

As already stated, there was no railroad south of Jackson, and not a mile of track east of Brandon. The railroad depot was on State street, near the present up-town freight depot, and the now prospering and booming West Jackson then afforded only a few residences, and a blacksmith shop.

The Eagle Hotel, where the Bowman House afterwards stood, and where Judge Campbell's residence now stands, the Mansion, or Slaughter House on State street, and the Union Hotel on Capitol street were the principal hotels. (The very tragic death of Col. A. K. McClung in the Eagle Hotel was then a local topic) . . .

"Cheapside" was then the headquarters for dry goods and groceries, and Pearl street went by the then very appropriate name of "Greasy Row."

The newspapers were: The Flag of The Union, Mississippian, Mercury and True Witness . . .

The Mississippian was published by Barksdale & Jones. F. C. Jones retired in 1855, and established "The Mercury" as the organ of the American or Know Nothing party. From that time until the war period the Mississippian was edited by Ethelbert Barksdale. It was printed at the corner of Capitol and President streets in a building that was the former State Capitol . . .

Thus stood Jackson in 1855. About mid-summer the yellow fever broke out, and there were about thirty deaths before it disappeared. Those who did not choose to remain in town removed quietly to the surrounding country, and ingress and egress was uninterrupted. It was thought that a person might visit Jackson and even see patients, between the hours of 10 and 4 daily. There was no fright, no panic, no shotgun quarantine—no hindrance to getting away and no obstacles to returning. The epidemic of that year, it was thought, originated from a mattress used by a patient the preceding year.

J. L. Power
Daily Clarion-Ledger
December 14, 1895

Andrew Jackson had carried Mississippi in every presidential election in which his name appeared on the ballot. His hand- picked successor, Martin Van Buren, won Mississippi in 1836. But the economic depression that gripped Mississippi during Van Buren's administration drove Mississippians into the arms of Clay's Whig Party in 1840. Clay, however, was not the nominee that year. The more folksy William Henry Harrison was chosen over Clay by Whig leaders who hoped to appeal to Jackson's supporters. The depression had not completely dissipated in 1843, and Clay wanted to be the nominee and to hold the state for his party.

Clay went to New Orleans for the winter of 1842–43. He was then sixty-five years old and suffering from the normal aches of his years, which, he believed, could be eased by the moderate climate of the South. More important, he needed to attend to some personal business affairs. Clay was then heavily in debt, and he sought to collect some notes that were due him. Also, he had recently begun the production of hemp (for bagging cotton bales), and he hoped to make contracts to supply planters in the lower South with hemp bagging and rope. While Clay's aims were mainly commercial, politics was never far from his attention, and he also wanted to encourage his Whig friends in Mississippi and Louisiana.[33]

On his way downriver in December 1842, Clay visited friends in Vicksburg and Natchez. In Vicksburg he stayed for a few days with Seargent S. Prentiss's law partner William C. Smedes, and in Natchez he was the house guest of William St. John Eliot of Devereaux, president of a Natchez insurance company.[34]

After Clay's arrival in New Orleans, a committee of his supporters from Jackson, led by William C. Richards, president of the Planters Bank, decided to invite Clay to visit Mississippi's capital on his way home to Kentucky. A delegation of three— Richards, Thomas J. Coffee, and S.S. Erwin—traveled to New Orleans to deliver the message in person. Clay immediately accepted. He planned to stop in Vicksburg to visit friends, and he promised to make a short excursion to Jackson to meet his supporters there "without ceremony and without parade." Clay explained that his entire trip had been undertaken for private business reasons, and he did not want to be "drawn into any public discussions or political entertainments."[35]

Clay arrived at Vicksburg aboard the steamboat *Ambassador* on Monday morning, February 20. After spending the night there, on Tuesday morning he took the train for Jackson, the line having been extended to the capital city since Andrew Jackson's visit three years earlier. Clay arrived at the depot in west Jackson around noon and rode up Capitol Street with Richards and Seargent S. Prentiss. In front of the capitol, Clay was welcomed to Jackson by Judge Daniel Mayes, one of the town's leading attorneys who had been an old friend of Clay's in Kentucky before moving to Mississippi in 1838.[36]

After thanking Judge Mayes, Clay spoke from the front of the capitol for an hour. Unlike his appearances elsewhere, wrote C.M. Price, the hostile Democratic editor of the *Mississippian*, Clay "launched into a sea of politics" devoting much of his talk to the need for a national bank. Clay avoided mention of his support for the tariff, which, according to Price, "robbed" the South "to enrich the manufacturers of New England." The "harangue" was "indifferent—hackneyed—stale" said the editor. M.R. Dudley, editor of the Whig paper, the *Southron*, was more charitable, noting that after the speech the "multitude thronged around [Clay] to give him the hearty welcome and shake of the hand."[37]

After dining with William C. Richards at the Planters Bank, Clay spent the afternoon receiving visitors at the Governor's Mansion. In the evening he attended a ball given in his honor at the city theater. Clay departed by train for Vicksburg the next morning, Wednesday, February 22.[38]

Clay was impressed with his reception. A month later, back home in Kentucky, he wrote that he had gone to Mississippi with little hope of holding that state for the Whigs in the upcoming presidential election. His visit, however, had given him "strong hopes." He expressed similar sentiments to Mississippi Whig leader Seargent S. Prentiss. The corruption of Mississippi Democrats, exemplified by their repudiation of the Union Bank bonds and the defalcation of State Treasurer Richard S. Graves, Clay predicted, boded ill for the Democrats and strengthened the appeal of the Whigs.[39]

Mr. Clay was mistaken. In the election of 1844, Democrat James K. Polk of Tennessee defeated Clay in Mississippi by a vote of 25,126 to 19,206.

The Town and the Old Capitol Before the War

Measured against its own tentative beginnings, Jackson enjoyed modest growth in the two decades before the Civil War. The state house, sitting imposingly at the junction of the town's two main streets, not only symbolized government, Jackson's sole reason for being, but also served as a community center for meetings, ceremonies, and celebrations.

In 1840 Jackson had about 900 inhabitants. By 1850 the number had doubled to 1,881, and by 1860 the population almost doubled again to 3,191. Impressive as that growth was, in 1860 Jackson still ranked only fourth in size among Mississippi towns, behind Vicksburg (4,591), Natchez (4,434), and Columbus (3,308). The town had merchants, banks, a literary society, a theater,

dentists, doctors, a host of lawyers, a school for males and another for females, saloons without number, militia companies, and a fire company.

In the decade before the Civil War, Jackson promised to become a small city with a diverse economy and some cultural sophistication. Prosperity had returned after the depression of the previous decade. The townspeople were emerging

of which queries Mr. K. was the reputed author.
I am informed that Governor Runnels who was
himself armed with pistols and bowie knife, told
Mr. Kearney to go and arm himself preparatory
to a street fight. Mr. Kearney did prepare himself, but was arrested and held to bail; Governor
R., I am told, bid defiance to the sheriff. I am
also informed that one of the members of the
house of representatives took part in this dis-
creditable fracas. Public opinion, it is to be
hoped, will frown down all such conduct, as
tending to produce honor on the state.

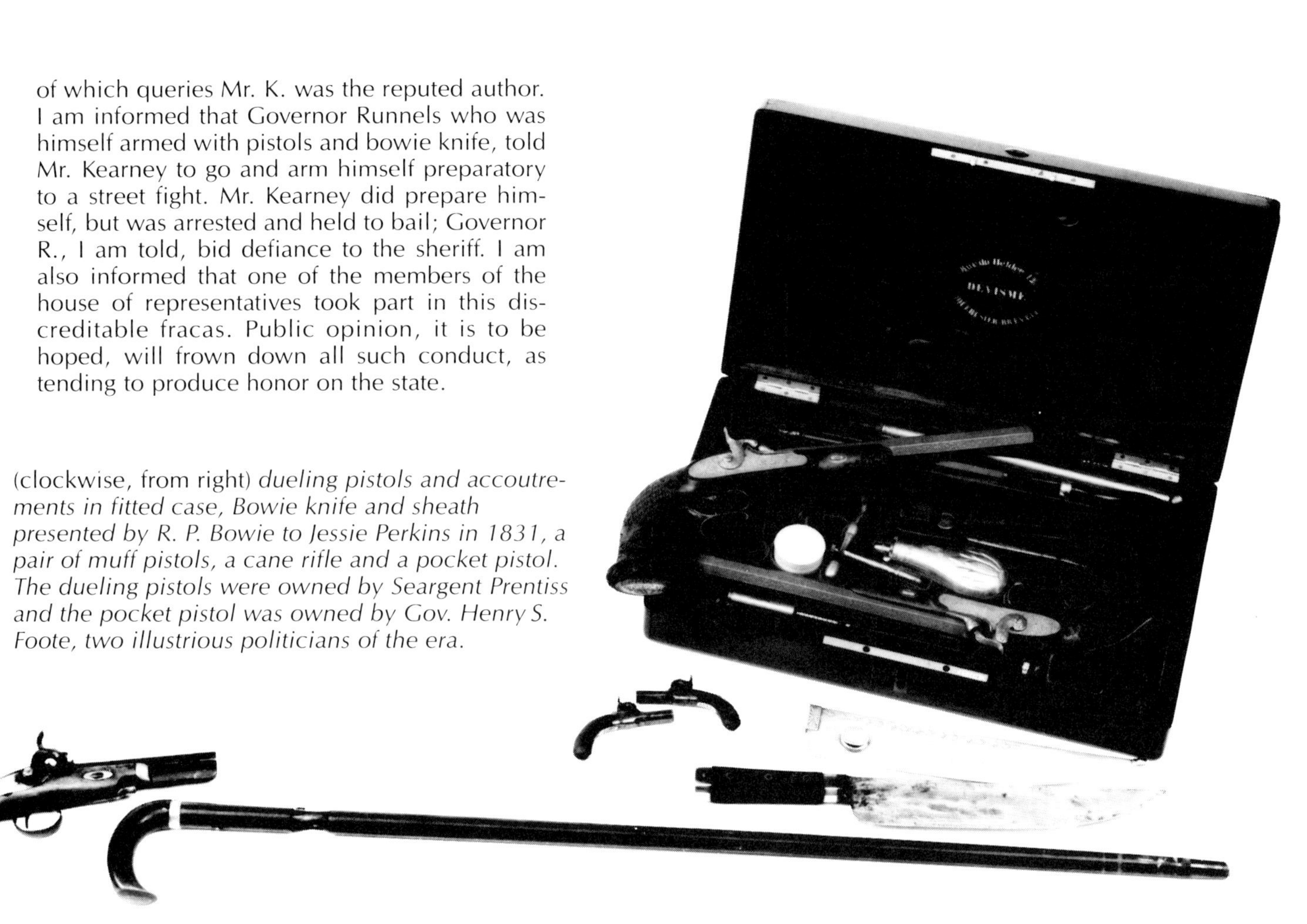

*(clockwise, from right) dueling pistols and accoutre-
ments in fitted case, Bowie knife and sheath
presented by R. P. Bowie to Jessie Perkins in 1831, a
pair of muff pistols, a cane rifle and a pocket pistol.
The dueling pistols were owned by Seargent Prentiss
and the pocket pistol was owned by Gov. Henry S.
Foote, two illustrious politicians of the era.*

from the raw, transient, frontier style of life that
had prevailed since the town's founding, and they
were taking on a more settled and civilized life-
style.

Industries and public services were established. The Pearl River Cotton Mills began
manufacturing cloth in 1858. The Jackson Foundry
and Machine Shop built machinery for sawmills,
and the Southern Agricultural Implement Factory
built farm equipment for the planters. Forty merchants sold dry goods, drugs, groceries, hardware,
and sundries to Jacksonians and planters from the
surrounding countryside. Most of the stores were
located near the capitol, principally in the three
blocks along South State immediately to the south.
There were also stores located along Pearl between

John Quitman and the Brass Cannons

In the summer of 1846, John Anthony Quitman—Natchez planter and lawyer, former legislator, governor and state chancellor—left for the Mexican War as a brigadier general. Late in 1847, he returned home a major general who had distinguished himself both in Zachary Taylor's conquest of Monterrey and in Winfield Scott's capture of Mexico City. Scott named Quitman military governor of Mexico City after the capital city's surrender.

Quitman arrived in Natchez on December 10, 1847, to a hero's welcome. He was banquetted, praised, and memorialized. Two brass Mexican cannons, trophies of war brought home by Quitman, were fired from the bluffs in his honor. He was invited to receive the honors of the state at Jackson, but he declined, pleading that he needed to rest before undertaking a trip to Washington.

Upon his return from Washington, he visited Jackson in early May 1848 to receive a belated welcome from his state. He was escorted to the Governor's Mansion to be received by Governor Joseph W. Matthews. Meanwhile, a procession of veterans and dignitaries formed at the corner of West and Capitol streets. Joined by Quitman and the governor, the procession moved up Capitol Street and into the Capitol grounds where the gen-

eral was welcomed by school children singing patriotic songs and dignitaries giving speeches.

The two brass cannons that Quitman had brought home and that had been earlier fired in welcome from the Natchez Bluffs had been captured by the United States Navy at Vera Cruz and presented to Quitman as trophies. Quitman now presented the cannons to the state of Mississippi, and they were positioned inside the front entrance to the Old Capitol. They disappeared during the Civil War, either pressed into service by the Confederates or carried off by the Yankees.

Saddlebags captured from Mexican General Valencia and brought back by Quitman as a trophy of war.

President and State and along both sides of Capitol Street in front of the state house. "West Jackson," another small cluster of businesses, sprang up around the railroad depot during the two decades before the Civil War.[40]

Hotel accommodations improved, and by the early 1840s several restaurants catered to the increasingly discriminating palates of Jacksonians. In 1856 the old, delapidated Eagle Hotel building across Amite Street from the northern end of the capitol was demolished. On the site rose the Bowman House, a large four-story brick structure that soon became the center of social life for the town. Hypolyte Savalle opened a restaurant on Capitol Street in 1842, where he dispensed French liquors, oysters, redfish, and game. Later, he moved to State Street and broadened his menu to include fresh salmon, lobster, and good wines. In the late 1850s, Angelo Miazza's restaurant surpassed Savalle's in popularity.[41]

Despite the outward refinements, however, frontier manners sometimes still prevailed. One aristocratic Adams Countian complained at the Bowman House in 1858 that the guests crowded around the doors of the dining room before meal times, and when the doors were opened rushed for the tables "like a set of hungry wolves."[42]

By European standards Jackson's finest accommodations were indeed shabby. Theresa Pulszky, who accompanied Hungarian patriot Louis Kossuth on a visit to Jackson in 1852, found her hotel "a wretched abode" that "showed attempts at finery, but the ceiling and walls looked as if they could not resist a strong wind." Nor did she find the food or sanitation any more pleasing. "The supper," she complained, "was in the western style, and the coloured girls who served it looked like the dishes: untidy and neglected." After supper she wandered out back where the servants were washing dishes. "They were all sitting before the water tubs, and little boys were running to and fro, handing to them the plates and saucers, and carrying them back, after they had been carelessly dipped into the water." She was, however, impressed with Governor Henry S. Foote, whom she thought "liberal-minded and well bred" with the looks of "an English gentleman." She pronounced the capitol "the only building of importance" in the town.[43]

In fact, aside from the city hall, completed in 1855, for the people of Jackson the capitol *was* the most important building in the community, not only for its governmental functions, but because it served as a geographical and cultural centerpiece for the town.

A sampling of activities during the two decades before the Civil War illustrates how Jacksonians used the building as a sort of town parlor and community front yard. In early November 1842, the Mississippi Agricultural Society held a fair at the capitol. Handicrafts and farm machinery were exhibited in the rotunda, while poultry and livestock exhibits were set up in the grove behind the building. In 1847, with help from the state legislature, the town of Jackson bought a new fire engine. The volunteer firemen named it the Magnolia, and they were so pleased with their new equipment that they put it on display in the rotunda of the capitol.[44]

Records indicate that local organizations held almost as many meetings in the capitol as the legislature did. Even as the building was being finished, the Mississippi Association for the Promotion of Education met in the senate chamber in mid-January 1839 to formulate a statewide education plan. On February 23, 1843, Capitol Lodge No. 11, Independent Order of Odd Fellows, held its organizational meeting in the capitol.[45]

Jackson College was formed in 1845 and began operations in the building of the old Eagle Hotel. The college closed in 1846 after its only annual commencement exercises were held in the chamber of the house of representatives. Four graduates received bachelor of arts degrees. Eleven years later, on July 2, 1857, another cultural event occurred in the house chamber: the Jackson Literary Association met the Brandon Lyceum in debate on the question "Is England's Glory Greater than Her Shame?"[46]

The capitol grounds were also put to good use by the people of Jackson. Fourth of July celebrations were usually there. On Independence Day 1842, the Jackson volunteer firemen put on a "collation" (a gathering to hear readings and to eat a light meal) at "Lake Spring," a favorite picnic site apparently in the woods behind the capitol. Afterwards, many citizens gathered in the grove to the rear of the capitol "where they spent the afternoon in social conversation and gymnastic exercises." The 1843 celebration was much grander. The "Capitol Guards," Jackson's premier militia unit, the volunteer fire company, and the "Washington Blues," a company of boys, accompanied by the governor, the high court judges, and other state officers, paraded up Capitol Street to the state house. They gathered in the house chamber to hear D.S. Jennings, an attorney who had come to Jackson in 1839, read the Declaration of Independence. Following that, Charles Scott, another prominent attorney who had come to Jackson from Tennessee, gave a one-hour oration. The celebrants then proceeded to Lake Spring for toasts and a barbecue.[47]

Though there were two slave markets in Jackson, both located on South State Street near the capitol, private slave sales were sometimes held in front of that building. On January 20, 1853, Mary A. Skipwith, executrix of the estate of George G. Skipwith, advertised "thirty-five acclimated Negroes, nearly all of them good working hands, and a large proportion likely young men from 18 to 25 years old" for sale in front of the capitol on Monday, February 21, 1853.[48]

Because of oil lamps, candles, and open fireplaces, fire was an ever-present hazard. The safety of public buildings depended on Jackson firefighters, and the legislature frequently appropriated money to help support the city's volunteer fire company. Thus, in 1852, not altogether for altruistic motives, the legislators appropriated $1,500 to build the city a firehouse on the grounds of the capitol. The station was put on Capitol Square just opposite the end of North Street (present site of War Memorial Building).[49]

EXECUTOR'S SALE.

By virtue of an order of the Probate Court of Hinds County, State of Mississippi, granted to the undersigned at the January Term, 1853, of said Court, I will, on

MONDAY, THE 21st DAY OF FEBRUARY NEXT,

in Front of the Capitol, in the City of Jackson, proceed to Sell, on the terms and within the hours prescribed by law,

Thirty-five acclimated Negroes, nearly all of them good working hands, and a large proportion likely Young Men, from 18 to 25 years old.

The Terms of Sale are a Credit of Ten Months, on Bonds with good and approved security, or good accepted bills.

MARY A. SKIPWITH,
Executrix of GEORGE G. SKIPWITH, deceased.

January 20th, 1853.

William L. Sharkey

The Jackson Convention

The first public debate in the south over southern secession was held in the Old Capitol.

A statewide convention met in October 1849 to discuss Mississippi's response should California be admitted to the Union as a free state and should Congress prohibit slavery in the newly acquired Mexican territories. The convention upheld the rights of slaveholders, but under the cool-headed leadership of Judge William L. Sharkey, a Unionist, the October convention stopped short of recommending secession. It called for a regional convention to be held in Nashville in June 1850 to discuss and protect the welfare of the slaveholding states. Judge Sharkey also presided over the Nashville Convention which recessed when the U.S. Congress began to piece together the Compromise of 1850 that summer.

All of Mississippi's congressmen except Senator Henry S. Foote opposed the Compromise of 1850. Foote, a Unionist with Sharkey, brought the issue to the voters of Mississippi by running for governor in the 1851 race in which he defeated Jefferson Davis. In the following decade, however, the secession movement continually gained strength in Mississippi.

If the city received some free benefits from the presence of the capitol, perhaps it was because Jacksonians considered the building to be a part of the town. In 1847 the city fathers arranged for a town clock to be installed on the front of the capitol above the portico. The clock was installed, and on December 29, 1847, they paid twenty-five dollars of the seventy- five dollar cost. The city fathers, however, delayed paying the other fifty dollars; they preferred to wait six months to see that the clock kept good time.[50]

The War Years

The promise that Jackson held in the two decades before the Civil War was not fulfilled. The onrushing war slammed the door on development and growth and almost ruined the town's future. The capitol, which witnessed the jubilation of Mississippi's secession in 1861, was four years later the scene of Mississippi's defeat and occupation. The building was abandoned by state government after mid-1863; for short periods it housed both Union and Confederate military headquarters, and at various times Union soldiers bivouacked on the grounds. A temporary post office was installed in the governor's office for a time. The town of Jackson was sacked and burned by Union troops on three occasions during the last two years of the war, but, except for natural deterioration and damage to furnishings, windows, and doors, the capitol remained largely unharmed throughout the war.

Even as the Civil War began, the twenty-year-old building was in dire need of expensive renovation. In 1860 Governor John J. Pettus engaged architect G.J. Larmon to evaluate the condition of the building and to recommend repairs. Larmon found the roof still leaking, despite the repairs made in 1844–45, and the water had begun to rot the roof timbers. New tin, coated with new roofing

paint, needed to be installed. The cornices and
gutters needed repairing, and about twenty window sills and lintels needed to be rebuilt. Larmon
also recommended that the entrance on the north
end of the building be rebuilt because "the frontis-
piece is about to fall." The walls, he noted, were
"badly cracked" and should be "secured with iron
anchors and ties and the brickwork repaired."
Much of the interior needed replastering, and the
whole building needed repainting inside and out.
Larmon also recommended repairing the iron and
stone fence and extending it to enclose the
grounds north and south of the building as well as
paving all the walkways with brick. All this, Larmon informed the governor, would cost $18,500.
The building, Larmon warned, was "receiving injury by every wet spell," and should the repairs be
delayed more than two years, the building "would
be past repairing." Four months later Larmon was
paid a fee of twenty dollars. When contractors
furnished individual estimates for the repairs, the
total came to almost $21,000.[51]

The 1860 legislators appropriated $10,000
for repairs, but when the next legislature convened
in November 1861, none of the allocation had
been spent. Deeming the earlier amount "fully
sufficient," the legislators refused to appropriate
more. At the time of the original appropriation,
the legislators had allowed $500 for building "suit-
able cisterns at accessible points to protect the state
capitol in case of fire." Although the cost exceeded
the appropriation by almost a thousand dollars,
these were constructed.[52]

There is no evidence, however, that the
$10,000 appropriation was ever used or that the
needed repairs were made. On the eve of the Civil
War, age and the elements were seriously undermining the Old Capitol. During the war,
abandonment and neglect added to the building's
decay and deterioration.

When the secession convention gathered on
January 7, 1861, in the house chamber to declare

Jackson's City Hall, c. 1869.

that "all the laws and ordinances by which the . . .
State of Mississippi became a member of the
Federal Union of the United States of America . . .
are hereby repealed," the Old Capitol was a dingy
and cracked relic of William Nichols's graceful
Greek Revival structure, so admired by Mississippians two decades before. Two months later, when
the convention reassembled to ratify the Confederate Constitution, a northern reporter from the
New York *Tribune* reported his impressions to his
readers. The delegates seemed handsome, direct,
dignified, and serious, but he was less impressed
with their capitol, calling it "a faded, sober edifice" with crumbling plaster and furnished with
shabby delapidated furniture. The curtains were

old and drab, and the chandelier in the house chamber was "festooned with cobwebs."[53]

Three months later another reporter described his impressions of the capitol. In June 1861, William Howard Russell, war correspondent from the London *Times*, visited Governor Pettus. The governor's office, the Englishman noted, "was of more than republican simplicity." The room was "surrounded by some common glass cases." Other furniture was sparse and simple, the carpet "ragged," the windows "cracked and broken," and "the walls and ceiling discolored by mildew."[54]

The first two years of war brought no threat to Jackson or to the capitol. Life in the town and government in the building went on with little outward change. The legislators convened on regular schedule, and state officers went to their capitol offices according to their usual routines. Only the work of government changed. Both legislators and executives were consumed with the work of war, and military affairs occupied the attentions of all.

In the spring of 1862 Union military threats to Mississippi concentrated around Corinth in the extreme northern part of the the state. In the summer of 1862 a Union fleet under Admiral David Farragut came upriver from the Gulf after forcing the surrenders of New Orleans, Baton Rouge, and Natchez. A fleet of riverboats under Admiral Charles Davis soon came downriver from Memphis to join Farragut's fleet of ocean-going vessels. Together, Farragut and Davis bombarded Vicksburg and demanded the town's surrender. In July the appearance of the Confederate ironclad *Arkansas*, falling water in the river, and the lack of a strong landing force to subdue the town caused the two fleets to retire.

But Vicksburg remained the prime Union objective in the western Confederacy, and in the fall of 1862 General U.S. Grant gathered an army in western Tennessee to take it. In November 1862 Grant divided his army to move on two fronts against Vicksburg. General William T. Sherman took a force down the Mississippi and assaulted the bluffs along the Yazoo north of Vicksburg. Meanwhile, with his main force Grant moved down the center of the state to attack Vicksburg from the rear. So serious was the threat that Governor Pettus issued an invitation to President Jefferson Davis to come home and "inspire confidence" among Mississippians "at this critical juncture." He pointedly mentioned the frequency with which Davis had visited Lee's army. When he received Pettus's invitation, Davis was already considering a trip into the western Confederacy. The president left Richmond on December 9, 1862, and after visiting General Braxton Bragg's army near Murfreesboro, Tennessee, Davis proceeded to Jackson. General Joseph E. Johnston, newly appointed commander of all western armies, including Bragg's in Tennessee and Pemberton's in Mississippi, accompanied the president. The party stopped only briefly in Jackson before traveling to inspect the defenses at Vicksburg. The president and his new western commander then went north to Grenada to inspect the forces that had been emplaced there to block Grant's southward march.[55]

By Christmas Day Davis was back in Jackson, and on December 26, 1862, the Confederate president delivered a speech to a large and emotional crowd in the house chamber of the capitol. His speech was designed to bolster sagging morale in his home state. He laid heavy emphasis on explaining the unpopular conscription law; he called for unity and emphasized that Vicksburg must be held. General Johnston was called by the crowd, but he spoke only a few words. He promised to be "indefatigable" in his defense of Mississippi—a vow that Jacksonians would remember five months later when he evacuated the capital rather than fight Grant's superior force.[56]

Davis's speech failed to save either Vicksburg or Jackson, nor did Johnston prove aggressive in his campaigns against Grant. Only four months later, in late April 1863, Grant's army came across the Mississippi River near Port Gibson. Instead of moving directly on Vicksburg as he had originally planned, Grant chose instead to drive toward Jackson to keep Johnston's and Pemberton's forces from concentrating against him.

During the last days of April and the first days of May, in addition to his worries about state government, Pettus found himself acting almost in the capacity of a military commander. He struggled to mobilize state militia and to obtain weapons and ammunition to equip it. Personal worries plagued him as well. As he was preparing to evacuate his family from the capital, he received word that his brother, Lieutenant Colonel Edmund W. Pettus, an officer of an Alabama regiment in Pemberton's army, had been captured by the enemy. He quickly learned, however, that his brother had managed to escape his captors and was safe.[57]

On May 2, 1863, General Pemberton advised Governor Pettus to remove the state records from Jackson. Grant, he warned, was "crossing nearly his whole force," and "very likely he will move on Jackson." Three days later Pettus issued an order to all state officers that they must be prepared to move their offices with the records necessary to carry on business "at a half an hour's notice." He planned to move to Meridian or to some other secure point on the Mobile and Ohio Railroad.[58]

Meridian lacked enough space to house the government, and Enterprise, a town on the railroad just south of Meridian, was chosen instead. Pettus remained in Jackson until the last minute, while he sent Adjutant General Jones S. Hamilton ahead to secure facilities. Pettus's family arrived at Enterprise on May 9. Pettus himself abandoned the capital just ahead of the advancing Federals.[59]

One of the last duties that Pettus performed before fleeing for Enterprise was to pay the bill to the Jackson Gas Light Company. Records fail to indicate whether he turned out the lights before leaving.[60]

By the morning of May 14 Grant's army was in sight of the capitol dome, but the building was empty of state authority. Grant's forces advanced on Jackson in two columns. Sherman's corps came up the Mississippi Springs (Raymond) Road, while McPherson's advanced on the Clinton Road (West Capitol). Johnston had already decided that his outmanned force would evacuate Jackson, and he only fought a delaying action to gain enough time to get his supplies out of town. The main fight occurred at C.P. Wright's farm (near present-day Livingston Park). Johnston's army escaped north toward Canton just as Sherman's troops were entering town from the south and McPherson's from the west.[61]

The Fifty-ninth Indiana Infantry, First Brigade, Seventh Division, XVII (McPherson's) Corps, planted its United States flag on the dome of the capitol. The flag remained there until the next day when that unit marched off towards Vicksburg. In his report, Colonel Jesse I. Alexander emphasized that his unit's colors "were the first and only colors planted on the capitol of Jackson during the May occupation."[62]

When the Fifty-ninth Indiana Infantry raised its colors over the capitol, Grant and Sherman were already there. One of Sherman's units had located an unmanned line of entrenchments at the railroad between the Mississippi Springs Road and the Pearl River. They came unopposed up the railroad into town. Grant, closely followed by Sherman, went directly to the capitol. McPherson also soon arrived.[63]

The three commanders held a conference at the Bowman House about four in the afternoon. They had little time to savor capturing the capital of Jefferson Davis's home state. Johnston's army had escaped. Should Johnston move rapidly enough (which he did not), the Confederate gen-

The five-story building in the photograph is the famous Bowman House facing Amite Street. In its brief history, 1857–1863, the hotel was a gathering spot for politicians and, during one hectic week in 1863, it housed Confederate as well as Union generals.

In the corner is the Jackson Fire Company station with the members gathered in front of it. For training purposes, it was customary to bring out the pumper each month and give the Old Capitol dome a good washing. Plaques (right) from the company's first engine, the "Thomas Green," are in the Old Capitol museum collection.

B. L. C. Wailes and the Historical Society

The Old Capitol was the birthplace of the Mississippi Historical Society as well as the Department of Archives and History.

The Mississippi Historical Society was organized in 1858 by B. L. C. Wailes of Natchez. It was the first effort in the state to systematically collect and preserve historical resources.

That first organization had a short life but the foundation was laid for its successor, a revived Mississippi Historical Society, chartered in 1890 in the Secretary of State's office on the ground floor. It was this incarnation of the organization that spearheaded the move to establish the Mississippi Department of Archives and History. After accomplishing that goal in 1903, the Historical Society faded away in 1914, not to be reborn until 1952, when the current Mississippi Historical Society was formed.

The Founder

B. L. C. Wailes, a native of Georgia, emigrated with his family to Washington, Mississippi, in 1810 when he was 13. He attended Jefferson College, married Rebecca Covington, and settled in Washington. He served on the Board of Trustees of Jefferson College and was founder and President of the Athenaeum Society.

Wailes had a life-long interest in his environment. He collected natural specimens and worked for agricultural progress as well as the advancement of education.

He served in the Old Capitol as a representative from Adams County, 1825–26, and in 1852 was appointed State Geologist. He toured the state and submitted to the legislature in 1854 his *Report on the Agriculture and Geology of Mississippi, Embracing a Sketch of the Social and Natural History of the State.*

Wailes died in 1862.

Portrait of B. L. C. Wailes sketched by John James Audubon.

eral could get across the Big Black River and join Pemberton. Then Grant would have to face a superior force deep in enemy country with no means of escape. Grant faced a desperate race to get between his adversaries before they could unite. But he also wanted to destroy Jackson as a manufacturing and transportation center.[64]

Grant ordered McPherson's corps to move out the next day. Sherman was allowed one day for the task of destruction, which, according to Grant, he did "most effectually." Then Sherman also would move quickly towards Vicksburg. Sherman assigned a brigade of infantry and two companies of cavalry as the provost guard for the town. The brigade commander, Brigadier General Joseph A. Mower, made his headquarters in the capitol, and his troops bivouacked on the capitol grounds.[65]

The next morning Sherman ordered Mower to burn by ten o'clock all public property not needed by Union forces and to be ready to move out for Vicksburg by one o'clock that afternoon. "Be sure," Sherman ordered, "to destroy all tents by burning them in a pile to the rear of the State-house tomorrow about noon."[66]

As the troops set about their work of destruction, Sherman was informed that Union soldiers were looting the stores. "This, if true, is wrong," he warned Mower. "Take only what is necessary. . . . The private rights of citizens should be respected," he continued. "The feeling of pillage and booty will injure the morals of the troops and bring disgrace on our cause."[67]

The destruction at Jackson, expected by Grant to be limited to facilities and supplies that supported the Confederate war effort, offended even Sherman's coarse sensibilities. Railroads were pulled up and bridges burned for several miles in each direction. Foundries, arsenals, and cotton mills were burned. But so was the penitentiary (the fault of convicts, according to Sherman), churches, hotels, private residences, hospitals, and stores. Sherman blamed the excesses on "camp-followers"

and on "the effect of some bad rum." He admitted that the destruction "was not justified by the rules of war," but he took no disciplinary action. All of his troops were gone from Jackson by the evening of May 16.[68]

The Bowman House escaped destruction during the pillage that followed the May 14–16 occupation of Jackson by Grant's army. Ironically, the hotel was completely destroyed by fire, apparently by accident, on June 10, 1863.[69]

Inexplicably, the Old Capitol, the Governor's Mansion, and City Hall all escaped destruction. The furniture in the capitol "was badly abused" and the pieces in the mansion "demolished."[70]

After the capture of Jackson on May 14, 1863, no Federal troops remained in Jackson for more than two days, and most of them were gone the next day. For the next six weeks all Union attentions focused on Vicksburg. While Johnston's main force did not return to Jackson until early July, Confederate scouts reentered Jackson only days after Sherman left.

Governor Pettus also returned to Jackson soon after the last Federals departed. On May 20, Major James Smylie telegraphed Pettus at Enterprise asking the governor to provide a provost guard of fifty state troops "to establish order in the city and collect [the] large number of straglers [sic] who are now pillaging and destroying everything they can lay hands on." Three days later General Joseph E. Johnston wired Pettus from Jackson advising the governor that "if you were in Jackson you could aid us greatly." Apparently, Pettus hastened to Jackson, for Johnston telegraphed the governor from Canton on May 24 that he would visit Jackson the next morning, presumably to meet with the governor.[71]

Pettus's correspondence indicates that as late as July 9 he was still in Jackson, though neither his family, nor, apparently, any other major government officers accompanied him. But even as Pettus had returned to Jackson, he was scouting for other locations for the state government. Adjutant General Hamilton had felt insecure in Enterprise from the beginning, and even as Pettus returned to Jackson, another aide, J.H. Rives, recommended Macon, which, he said, had ample accommodations for all state officials and enough troops in the area to protect the town from raids. Pettus moved his family there in early June.[72]

Meanwhile, Pettus and Johnston awaited the next blow. Vicksburg fell on July 4 just as Johnston was reoccupying Jackson. Grant wasted no time in dealing with Johnston's threat to his rear. He assigned Sherman to march to Jackson and destroy or drive away Johnston's army. Sherman arrived on July 9 and faced Jackson defenses that were much stronger and better manned now than in May. The town was ringed with earthworks anchored on the Pearl River both north and south of town. Johnston also had heavy caliber, long-range artillery. Sherman settled down for a siege. Johnston feared, however, that Grant's entire army was gathering against him, and on the night of July 16 he began a withdrawal across the Pearl River burning the bridges behind him.

The Federals occupied Jackson on July 17 for the second time. Sherman recorded that Jackson was "simultaneously entered at several points, a brigade of Potter's Division, Parkes' Corps being the first to reach the State-house and plant its colors thereon." Sherman assigned Major General Frank P. Blair's division to guard the town. Blair's orders were to guard private property and to prevent looting—a mission, apparently, that Blair failed to perform with enough energy.[73]

On this visit the Federals stayed six days, from July 17 to July 23. Jackson was again sacked, plundered, and burned. This time the pillaging was concentrated on private homes and private property. In a lengthy report to Grant, Sherman condemned the lack of discipline "that relects discredit on us all," but he hastened to add that the conduct was "confined to a few men." He took

The Mississippi Convention

In March 1861 a *New York Herald* reporter filed this description of the Mississippi Convention that reconvened to ratify the Constitution of the Confederate States of America:

"The Mississippi State House, upon a shaded square in front of my window, is a faded, sober edifice, of the style in vogue fifty years ago, with the representative hall at one end, the senate chamber at the other, an Ionic portico in front, and an immense dome upon the top. Above this is a miniature dome, like an infinitesimal parasol upon a gigantic umbrella. The whole is crowned by a small gilded pinnacle, . . .

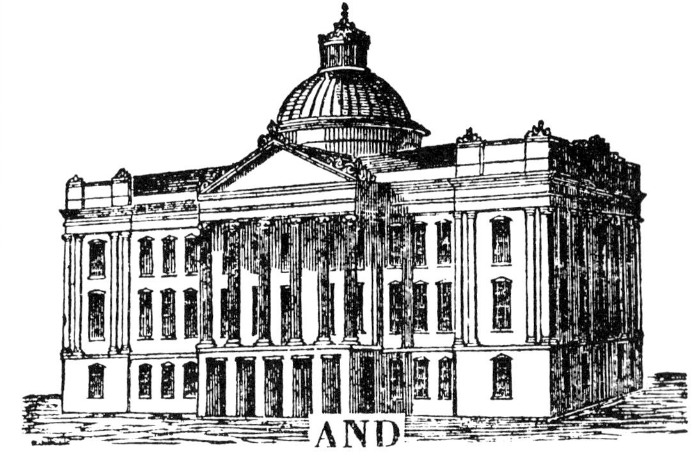

Ascending a spiral stairway, and passing along the balustrade which surrounds the open space under the dome, you turn to the left, through a narrow passage into the representative hall. Here is the Mississippi Convention.

At the north end of the apartment sits the president, upon a high platform occupying a recess in the wall, with two Ionic columns upon each side of him. Before him is a little, old-fashioned mahogany pulpit, concealing all but his head and shoulders from the vulgar gaze. In front of this, and three or four feet lower, at a long wooden desk, sit two clerks, one smoking a cigar.

Before them, and still lower, at a shorter desk, an unhappy Celtic reporter, with dark shaggy hair and eyebrows, is taking down the speech of the honorable member from something or other county. In front of his desk, standing rheumatically upon the floor, is a little table, which looks as if called into existence by a drunken carpenter on a dark night, from the relics of a superannuated dry-goods box.

Upon one of the columns at the president's right hangs a faded portrait of George Poindexter, once a senator from this State. Further to the right is an open fire-place, upon whose mantel stand a framed copy of the Declaration of Independence, now sadly faded and blurred, a lithographic view of the Medical College of Louisiana, and a pitcher and glass. On the hearth is a pair of ancient and-irons, upon which a genial wood fire is burning. . . .

On the left of the president is another fire-place, also with a sadly blurred copy of the great Declaration standing upon its mantel. The members' desks, in rows like the curved line of the letter D, are of plain wood, painted black. Their chairs are great, square, faded mahogany frames, stuffed and covered with haircloth. As you stand beside the clerk's desk, facing them, you see behind the farthest row a semi-circle of ten pillars, and beyond them a narrow, crescent-shaded lobby. Half-way up the pillars is a little gallery, inhabited just now by two ladies in faded mourning.

In the middle of the hall, a tarnished brass chandelier, with pendants of glass, is suspended from the ceiling by a rod festooned with cobwebs. This medieval relic is purely ornamental, for the room is lighted with gas. The walls are high, pierced with small windows, whose faded blue curtains, flowered and bordered with white, are suspended from a triple bar of gilded Indian arrows . . .

They impress you by their pastoral aspect—the absence of urban costumes and postures. Their general bucolic appearance would assure you, if you did not know it before, that there are not many large cities in the State of Mississippi. Your next impression is one of wonder at their immense size and stature. Of them the future historian may well say: 'There were giants in those days.'

All around you are broad-shouldered, herculean-framed, well-proportioned men, who look as if a laugh from them would bring this crazy old

capitol down about their ears, and a sneeze, shake the great globe itself. The largest of these Mississippi Anakim is a gigantic planter, clothed throughout in blue homespun. You might select a dozen out of the ninety-nine delegates, each of whom could personate the Original Scotch Giant in a traveling exhibition. They have large, fine heads, and a profusion of straight brown hair, though here and there is a crown smooth, bald, and shining. Taken for all in all, they are fine specimens of physical development, with frank, genial, jovial faces. The speaking is generally good, and commands respectful attention. There is little *badinage* or satire, a good deal of directness and coming right to the point, qualified by the strong southern proclivity for adjectives . . .

The members, like all deliberative bodies in this latitude, are mutual admirationists. Every speaker has the most profound respect for the honest motives, the pure patriotism, the transcendent abilities of the honorable gentleman upon the other side. It excites his regret and self-distrust to differ from such an array of learning and eloquence; and nothing could impel him to but a sense of imperious duty."

—Albert D. Richardson, *The Secret Service,
the Field, the Dungeon and the Escape*
(Hartford, Conn., 1865)

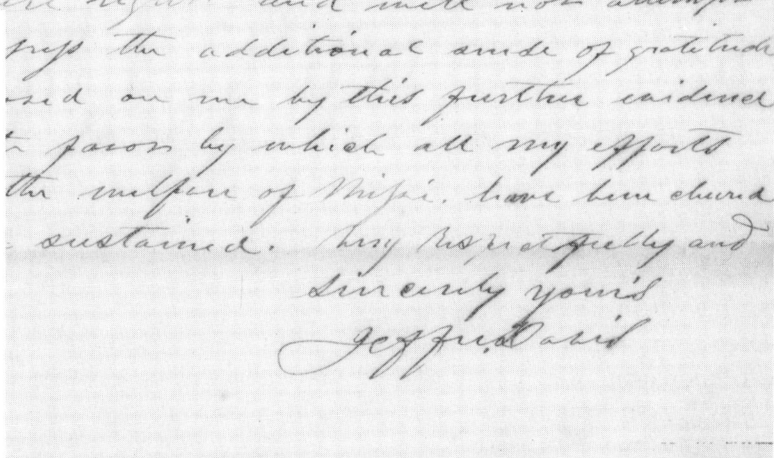

Executive Office,

Jackson, Miss. Feby 12 1861

Govr. J. J. Pettus

My dear Sir,

Circumstances of which you are aware render it necessary for me to tender to you my resignation of the office of Major Genl. of the Army of Mississippi which was conferred on me by the Convention of the Republic of Mississippi.

Proud of the station to which the too kind estimate of the people's representatives elevated me, I retire from it with sincere regret, and will not attempt [to express] the additional [sense] of gratitude [impos]ed on me by this further evidence [of favor] by which all my efforts [for] the welfare of Missi. have been cheered [and] sustained. Very respectfully and sincerely yours

Jeffn Davis

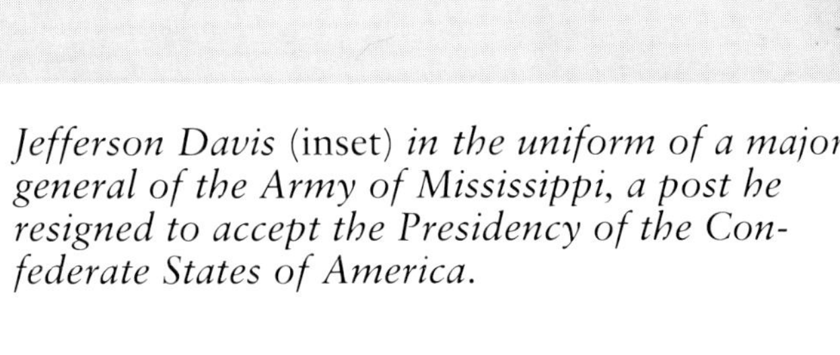

Jefferson Davis (inset) *in the uniform of a major general of the Army of Mississippi, a post he resigned to accept the Presidency of the Confederate States of America.*

no action, however, to restrain or to punish them; and in other statements, he seemed to gloat at the degree of destruction. In another report to Grant, he reported that "the inhabitants are subjugated. They cry aloud for mercy. The land is devastated for thirty miles around." To Sherman's credit, when the city leaders of Jackson and Clinton asked for food to feed the hungry, Sherman gave it, asking only that the food not be used to feed Confederate soldiers.[74]

But once again little harm came to the capitol or to the mansion; the latter was perhaps saved because Sherman used it as his headquarters. Despite the ruin of Jackson, Sherman remarked, as if he were amazed, "the State-house, Governor's Mansion, and some fine dwellings . . . remain untouched."[75]

Governor Pettus was again forced to flee Jackson just ahead of Union occupation. As Sherman besieged the capital, Pettus moved to Meridian, but on August 11, 1863, citing the unavailability of space for the officers and records of state government, Pettus ordered the government to Macon. Charles Clark, who in October was elected to succeed Pettus, also maintained the government at Macon, except for the two brief occasions when the legislature met at Columbus. For reasons unknown, Governor Clark's attorney general, T.J. Wharton, remained in Jackson and conducted business from the capitol, possibly because the state library remained there. Clark's 1864 and 1865 correspondence is filled with letters to Wharton at Jackson asking for legal opinions. Governor Clark also made occasional visits to Jackson, and a few government conferences continued to be held at the capitol.[76]

Until the fall of Jackson in May 1863, the legislature continued to convene at the capitol. The lawmakers met there in regular session in November 1861 and again in a called session in December 1862. By November 1863, the date for convening the next regular session, the executive

branch was firmly established in Macon, but space there for the legislators was limited. Just before going out of office, Pettus issued a proclamation ordering the upcoming session to meet at Columbus and calling on state officers to move there. Thus, at the beginning of the November 1863 session, newly elected Governor Charles Clark was inaugurated on the portico of the Lowndes County Courthouse. The senate met in the Christian Church and the house convened in the courthouse.[77]

In mid-December the session ended, and the government returned to Macon. Two called sessions of the legislature met in the Calhoun Institute at Macon in 1864, the first in March and the second in August. The final wartime meeting of the legislature met at Columbus in February 1865.[78]

Meantime, as the government traveled, the capitol at Jackson stood neither vacant nor totally neglected. Contrary to common belief, Jackson was not perpetually occupied after its conquest in May 1863. The town was captured three more times before the war ended, but the longest occupation on any of these occasions was six days (July 17–23, 1863). Thus, although the legislature did not meet in Jackson after December 1862 and state officers were successively in Enterprise, Meridian, Macon, and Columbus, in their absence the capitol was not constantly in Union hands. Keepers of the capitol continued to be elected, and during the last eighteen months of the war, Governor Clark made occasional visits to Jackson.

Mayor C.H. Manship wrote to Pettus in October 1863 about the capitol. The post office at Jackson had been destroyed, and since the retreat of General Johnston in July, Manship explained, he had been using the governor's office as a post office and "taking generally as much care of the capitol grounds as I could." He requested approval to continue the arrangement during the winter. The mayor promised "to take good care . . . both

"Raising the Stars and Stripes over the Capitol of the State of Mississippi."

of the offices and the building." Pettus's response was not recorded.[79]

When he received Manship's request, Pettus had just noted that "no one is in charge of the state library, capitol, and public grounds at Jackson," and he had appointed James M. Coates as librarian and keeper of the capitol. The November 1863 session of the legislature confirmed Coates's appointment. But Coates never served, and at the March 1864 session Governor Clark asked for the election of somebody else. He also asked the legislators to appropriate $10,000 for repairs to the building. The roof, he said, needed "extensive repairs," and so did the fence around the grounds. Although only $228 had been spent on capitol repairs between November 1, 1863, and December 31, 1864, the legislators refused to appropriate any money for the repairs. They did, however, elect F.A. Whiting to the position of librarian and keeper of the capitol.[80]

Whiting took the job, and on October 14, 1864, he telegraphed Governor Clark in Macon that "Genl Gardner is taking possession of auditor's office. What course shall I pursue." Whiting was referring to Major General Franklin Gardner, the new Confederate commander of the District of Mississippi and East Louisiana. Lieutenant General Richard Taylor, commanding the Department of Alabama, Mississippi, and East Louisiana, had just appointed Gardner to the command and ordered him to place his headquarters at Jackson. Apparently Gardner picked the vacant auditor's office in the capitol. Clark's records do not indicate his reply to Whiting's question.[81]

Early in 1865, Governor Clark issued a call for the legislature to convene at Columbus on February 20. In preparing for the session, Clark twice wrote Whiting asking for a report on the state library and on the condition of the capitol. On February 6, 1865, Whiting responded with a

Genl. Ulysses S. Grant's son who accompanied his father to the evacuated city of Jackson, May 14, 1863, witnessed the raising of the Union flag over the Old Capitol.

"Thinking the battle was ended, I rode off toward the State House, where the Confederate troops passed me in their retreat. . . . I saw a mounted officer with a Union flag advancing toward the Capitol. I followed him into the building and entered the Governor's room, which had been hastily abandoned. Finding what I supposed to be the Governor's pipe lying on the table, I confiscated it, primarily and ostensibly for the National service, but secondarily and actually for my own private and individual use. It had the advantage of being still loaded and lighted.

Returning to the street, I saw the officer whom I had followed in the act of raising the Union flag over the building."

—F. D. Grant
Outlook, July 2, 1898

two-page report. The library, he said, contained 10,912 volumes. A few unimportant books had been damaged by leaks in the roof, Whiting reported, and Union troops had done considerable damage "amongst the literary works and maps." The Federals had carried away many valuable books and stolen or mutilated most of the maps.[82]

As for the capitol, Whiting said that he had spent $2,000, "which I consider a fair and reasonable charge," to have the roof and gutters repaired. The repairs, though still in progress, had stopped "all of the principal leaks." He reported that much of the furniture had been broken and that almost all of the doors and locks had been broken or destroyed. The carpets in the governor's office had been "entirely destroyed" and those in the high court chamber and the library had been "greatly damaged." On the grounds "the arsenal houses have been burnt, and the remaining outhouses nearly entirely destroyed." The fence, he reported, had been "very greatly damaged." In addition, the north wall of the building needed "anchoring"—a repair that had been recommended in 1860 but apparently not done. He estimated the total cost of repairs at "$8,000 to $10,000 over and above the $2,000 already contracted to be paid for repairing the roof."[83]

On March 3, 1865, the lawmakers appropriated only $3,000 to cover Whiting's expenditures on the roof and to repair the locks and doors.[84]

It became clear to Governor Clark in early May 1865 that General Richard Taylor would soon surrender all his forces and that the war in Mississippi was effectively over. How should he begin the process of "reconstruction," the term already in use to describe bringing the states of the Confederacy back into the Union? After conferring with some leading Mississippians who for some time had favored rejoining the Union, Governor Clark decided to move the government back to Jackson and to call the legislature into session. He issued a proclamation calling the legislators to meet at the capitol on May 18.[85]

If the governor's motive was to preempt Union rule by quickly establishing a cooperationist state government, he was almost immediately disabused of that notion. Clark returned to Jackson and reoccupied the mansion and the capitol. On May 20, the legislature convened but adjourned almost immediately under threat of arrest by the military authorities. Even as the legislature dissolved, a letter from Brigadier General E.D. Osband was enroute to Clark's office. Osband informed Clark that "by orders received from superior headquarters based upon the instructions of the President of the United States, I am directed not to recognize the present civil government of Mississippi." Politely, but firmly, General Osband continued, "I must call upon you for the custody of the Records and Archives and Executive Mansion of the State of Mississippi." Osband designated May 22 "as the time and the State House as the place when

Brocade curtains were ripped from the Old Capitol building by a Union soldier during one of the several invasions of Jackson. The shirt made from the fabric was returned to the Museum by the soldier's descendants in 1979.

"Destruction of Rebel property at Jackson, Mississippi. May 15."

and where I will meet with you to consumate [*sic*] this arrangement."[86]

Clark replied that he was the duly elected governor of Mississippi, and, as such, he was charged with the custody of the records, archives, and executive mansion. Thus, Clark wrote, he could not "voluntarily surrender the archives and public property to anyone." The governor seemed interested primarily in recording a formal protest before yielding to the inevitable, for, he concluded, "I will not attempt to resist the armed force of the United States." He promised to be in his capitol office at nine o'clock on the morning of May 22.[87]

General Osband designated Captain Warren Miller, a member of his staff, to receive the property of the state. Clark delivered the great seal and other property in his possession and promised that all other state officials would do likewise. The mansion, he informed Osband, would be turned over by his private secretary. Clark even informed the general that some of the furniture belonging at the mansion was still in Macon. But again he lodged a courteous protest, saying that by this "enforced surrender" he had been relieved of his duties as governor, and "for the grave consequences that may result, the President of the United States has assumed the responsibility."[88]

Over the next several days, Captain Miller visited the other state officers and took possession of their records also. He meticulously presented itemized receipts for the property that he received.[89]

The next day, May 23, Governor Clark was given permission to return to Macon. He gave his oath to appear before Federal authorities to answer any charges that later might be brought against him; then he went back to Macon. Five days later, on orders from Secretary of War Edwin Stanton, the Union commander at Macon arrested Clark. The governor was transported to Mobile, where, again on orders from Secretary Stanton, he was transported by steamer to Fort Pulaski at Savannah, Georgia. He was confined there with other prominent state and Confederate officials.[90]

Governor Clark arrived at Fort Pulaski on June 25, 1865, and was held there "in close custody" until October 11, 1865, when he and a number of others were released by order of President Andrew Johnson. By then Clark had taken an oath of allegiance to the Union and requested pardon from the president.[91]

"*Re-occupation of Jackson, Mississippi, by the Confederates.*"

NOTES

[1] *Mississippi Free Trader and Natchez Weekly Gazette*, January 10, 1839.

[2] Proceedings; *Laws of Mississippi*, 1839, 244–245.

[3] *Laws*, 1840, 229.

[4] *Laws*, 1839, 74.

[5] *Hutchinson's Code*, 1848, 112, 115.

[6] *Ibid*. During construction and for some years following, officials referred to the ground or first floor as the "basement" and the upper floors as the "first" and "second" floors. The author has adopted current usage of first or ground floor, second and third floors.

[7] *Ibid*.

[8] *Ibid*.

[9] *Laws*, 1858, 137–138.

[10] *Hutchinson's Code*, 1848, 112–113; *Laws*, 1844, 117–118.

[11] *Laws*, 1844, 228–229; Proceedings, February 6, 13, 1845.

[12] John A. Quitman Papers, Z 66, Box 3, Folder 35, MDAH.

[13] McCain, 87, 192.

[14] *Laws*, 1857, 139.

[15] RG 29, Auditor, vol. 71, Expenditures for Mansion and Capitol Repairs, MDAH.

[16] *Ibid*.

[17] Sandra Moncrief, "The Mississippi Married Women's Property Act of 1839," *The Journal of Mississippi History*, 47 (May 1985), 110.

[18] Fisher v. Allen, 2 Mississippi Reports (Howard) 611.

[19] *Ibid*.

[20] *Ibid*.

[21] Moncrief, 117; Dunbar Rowland, *Encyclopedia of Mississippi History*, vol. 2 (Atlanta: Southern Historical Publishing Association, 1907), 989; J.F.H. Claiborne, *Mississippi as a Province, Territory, and State*, vol. 1 (Jackson: Power and Barksdale, 1880), 475–476.

[22] Moncrief, 119; Miles, *Jacksonian Democracy*, 165.

[23] *Laws*, 1839, 72–73.

[24] Jackson *Southern Sun*, December 3, 1839; McCain *Story of Jackson*, 136; Robert V. Remini, *Andrew Jackson and the Course of American Democracy, 1833–1845* (New York: Harper and Row, 1984), 455.

[25] *Senate Journal*, 1840, 25; *Laws*, 1840, 89–90; *Mississippian*, January 3, 1840.

[26] *Laws*, 1840, 246–247.

[27] Jackson *Enquirer*, January 10, 1840; *House Journal*, 1840, 155; *Senate Journal*, 1840, 171.

[28] Jackson *Enquirer*, January 10, 1840; Vicksburg *Sentinel*, January 6, 7, 1840.

[29] Remini, 458–459; Vicksburg *Sentinel*, January 28, 1840.

[30] Jackson *Enquirer*, January 25, 1840; *Mississippian*, January 24, 1840.

[31] *Ibid.*; *House Journal*, 1840, 155; *Senate Journal*, 1840, 171.

[32] *Mississippian*, January 24, 1840; Remini, 459.

[33] Glyndon G. Van Deusen, *The Life of Henry Clay* (Boston: Little, Brown and Company, 1937), 359, 362; Robert Seager, ed., *The Papers of Henry Clay*, vol. 9 (Lexington: The University Press of Kentucky, 1988), 790–792.

[34] Seager, *Papers of Henry Clay*, 790–792.

[35] Jackson *Southron*, January 5, 1843.

[36] *Mississippian*, February 23, 1843; Jackson *Southron*, February 23, 1843.

[37] *Ibid.*

[38] *Ibid.*

[39] Seager, *Papers of Henry Clay*, 805, 813–814. In 1842 Graves converted $165,000 of state funds to his own use. When discovered and arrested, he escaped and fled to Canada. Graves's wife later returned most of the money, but Graves never returned from Canada.

[40] Martha Boman, "A City of the Old South: Jackson, Mississippi, 1850–1860. *The Journal of Mississippi History*, XV (January, 1953). 2–8.

[41] McCain, 71; Boman, 16.

[42] McCain, 68.

[43] McCain, 69; Francis and Theresa Pulszky, *White Red Black: Sketches of Society in the United States*, vol. 2 (London: Turner and Company, 1853), 253–256.

[44] McCain, 116, 144.

[45] *Ibid.*, 115, 146.

[46] *Ibid.*, 105, 115.

[47] Jackson *Southron*, July 7, 1842, July 5, 1843.

[48] Boman, 6; Broadside, Natchez Trace Collection, University of Texas, copy in MDAH.

[49] McCain, 144.

[50] *Ibid.*, 185.

[51] RG 27, Governors Correspondence, vol. 35, Larmon's report to Pettus, January 19, 1860; RG 29, Auditor, vol. 71, "Expenditures for Mansion and Capitol Repairs and Furnishings," February 25, 1860—April 30, 1863.

These three buildings housed the state government in exile during the Civil War: (3) Lowndes County Courthouse, (1) First Christian Church, Columbus, and (2) Calhoun Institute, Macon. The collage was first printed in Dunbar Rowland's "Mississippi: Heart of the South" in 1925.

52 *House Journal*, 1861–62, 114; *Laws*, 1860, 298; RG 29, Auditor, vol. 71, "Expenditures for Mansion and Capitol Repairs and Furnishings, February 25, 1860—April 30, 1863." One of the cisterns was uncovered at the southwest corner of Capitol Green in 1970 during the construction of the Archives and History Building.

53 New York *Tribune*, April 9, 1861.

54 William Howard Russell, *My Diary North and South* (Gloucester, Massachusetts: Peter Smith, 1969,), 156. Originally published in 1863 and republished by Harper and Row in 1954 with an introduction by Fletcher Pratt. The edition cited is a reprint of the latter volume.

55 Hudson Strode, *Jefferson Davis, Confederate President* (New York: Harcourt, Brace and Company, 1959), 348–350; RG 27, Governors Correspondence, vol. 55, telegram, Pettus to Davis, December 2, 1862.

56 Strode, 350; Natchez *Daily Courier*, January 1, 1863; Vicksburg *Daily Whig*, December 30, 1862.

57 RG 27, Governors Correspondence, vol. 55, telegrams, Pemberton to Pettus and E.W. Pettus to John J. Pettus, May 6, 1863.

58 RG 27, Governors Correspondence, vol. 55, telegram Pemberton to Pettus, May 2, 1863; vol. 43, Pettus order, May 5, 1863.

59 RG 27, Governors Correspondence, vol. 55, telegrams, Hamilton to Pettus and Edward Malleu to Pettus, May 9, 1863.

60 RG 27, Governors Correspondence, vol. 51, vouchers, May 1, 1863.

61 An excellent source for the Civil War in Jackson is Horace Adams, "Military Operations in and Around Jackson, Mississippi, During the Civil War" (M.A. Thesis, University of Mississippi, 1950).

62 *Official Records, War of the Rebellion*, Series I, vol. 24, Part I, 722, 772, hereafter cited as *ORWR*.

63 U. S. Grant, *Personal Memoirs*, vol. 1 (New York: Charles L. Webster and Company, 1885), 506; William T. Sherman, *Memoirs*, vol. 1 (New York: Charles L. Webster and Company, 1892), 349; *ORWR*, Series I, vol. 24, Part I, 754.

64 Grant, *Memoirs*, 423–426.

65 *Ibid.*, 424; Sherman, *Memoirs*, 349; *ORWR*, Series I, vol. 24, Part I, 759.

66 *ORWR*, Series I, vol. 24, Part III, 314–315.

67 *Ibid.*, 315.

68 RG 27, Governors Correspondence, vol. 55, telegrams, R. Maxey to Pettus, Pettus to Davis, May 16, 1863.

69 *Mississippian*, June 11, 1863.

70 RG 27, Governors Correspondence, vol. 55, telegrams, Pettus to Davis, May 16, 1863, and Col. U. Bourne to Pettus, May 17, 1863.

71 RG 27, Governors Correspondence, vol. 55, telegrams, Smylie to Pettus, May 20, 1863; Johnston to Pettus, May 23, 1863; Johnston to Pettus, May 24, 1863.

72 RG 27, Governors Correspondence, vol. 55, telegrams, Jones S. Hamilton to Pettus, May 12, 1863; Rives to Pettus, May 22, 1863; Polka to Pettus, June 5, 1863.

73 *ORWR*, Series I, vol. 24, Part II, 536; Part III, 524–525.

74 *ORWR*, Series I, vol. 24, Part II, 536–537, 539–540.

75 *ORWR*, Series I, vol. 24, Part III, 531–532.

76 *Ibid.*; RG 27, Governors Correspondence, vol. 57, letter from James Lyon to Clark, January 17, 1865; letter from F.A. Whiting to Clark, April 26, 1865.

77 *Senate Journal*, 1863, 83; Dunbar Rowland, *History of Mississippi, the Heart of the South*, vol. 1 (Chicago-Jackson: The S.J. Clarke Publishing Company, 1925), 815.

78 *House* and *Senate Journals*, 1864, 1865.

79 RG 27, Governors Correspondence, vol. 52, Manship to Pettus, October 20, 1863.

80 *Senate Journal*, 1864, 12, 30; RG 27, Governors Correspondence, vol. 57, Auditor's Report, January 1, 1865.

81 RG 27, Governors Correspondence, vol. 60, telegram Whiting to Clark, October 14, 1864; *ORWR*, Series I, vol. 39, Part III, 788, 800.

82 RG 27, Governors Correspondence, vol. 57, Report, Whiting to Clark, February 6, 1865.

83 *Ibid.*

84 *Laws*, 1865, 14.

85 RG 27, Governors Correspondence, vol. 43, Executive Journal, May 6, 1865; Dunbar Rowland, ed., *Mississippi*, vol. 1 (Atlanta: Southern Historical Publishing Association, 1907), 443.

86 RG 27, Governors Correspondence, vol. 57, letter, Osband to Clark, May 20, 1865.

87 RG 27, Governors Correspondence, vol. 57, letter, Clark to Osband, May 22, 1865.

88 RG 27, Governors Correspondence, vol. 57, order appointing Captain Miller, May 22, 1865; letter, Clark to Osband, May 22, 1865.

89 *Ibid.*, various receipts.

90 *ORWR*, Series I, vol. 49, Part II, 879, 887, 926, 934, 952, 959–960.

91 *Ibid.*, Series II, vol. 8, 674, 723–724, 763–764.

ILLUSTRATION NOTES

P. 50   Photograph by E. von Seutter. MDAH.

p. 51   MSHM collections.

p. 53   Oil by Steve Moppert, 1978. From the original portrait ascribed to John Antrobus. Hall of Governors, MDAH.

p. 54   Photograph. MDAH.

p. 54   Engraving by Alfred Brennen. *Harper's New Monthly Magazine,* May, 1895.

p. 55   Pastel on paper by Jean Baptiste Adolphe LaFosse, 1839. MSHM.

p. 57   Carte de visite. MDAH.

p. 58   Engraving. John Warner Barber and Henry Howe, *Our Whole Country* (Cincinnati: Charles Tuttle, 1863) 2 vols.

82

p. 61   MSHM collections.

p. 62   MSHM collections.

p. 62   Etching from a painting by Alonzo Chappell, 1885. MSHM.

p. 64   Broadside. E. C. Barker Texas History Center, University of Texas.

p. 65   Engraving. *Frank Leslie's Illustrated Newspaper*, October 7, 1865. MDAH.

p. 66   Stereograph by E. von Seutter (detail). MDAH.

p. 69   Photograph, ca. 1860. Collection of Charles Galloway, Jr.

p. 69   MSHM collections.

p. 70   Pencil drawing by John James Audubon. Private collection.

p. 72   Masthead engraving. *Mississippian and State Gazette*, Jackson, Miss., October 20, 1898. MDAH.

p. 73   Engraving. Albert D. Richardson, *The Secret Service, the Field, the Dungeon and the Escape* (Hartford, Conn., 1865).

p. 74   Carte de visite by C. D. Fredericks, 1861. Library of Congress.

p. 74   MSHM collections.

p. 76, 77   Engraving: "Raising the Stars and Stripes over the capitol of the state of Miss." Harper's Weekly, June 20, 1863. MDAH.

p. 78   MSHM collections.

p. 79   Engraving: "Destruction of Rebel property at Jackson, May 15." *Harper's Weekly*, June 20, 1863. MDAH.

p. 80   Engraving: "The Civil War in America: Reoccupation of Jackson, Mississippi by the Confederates." *The Illustrated London News*, August 8, 1863. MDAH.

p. 81   Collage illustration. Dunbar Rowland, *History of Mississippi, Heart of the South* (Chicago-Jackson: S. J. Clarke, 1925), 4 vols.

Stereograph views of the Old Capitol, c. 1869 (above) looking south from North State Street showing corner of the Bowman House ruins, (below) looking north from South State Street.

From Reconstruction to Decay

The years from the end of the war in 1865 to the turn of the twentieth century spanned only a single generation. Yet in that brief time the Old Capitol, neglected throughout the war years, was rehabilitated during Reconstruction only to decay rapidly during the last quarter of the nineteenth century. Aged sixty years, by the turn of the century the building teetered on the edge of collapse. In 1900, the old building was shoved aside in favor of a new capitol, and in 1903, the Old Capitol was abandoned to become for a time a decaying relic.

In its late years as state capitol, the building witnessed dramatic events—military rule and the Constitutional Convention of 1868; the birth of Republican rule and its sudden demise in the legislative session of 1876; the last visit of Jefferson Davis to Jackson in 1884; the Constitutional Convention of 1890; the drive to build a new capitol. The first of these events took place in a refurbished building. The last occurred in a structure that was about to fall on the legislators and state officers who worked in it.

Reconstruction, 1865–1876

Of the largest of Jackson's public buildings, only the penitentiary was destroyed by the war. The others—the capitol, the mansion, and the state lunatic asylum—escaped largely unscathed except for damages to the furniture, windows and doors. Greater harm to these institutions came from inattention and from the workings of "Yazoo clay," the unstable material underlying the Jackson region that shifted the foundations and cracked the walls of large buildings.

The penitentiary, which became a munitions factory early in the war, was burned by Sherman during the May 1863 occupation of Jackson. The lunatic asylum, located two miles north of Jackson, was outside the Confederate defenses during Sherman's July 1863 siege of the town and thus received little damage from military operations. In fact, the facility continued to function throughout the war. But considerable damage resulted from the settling of the walls, and in 1866, a tornado and a fire added to the building's deterioration.[1]

In the fall of 1865, legislative investigators found the Governor's Mansion "entirely without furniture of any kind." They recommended a $2,000 appropriation to buy furniture and suggested that an agent be sent to Macon to bring back any pieces that had been moved there during the war. The legislative investigators recommended an additional appropriation of $5,000 to repair the mansion. To repair the capitol and the grounds, they said, would require an expenditure of $12,000. In addition, "a large number of negroes, not in Government employ" were living in huts on the capitol grounds. These newly freed slaves were illegally cutting timber on the grounds for firewood, the legislators complained, and should be removed.[2]

The legislators who made these recommendations were white Mississippians, and most of them only recently had supported the Confederacy. Since the removal and arrest of Governor Charles

Clark in May 1865, events had moved rapidly to reinstitute a loyalist civil government. Before his displacement by the military authorities, Clark had appointed William Sharkey and William Yerger, two old-line Whigs who had opposed secession, as emissaries to Washington. Their job was to meet with President Andrew Johnson and to determine how Mississippians could form a state government that would be satisfactory to the president and to Congress. President Johnson recommended that Mississippians who would take an oath of allegiance to the Union could elect delegates to a constitutional convention. He was certain that if the new government would renounce slavery by ratifying the Thirteenth Amendment and would grant some civil rights to the former slaves, Mississippi would be readmitted. Meanwhile, until a convention could meet and a government be formed, Johnson appointed Sharkey as provisional governor of Mississippi. So quickly did events proceed that he was destined to serve for only four months.[3]

President Johnson's choice of Sharkey was a shrewd one. William Lewis Sharkey was perhaps the most respected Mississippian of the prewar generation. He had come to Warren County in

Insane Asylum, Jackson

1803 from Tennessee, and over the next half century, he became Mississippi's most esteemed lawyer and judge. He served as Chief Justice of the High Court of Errors and Appeals from 1833 to 1851. A prewar Whig, Sharkey remained a Unionist throughout the war. Yet his reputation for wisdom, honesty, and selfless service was so great that he suffered little abuse. In 1865, secessionists were in disrepute among war-weary Mississippians, and prewar Unionists were looked to for leadership. Sharkey was the perfect choice to lead Mississippians toward Reconstruction; he was a staunch Unionist thoroughly trusted by the people.

Elections to the Constitutional Convention of 1865 were held on August 7, and the delegates convened in the capitol a week later. The delegates were overwhelmingly prewar Whigs who accepted the results of the war and desired quick accommodation with the national government. Nonetheless, they failed to do the things that President Johnson considered essential to undercut the growing power of the congressional radicals: they equivocated and temporized on the abolition of slavery, debating the prospect of compensation and questioning the legality of the Emancipation Proclamation, and they refused to grant even token civil rights to the freedmen. On October 2, 1865, former Confederate Brigadier General Benjamin G. Humphreys was elected to head the new government.

General Humphreys was one of many Mississippians who had opposed secession but had rallied to the defense of the Confederacy once the war began. He entered the United States Military Academy in 1825 in the same class as Robert E. Lee and Joseph E. Johnston, but in 1827, Humphreys was expelled along with a number of other cadets when a Christmas prank became a riot. When the war began, he organized a company of troops and left his Delta plantation for Virginia. Within months, Humphreys was made a

The ruins of Jackson was viewed from the north end (probably the roof) of the Old Capitol. This illustration was published in the October 7, 1865, issue of Frank Leslie's Illustrated Newspaper *with a report which referred to Jackson as "Chimneyville."*

regimental commander and promoted to colonel. After his brigade commander, William Barksdale, was killed at Gettysburg, Humphreys was given command of the Mississippi Brigade in Lee's Army of Northern Virginia. A serious wound in September 1864 ended his active service, and Humphreys served out the war on limited duty in south Mississippi. While he was a realist and an accommodationist, Humphreys was also a proud man who had fought well and wanted no humiliation.

The legislators convened at the capitol in October 1865 in no mood for political or social experiments. They were under the illusion that "Reconstruction" had been accomplished. Thus, they wished to concentrate on matters of economic recovery, and they mistakenly believed that the state would be allowed to set the postwar status of the freedmen. In holding this belief, they under-

estimated the determination of the congressional radicals. When the legislators refused to grant civil rights to the freedmen, passed the proscriptive "Black Code" to restrict the social and economic rights of the ex-slaves, and even refused to ratify the Thirteenth Amendment abolishing slavery, they set the stage for the congressional radicals to supplant Johnson's moderate policies of reconstruction with far harsher policies.

The legislators of 1865 were also in a mood of fiscal retrenchment. They faced the prospect of mammoth expenditures to rebuild state properties and public services, yet they had to exact the necessary money from an economically prostrate citizenry. To begin dealing with the repair and rebuilding of state properties, the lawmakers empowered Governor Humphreys to employ a state architect. He chose Captain A.J. Herod, a former Confederate captain of artillery.[4]

As a youth of nineteen, Herod had served in the Mexican War with Jefferson Davis's Mississippi Rifles. He volunteered for service in the Civil War and was immediately elected Captain of Company B, First Regiment, Mississippi Light Artillery. Herod served at Port Hudson from October 1862 to the fall of that bastion on July 9, 1863. He was captured there and spent the next fifteen months as a prisoner of war. Exchanged in October 1864, Herod was furloughed home to Hinds County. He soon returned to Confederate service under Lieutenant General Richard Taylor and was again captured in April 1865. He signed a parole on May 17, 1865, upon Taylor's surrender of his army.[5]

Whether Herod ever encountered or served with Brigadier General Humphreys during the war is uncertain. Possibly, Herod encountered the future governor during Herod's brief service in Virginia in 1864 or in 1864–65 when both men were on duty in Taylor's military Department of Alabama and Mississippi.

Despite the state's straitened circumstances, the legislators appropriated $19,000 for repairs to the capitol and the mansion and for furniture for the mansion: $12,000 for the capitol, $5,000 for the mansion, and $2,000 for furniture. These were the exact amounts recommended earlier by the Joint Standing Committee on Public Buildings.[6]

Herod went immediately to work drawing estimates and specifications for all the public buildings. His largest jobs were the repairs to the penitentiary and the lunatic asylum, so he did not file his report on the condition of the capitol with Governor Humphreys until February 23, 1866. Herod found the same defects that had been noted by Larmon in 1860 but that apparently had never been repaired. Crumbling walls and a badly leaking roof were the chief problems. Herod recommended running iron anchor rods through the building "to prevent the cracked and crumbling walls from tumbling to pieces."[7]

The leaking roof and the damage done by the water over the years was a much greater problem. Herod wanted to take up the old copper roofing that covered the portico and the rooms behind the rotunda and cover them with new tin. The old copper could then be used to make repairs on the dome. More serious, however, was the condition of the roof over the house and senate chambers. Water had rotted the roof timbers, and it would be dangerous to cover the roof with new metal without repairing the roof supports. Heavy timbers ran along the walls, and crosspieces rested on these. These crosspieces bore the weight of the roof. Both the wall timbers and the ends of the crosspieces were badly decayed. Herod recommended installing temporary supports while workmen replaced some of the old timbers and repaired others with splices or iron bolts. The only other alternative, according to Herod, was to remove the roof entirely, but that would inevitably loosen the ornamental ceilings in the house and senate chambers.[8]

The building, Herod concluded, was "without exception the most improperly contructed edifice that I have ever examined." The building materials were not durable, and little thought had been given to their weight-bearing qualities. If the repairs were not done immediately, he warned the governor, "the State of Mississippi will be under the heavy task of building another State House." On the other hand, if the state acted quickly, "the Capitol Building may be so repaired and strengthened that our Legislators will be able to use the building for half a century." A few thousand dollars, Herod concluded, would "preserve a building that has cost our state over half a million."[9]

Evidently, Governor Humphreys gave permission and Herod started to work, for the records indicate that carpenters and brickmasons were busily engaged at the capitol throughout 1866, apparently making the necessary repairs to the roof timbers. In March 1866, Herod added to his schedule repairs on the fence surrounding the capitol that had been put in place by Nichols. It was almost 700 feet in length and consisted of a brick wall eighteen inches high topped by iron pickets. The fence had suffered considerable damage during the war, and Herod suggested repairing it by lowering the brickwork to eleven inches and replacing the missing pickets.[10]

After working on the building for a year, Herod and Humphreys had to go before a special session of the legislature in October 1866 and

request additional money. Governor Humphreys delivered the bad news to the legislators in his opening message. Expenditures on the mansion had already exceeded the allotment by more than $7,000 with an estimated $24,000 still needed to finish the job; the penitentiary appropriation had been $30,000, and the governor asked for an additional $65,000. The $12,000 appropriation for the capitol had been exceeded by $12,500, and an additional $24,000 was still needed to finish the work.[11]

The figures shocked the lawmakers. The house passed an additional appropriation, but when the bill reached the senate, the senators amended the bill to abolish the office of state architect and to require the governor to solicit other bids for the work on the capitol. However, the amended bill failed final passage in the senate, and no legislative funds for capitol repairs were provided at the 1866 session.[12]

How Herod and Governor Humphreys covered their excess expenditures is unknown, but they did, for the records indicate that work on the capitol continued into 1867. In February 1867, the legislators partially remedied their parsimony of a year earlier by appropriating $10,000 for capitol repairs. By mid-1867, work on repairing the roof timbers was apparently complete, and the workmen were ready to lay on the new metal roof. In early June, Herod made a trip to the North to arrange for the purchase and shipment of sheet metal to cover the roof. Painting began in the spring of 1867. By the end of 1867, the work was complete.[13]

As the 1867 session of the Mississippi legislature adjourned, the United States Congress took control of Reconstruction policy and put the ex-Confederate states under military rule. Major General Edward O.C. Ord, one of Grant's three corps commanders at Vicksburg, was appointed to head the Fourth Military District consisting of Mississippi and Arkansas with his headquarters at Vicksburg. He was empowered to keep peace and order until loyal civil governments could be established in the two states under his authority. Ord did not remove Humphreys and his administration, but for the next year, the officers of civil government became mere figureheads. Ord's chief duty was to conduct a new registration of voters, and he was specifically ordered by Congress to enfranchise freedmen. A new more stringent oath made ex-Confederate leaders ineligible. The newly registered voters would then elect delegates to a constitutional convention, form a government, and be readmitted to the Union.[14]

Although Ord had the authority to remove

Hiram Revels, United States Senator

Hiram Revels being sworn in on the floor of the U.S. Senate, February 25, 1870.

In 1870, Hiram Revels of Mississippi became the first black American ever to sit in the United States Senate. He was, at the time of his election, a relatively obscure and reluctant political figure. Born of free parents in North Carolina, Revels was educated as a Methodist minister and teacher. He came to Mississippi after the Civil War as chaplain to a black regiment in the Union Army. He took up the ministry at Natchez. There, in 1869, he was drafted into Republican politics as a compromise, dark horse candidate for the state senate and was elected.

Upon his arrival at the Old Capitol in January 1870 for Mississippi's first Republican legislative session, Revels was called upon to deliver the prayer opening the senate session. So eloquent was his prayer that it brought Revels immediate respect and fame, and, according to one of his colleagues, the prayer made Revels a United States senator. Again as a compromise candidate, Revels was chosen by the state legislature to take Jefferson Davis's unexpired term which ran until March 1871.

After leaving the United States Senate in 1871, Revels was named as the first president of newly established Alcorn University.

the Humphreys administration, he did not do so, and Humphreys continued in office until June 1868. While Humphreys retained his title and continued to occupy his capitol office and to live in the mansion, he was practically powerless. All gubernatorial appointments were subject to military veto, and many offenses, especially those against freedmen, were tried in military courts.

By the fall of 1867, the new voter registration lists were complete, and of 137,561 registrants, 79,176, or fifty-seven percent, were ex-slaves. Almost all were Republicans. So discouraged were the Democrats that they offered no candidates for convention delegates, and Democratic voters refused to go to the polls in the elections. The result was a constitutional convention made up overwhelmingly of Republicans (although only eighteen were blacks) and dominated by the radicals (although the moderates outnumbered them).

The convention opened in the house chamber of the capitol on January 7, 1868, amidst much rancor and discord. The Democratic press throughout the state attacked the convention with bile and contentiousness perhaps unmatched in the history of the state. The acrimony, both at the convention and among the people of Mississippi, came from two issues—the constitutional status of the freedmen and the requirements for voting and for holding office.

The convention remained in session for more than four months; the members adjourned from their labors on May 18, 1868. They produced a constitution in many respects far more conservative than the Mississippi constitution of 1832. The governor's term was increased from two to four years, and the limitation on tenure for the governor was removed. The chief executive's appointive power was vastly enlarged, especially regarding judgeships. Whereas the 1832 constitution had mandated the election of all judges, the new constitution authorized the governor to appoint them all. On the other hand, the delegates also created Mississippi's first statewide, tax-supported system of free public schools. Arguments erupted when one conservative tried to write segregated schools into the constitution, but his effort failed. However, there was little sympathy among the delegates for mixed schools, and that issue was left to the legislature to decide. In the law establishing the public school system, the 1870 legislature remained silent on the issue, and separate schools for blacks and whites were established by local authorities.[15]

The issue that produced the most rancor at the convention was the article on the franchise and qualifications for holding office. The radicals were convinced that the spirit of rebellion still smouldered among many unreconstructed Mississippians, and they wished to keep government in the hands of loyal Republicans. Thus they suggested even tighter restrictions on the franchise than those required by Congress. Not only would the radical measures disfranchise former officeholders from the war years, but prospective voters would be required to admit under oath "the political and civil equality of all men," and nobody who had supported the Confederacy would be eligible for office. The latter provision would prevent most Democrats from holding office; it would also proscribe many Mississippians who had joined the Republicans—even some convention delegates.[16]

So heated did the arguments become that a sensational fight over the issue occurred at the capitol. Ex-Union Brigadier General Beroth B. Eggleston, an upstate New York native by way of Ohio, had arrived in Columbus in 1865 after serving as military governor of Atlanta. Three years later, he was chosen president of the constitutional convention. Elected as a moderate, he sided with the radicals and packed key committees with them. In the heat of the debate over the franchise article, Charles H. Townsend, a conservative carpetbagger who later deserted to the Democrats, called for a roll call vote. Eggleston refused, and Townsend "in uncomplimentary terms denounced Eggleston." In turn, defenders of Eggleston denounced Townsend. The principals then retired to the capitol grounds, where Eggleston and his friends attacked Townsend, and Townsend's friends retaliated. The melee that ensued had to be broken up by the town police.[17]

The fight symbolized the bitter resentment and animosity that pervaded the state as the convention adjourned. The convention ordered that the constitution be put to a vote of the people for ratification. In the same election, voters would choose legislators, congressmen, and state officers. Opponents vowed to defeat the constitution at the polls when it came up for ratification. They chose Governor Humphreys as their candidate for chief executive, and he began campaigning aggressively against the constitution. Major General Irwin McDowell, who had become military governor in June, forcibly barred Humphreys from his capitol office for "obstructing Reconstruction" and appointed young Brigadier General Adelbert Ames as provisional governor. Several days later, Ames forcibly ejected Humphreys and his family from the mansion. These blunt moves redounded to the political benefit of the opponents of the constitution.

On election day, the constitution failed by 7,000 votes, Humphreys defeated Eggleston by the same margin, and the Democrats won both houses of the legislature. The latter victories, of course, were moot, for with the rejection of the constitution, there were no offices to fill.

The Republicans cried intimidation, and their leaders considered simply declaring a Republican victory. At that prospect, even the normally steady-tempered ex-governor Sharkey became enraged and charged into the capitol to confront the Republican leaders. Cooler heads prevailed, however, and the problem was dumped onto Congress. For a year the problem languished, and Mississippi continued under military rule—a military rule carried out by a man who could hardly have been more ill-suited for the task of governing a people so fractious and divided.[18]

Adelbert Ames was a New Englander and a soldier. He combined the moral certainty of a Puritan with the political inflexibility of a soldier. He was also the son-in-law of Benjamin "Beast" Butler, perhaps the most hated Yankee general of the war and now an equally despised radical congressman. Ames was thirty-two years old when he was appointed provisional governor. Since leaving his native Maine to enter West Point in 1856, he had been in the army. A brilliant record during the Civil War earned the young officer promotions from lieutenant in 1861 to brevet major general in 1865. In 1866, after the Union army was demobilized, Ames returned to his permanent regular army rank of lieutenant colonel and took service with the troops occupying Mississippi.

Their election loss in 1868 threw the radical Republican faction into momentary retreat, and when the Constitution of 1868 was resubmitted in 1869, the voters ratified it without the harsh restrictions against ex-Confederates for voting and holding office. The elections of 1869 also swept into state office a full slate of Republicans headed by Governor James Lusk Alcorn.[19]

Alcorn personified the shift towards moderation in the Republican leadership. A Coahoma County lawyer, planter, and political leader since the mid-1840s, he had served as a Whig representative in the antebellum legislature and had been a delegate to the secession convention. Although he argued against secession, Alcorn had eventually signed the secession ordinance. He rose to the rank of brigadier general of state troops, and although he remained a Unionist at heart and an anti-slavery slaveholder, he refused to take the oath of allegiance to the Union until the end of the war. After resigning his commission, Alcorn served his county in the wartime legislatures of 1863 and

"Cotton and its Capitol, Jackson, Mississippi" Mississippi was the center of America's cotton belt from the time the Old Capitol was built through the rest of the 19th century. Cotton was the source of the state's prosperity as well as most of her problems throughout this time.

1864. After the war, hoping to ameliorate the policies of the radical element in the party, he became a Republican. In 1869, with the tacit support of many Democrats, he was elected the first governor under the Constitution of 1868.

Alcorn's administration in 1870 faced many problems— financing the new system of public education, establishing stable local governments after years of instability and turmoil, reestablishing and repairing public services. In attacking the latter problem, Alcorn's administration began the most extensive renovation of the capitol since its construction.

In addition to the economic depression after the war, continuing efforts by some legislators to move the capital out of Jackson had handicapped efforts to spend large sums on rehabilitating the building. In 1866, some support emerged in the legislature for moving the capitol to an unspecified site in north Mississippi. The Consitutional Convention of 1868 appointed a committee to examine the possibility of a move to Attala County. The committee recommended inserting a provision in the new constitution requiring that the capital be moved to Kosciusko in 1875, but the convention refused to adopt it. In 1870, the Republican-dominated legislature received an invitation from Vicksburg leaders to make their city the capital. They reminded the legislators that Vicksburg was already the commercial capital of the state.[20]

Remodeling the House Chamber

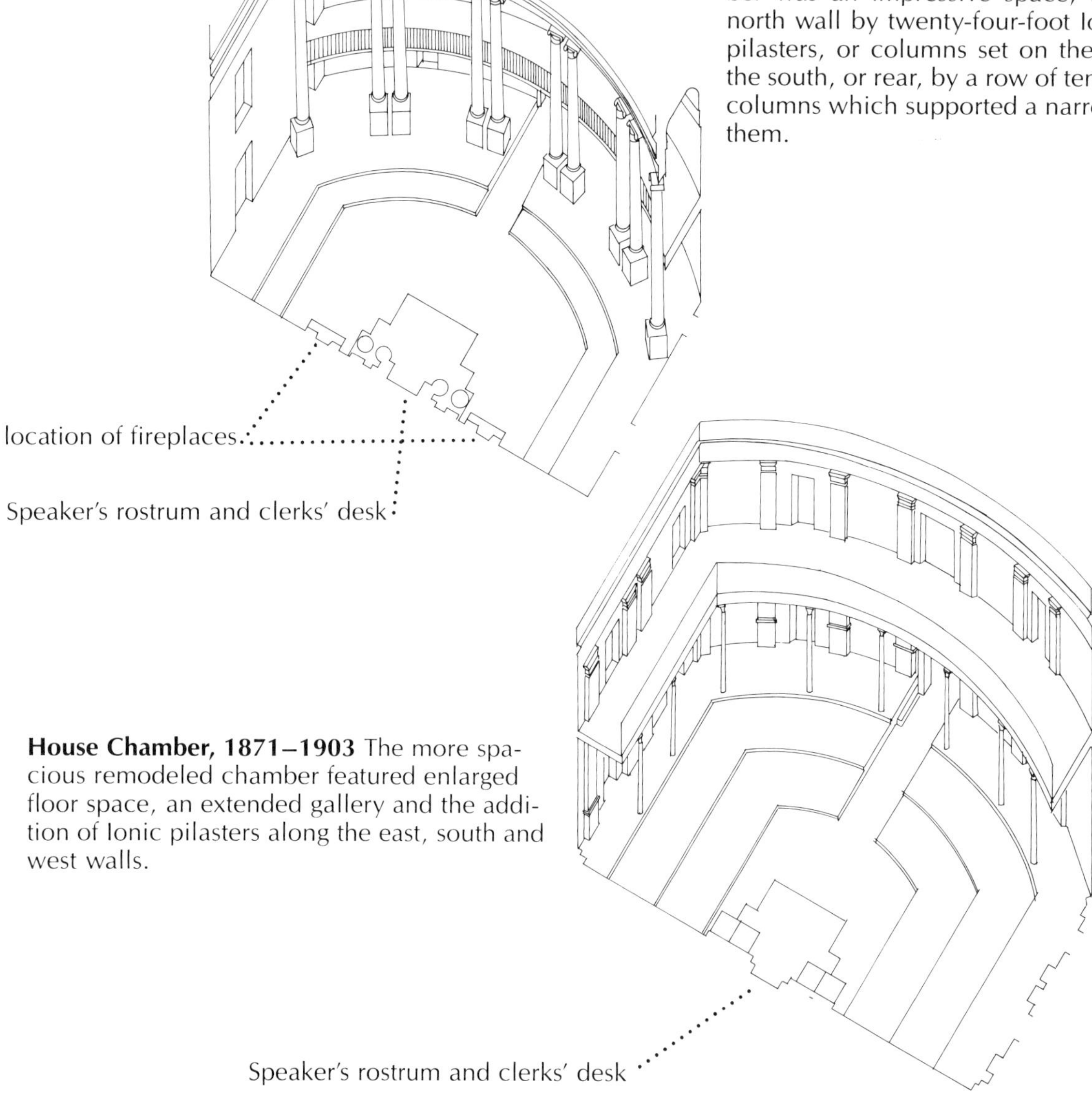

House Chamber, 1839–1870 The original chamber was an impressive space, bound across the north wall by twenty-four-foot Ionic columns and pilasters, or columns set on the wall, and across the south, or rear, by a row of ten equally tall Ionic columns which supported a narrow gallery behind them.

House Chamber, 1871–1903 The more spacious remodeled chamber featured enlarged floor space, an extended gallery and the addition of Ionic pilasters along the east, south and west walls.

This photo, c.1903, shows the house chamber as Willis remodeled it in 1870 and was a guide for the 1959 restoration.

Nothing came of Vicksburg's effort, and the legislators must have considered the matter settled—that the capital would remain at Jackson—for the 1870 session of the legislature appropriated $70,000 "for the repairing of the State Capitol, to make the same safe and tenable for the occupants thereof." They also made large appropriations for the mansion and for the state lunatic asylum. The legislators appointed the Standing Committee on Public Buildings consisting of five members, F.E. Franklin, J.M. Stone, W.H. Gibbs, J. Aaron Moore, and Joseph Bennett to administer the repairs. Franklin was chosen chairman, and Bennett was made secretary. Franklin, a physician and lawyer from Ohio, had enlisted in the Union army as a private and had finished the war as a colonel. After the war, he had settled in Yazoo County, and in 1870, he was chosen Speaker of the House in the first Republican legislature. In September 1870, just as the committee was beginning to award contracts, Franklin suddenly died, and John Marshall Stone was named chairman.[21]

Although the legislature had not provided for an architect, the committeemen immediately saw the need for expert advice. Hoping that they could convince the next session of the legislature in 1871 to approve, they hired Joseph Willis to supervise the repairs to the capitol and to oversee the construction of a major addition to the lunatic asylum. In 1870, Willis was living and working in Memphis, but during the decade before the Civil War, he had done some important architectural work in Jackson. In fact, after taking over an unsuccessful start by architect William Gibbons, Willis had been the architect on the construction of the lunatic asylum from 1850 to 1855. In 1854, he had served as architect for repairing the mansion, and about the same time he had supervised the construction of an addition to the Jackson City Hall.[22]

The 1870 legislature did not adjourn until mid-July, but the Committee on Public Buildings started work immediately. Willis's first major task was to draw the plans and specifications for the repairs so that contractors could make their bids. The new state architect planned the most extensive renovation of the building since its construction thirty years before. Over the years the building had become structually unstable—the walls had cracked in many places, and the north and south walls were pulling away from the front and back walls. The local stone that had been used by Nichols for the first story was soft, and it had broken in numerous places. The stone entryways at the front were sagging under the weight of the portico above. The stone lintels and frontispieces over the north and south entrances had cracked and were about to fall.[23]

Willis's specifications called for a system of rods and anchors to tie together and stabilize the walls. A few iron rods had been run through the building by A.J. Herod in 1866–67. Willis planned to leave those in place and add a more extensive network. Two iron rods more than an inch in diameter would be run through the entire length of the building just inside the back wall at the top and bottom of the second story. Inside the front wall, matching rods would run from both ends of the building to the rotunda. Herod had put rods across both ends of the building, so Willis suggested only one additional rod at each end. He called for additional iron rods to run entirely across the building under the floors and just under the galleries at the rear of the house and senate chambers. All of the rods would have ten-inch washers and bolts on each end and turnbuckles in the centers "so that they can be screwed up perfectly tight."[24]

The walls would also be anchored at both rear corners by eight iron corner brackets. The brackets would be set inside and outside both rear corners and bolted together through the walls. Two four-inch iron bands would be run around the circular wall on the rear of the building at the top and bottom of the second floor. The bands would be held in place by rods attached to the floor joists. Finally all cracked and broken walls were to be repaired with new bricks.[25]

Nichols's stone window sills and lintels were also giving way. Willis called for removing all of them except those under the portico and replacing them with iron lintels and sills that would be painted to resemble stone. The few good stone lintels and sills could be used to repair the windows under the portico. Willis specified that the stone lintels over the north and south entrances be replaced with iron and that the stone frontispieces over the entrances also be replaced by iron. The entryways under the front portico were rectangular and made of stone, and the stone had begun to sag and crack under the weight above. Willis wanted to tear out the old stone and build brick arches that would be stuccoed and painted to look like stone.[26]

Willis also was forced to address the continuing problem of the roof. Once again, for the second time in five years, rafters and roof beams needed replacing and repairing, and a badly leaking roof needed patching. Willis called for a repair job similar to that done by Herod only five years earlier. He planned to jack up the main timbers over both the house and senate chambers and splice or replace defective beams. Although Willis called for an entirely new system of gutters, he initially planned only to patch the roof; in fact, he had to replace the entire roof with new tin.[27]

In his repair of the house chamber, Willis significantly modified its design. The number of representatives in the house had increased dramatically, and Willis had to find more floor space to seat them. Nichols had originally built the chamber with pilasters only on the north wall. These pilasters had matched a row of columns across the rear that rose from floor to ceiling. The columns also supported the gallery across the rear of the chamber. The space between the columns and the back wall formed a kind of lobby. Willis specified that the columns, along with the entablature and cornice over them be removed, thus allowing additional rows of desks across the rear of the chamber. The gallery was to be extended along both sides of the hall and supported "by iron bearers extending through the walls" and by iron brackets underneath. The ceiling was to be made plain except for Nichols's ornamental center medallion. Pilasters, to match those on the front wall, would be added along the side walls. The floor where the columns had been located would be raised five inches and made level to the rear of the chamber. The fireplaces in both the house and the senate were "to be stopped up, and the mantles and projections to be removed, and flues fixed for stoves." Four large coal stoves were to be put in the house and two in the senate.[28]

Over the years, a list had accumulated of smaller repairs that needed to be done—painting, repairing doors and door frames, laying new flagging in the rotunda, putting in new pavement and fencing around the building, installing an iron railing between the columns on the portico, and building new front steps.[29]

The Committee on Public Buildings acted with extraordinary speed. The $70,000 appropriation for capitol repairs was approved on July 21, 1870, and the members of the committee held their first meeting on July 22. In early August they advertised for bids in Jackson, Vicksburg, Meridian, Holly Springs, Memphis, Chicago, St. Louis, and Cincinnati. A month later, on September 6, they opened the bids and awarded the contract to Keary, Stanton and Company of Vicksburg. Their initial contract was for $59,700. However, in three separate supplemental contracts covering additional work not foreseen by Willis in his initial specifications, Keary and Stanton's contract was increased to $69,500. The supplemental contracts included painting and papering in the offices on the first floor, an entirely new roof rather than the

Senate desk and chair, purchased following the 1870 renovation of the building.

anticipated patching, and various other small repairs on the interior of the building. Among the latter was a new "iron cap . . . put on the balustrade in the rotunda, as the wooden cap had been cut to pieces, or hacked a good deal." Whether the "hacking" had been done by the pocketknives of idle legislators or the sabers of Yankee soldiers, Willis did not say.[30]

Willis indicated in a report written late in 1870 for the Committee on Public Buildings that the interior repairs would be complete by the time the legislature convened in January. Within a few weeks of the legislature's convening, he promised, everything would be done. "The plastering is

(overleaf) *Stereograph views of Jackson street scenes* (clockwise, from top) *South State Street across from the Old Capitol; South State Street, looking south from the Old Capitol; Spengler House and North State Street looking north from the Old Capitol; Old Capitol and Capitol Street looking east; Pearl River Bridge, probably at Silas Brown Street; a residence at North State Street and Amite Street, looking west.*

nearly all completed," Willis reported, " and the painters are at work with a big force." J.M. Coats had been granted a contract to build seven water closets, four in the north end of the building and three in the south end. Pumps and pipes would carry away the sewerage into "sinks" behind the building. These, too, Willis said, should be ready for the legislators.[31]

The contractors had kept on schedule despite finding the roof in much worse condition than originally anticipated, making it necessary to put on an entirely new metal roof. The new roof should end the chronic leaking, Willis said, provided that the gutters and downspouts were kept clean and the roof was repainted every three years. He also suggested that "the door opening out of the dome onto the roof should be kept locked to keep the boys from running over the roof, for nothing injures a roof more than running over it; and I am told that the roof has frequently been the playhouse for a large number of boys."[32]

Willis concluded by making three additional recommendations to the lawmakers; all were endorsed by the members of the committee. First, he suggested remodeling and rebuilding the spiral staircases. The steps were too narrow and too steep, he said, and the style was "an eye-sore." They should be built of iron "in the modern style." Second, the iron fence in front of the capitol should be removed and replaced with another more "modern" iron fence. The old one could be used, he suggested, to replace the decaying board fences at the north and south ends of Capitol Green. Apparently, the repairs to the fence that Herod had advised in 1866 had not been done. Willis also recommended that the water closets in the rear of the building be enlarged by "bringing them out further from the rear wall, as, at present, they are too narrow and contracted." Finally, he said, a small coal house should be built behind the Old Capitol to store coal for the new stoves and coal grates that had replaced the old fireplaces.[33]

The Committee on Public Buildings headed by future governor John Marshall Stone, architect Joseph Willis, and contractors Keary and Stanton had accomplished a remarkable feat. The contract had been awarded in September 1870; by February 1, 1871, the repairs to the interior of the building were complete. By mid-May, the work on the exterior also was complete. The work went fast in part because priority was given to the capitol over the much larger and more complex construction effort at the lunatic asylum. Perhaps more remarkably, the capitol repairs were done within the $70,000 appropriation. Keary and Stanton collected $69,500 for their work, and J.M. Coats was awarded $500 for work on the water closets. The Republicans, who were constantly lambasted by their Democratic opponents for graft, corruption, and inefficient government, conducted the repairs on the capitol with honesty and dispatch.

Neglect, 1876–1903

The refurbished capitol served as the scene in 1876 for the ouster of the Republican government and the restoration of the Democrats to power. The underlying tensions in the Mississippi Republican Party between radicals and moderates, personified by the political and personal enmity between moderate James L. Alcorn and radical Adelbert Ames, in 1873 broke out into open factional warfare. Both Alcorn and Ames came home from their Senate seats in Washington to seek the Republican gubernatorial nomination. The contest accentuated the natural divisions that had existed in the party from the beginning of Reconstruction. Ames and his supporters, mostly carpetbaggers and newly enfranchised blacks, distrusted the sincerity of the ex- Confederates and believed that the newly won civil rights of the freedmen could be guaranteed only through radical domination and federal protection. The

100

moderate faction led by Alcorn wanted to guarantee the Republican Party's future by enlarging its base among Mississippi whites. As long as the party depended almost wholly on black votes, the moderates argued, Mississippi's politics would remain racially polarized. The moderates were also less enthusiastic about full and immediate equality for freedmen than were the radicals. Thus, the Ames faction viewed the moderates as being soft on civil rights.

Ames, largely through control of the black vote, won the Republican nomination in August 1873, and despite Alcorn's entry into the race as an independent, Ames won the governorship in November. The Ames administration simultaneously marked the high point of Radical Republicanism in Mississippi and its demise. Many blacks were elected to office with Ames, and the new governor refused to extend his hand either to the Democrats or to the moderate faction of his own party. Tax rates increased, and Ames was soon embarrassed by corruption among his allies, especially Lieutenant Governor Alexander K. Davis, and in the radical-dominated governments of Vicksburg and Warren County. In answer to complaints, Ames charged Democrats and moderate Republicans with racism and disloyalty.

The catalyst for Ames's failure and the return to power of the Democrats was soaring taxes coupled with economic stagnation. The crisis came first in Vicksburg and Warren County in late 1874, when white conservatives rose up and in a violent confrontation threw the radicals from power. Federal troops later restored the Republicans, but a pattern had been set. In the elections of 1875, capitalizing on the widespread disgust with high taxes and corruption and using the same tactics of violence and intimidation that had worked a year earlier at Vicksburg, the Democrats gained control of the legislature.

When the new Democratic legislature convened in early January 1876, the lawmakers set about the task of driving Ames and his administration from office. The corrupt Lieutenant Governor Davis was impeached and removed from office. Superintendent of Education Thomas W. Cardozo, a member of the corrupt radical machine that ruled Vicksburg and Warren County, resigned under threat of impeachment and removal. Governor Ames was at first inclined to fight the Democratic legislature, and he hired lawyers to do so. But after the legislators drew up charges of impeachment and after it became apparent that he would be removed, Ames resigned. The Democrats had agreed that he could do so with no stain on his integrity.

The Democrats had unseated the Republicans with a platform of fiscal retrenchment—lowering taxes and cutting state expenditures. In 1876, they set about their fiscal program with a will. The Democrats slashed taxes; they fired many government employees and lowered the salaries of the rest; they drastically cut back state expenditures for public schools and other public services. In 1875, the Republicans spent $1,400,000. Within the next decade, the Democrats reduced annual expenditures to $600,000.[34]

Soon after Joseph Willis's 1871 repairs to the Old Capitol, a traveler to Jackson pronounced the building "solid and not unhandsome." Like the other public buildings in Jackson, he noted, the capitol was "well built and commodious." Twenty years later, in 1895, another traveler reported his impressions of the building. The capitol, he observed, was "a pitiful object of neglect." The clock on the portico put there by the city of Jackson a half century before was "a great plate of rust." The roof over the senate chamber was supported by "rough trusses of raw wood," and the "statues of Bacchus and Venus in the once noble lobby beneath the dome now stand ridiculous in a scene of untidiness and slow decay." The once-beautiful house chamber, he lamented, "is ornamented with the advertisement of an insurance company, the faded banner of a lodge of Confederate veterans," and "a cheap portrait that dangles threateningly overhead."[35]

The Republican repairs of 1870–71 had saved the Old Capitol from utter ruin. Democratic retrenchment over the next two decades doomed the building's future as the state capitol. By 1900, neglect and stingy appropriations had allowed the Old Capitol to fall to pieces. Between 1876 and 1880, an average of $800 annually was spent on capitol maintenance and repairs. In some years even that small amount had to be drawn from the governor's contingency fund because the legislators failed to appropriate any money for capitol expenses. Relatively inexpensive repairs like replastering ceilings and repairing cracks in the walls remained undone.[36]

By 1880, however, major structural problems were apparent— problems so threatening that they could not be ignored. The Senate Committee on Public Works and the House Committee on Public Buildings and Grounds investigated the condition of the capitol. They found that the south end of the building had settled eight inches lower than the north end and that the south wall had "sprung out at least from eight to twelve inches from a plumb line." The wall was kept from falling only by the anchors that Willis had installed in 1871. The roof was leaking once again. Because the building was settling toward the southeast corner and the south wall was leaning outward, water ran to the south end of the building and seeped down between the walls, weakening the brickwork and further undermining the foundation at that end of the building. Moreover, the dome over the senate chamber was hung from the roof trusses and threatened to come crashing down on the heads of the senators.[37]

The problems seemed to the lawmakers so serious that they appropriated $8,000 for repairs—the largest amount since the $70,000 repairs by the Republicans nine years earlier. Yet only a fraction of the appropriation was spent. In February 1881, a storm tore off a portion of the roof, further damaging the building. Governor John Marshall Stone spent $1,620.97 to repair the storm damage and to make other minor repairs, but he refused to spend the money on major structural repairs. He admitted that the building was "greatly in need of repairs"; the only solution, however, was to take down some of the walls and to rebuild them, a job that would require a much larger appropriation than $8,000.[38]

Probably at this time, wooden pilings were put in to support the sagging dome over the senate chamber. Later records reveal that these supports ran from the ground floor in the offices of the governor and secretary of state to the roof over the senate chamber. These pilings were noted in an architect's evaluation of the building in 1896.

Apparently, the legislators considered their $8,000 appropriation in 1880 ample to run the capitol as well, for they allocated nothing during the biennium 1880–81 for capitol expenses. Again, as in 1876, these routine expenses had to be paid from the governor's contingency fund. An appropriation was made for capitol expenses in 1882, but the amount was insufficient to cover needed repairs, and the difference had to be made up from the contingency fund. The "delapidated" governor's office was renovated, plastered, painted, and carpeted. The office of the secretary of state also received new plaster, paint, and carpets. Some repairs on the roof were also necessary.[39]

With the inattention to the fundamental structural problems afflicting the Old Capitol, the building got steadily worse. The foundation continued to sink on the south end, cracks in the walls widened, and the walls leaned more and more out of plumb. The cracks and the leaning walls admitted great quantities of water, rotting the roof timbers and ruining the plaster on the walls and the ceilings. After reporting in 1886 that some repairs had been made to the roof, the fences, and some of the offices during the previous two years, the keeper of the capitol, Mary Morancy, pled with the 1886 legislators to reach "some positive conclusions as to the repairs necessary to put the capitol in good order." The building, she concluded, was "in a dreadful condition."[40]

During the spring of 1886, a storm again blew the roof off the south end of the building, and tarpaulins had to be rented from New Orleans to cover the roof until repairs could be made. The keeper's report of 1888 carried a panicky tone. "This building," she said, "is in imminent danger of falling, the walls are constantly sinking and cracking, the ceiling falling and the roof springing

John Marshall Stone and the Old Capitol

John Marshall Stone returned home to Tishomingo County from the Civil War a colonel who had fought with Lee in the Army of Northern Virginia. For the next thirty-five years until his death in 1900, Stone's career was bound up with the Old Capitol. For twelve years, 1876–1882 and 1890–1896, Stone occupied the governor's office, longer than any other chief executive in the history of Mississippi.

Stone's identification with the Old Capitol building began in 1870 when he went as a Democrat to the Republican-dominated legislature. He was immediately appointed to the joint committee on public buildings formed to repair and refurbish the Old Capitol. Republican Speaker F. E. Franklin was named chairman of the committee, but he died before the work began, and Stone was chosen committee chairman. Ironically, the expensive Republican-sponsored repairs in 1870–1871 were overseen by an ex-Confederate colonel and future Democratic governor.

In fact, as president pro tempore of the state senate, Stone succeeded to the governor's chair when Governor Adelbert Ames along with his administration, was forced from office in 1876. Elected to a full term in 1877, Stone served until 1882. He served from 1886 to 1890 on the Railroad Commission before being chosen in 1890 for another term as governor. The terms of state officers were extended for two additional years by the new Constitution of 1890, so Stone stayed on as governor until 1896.

Stone's first political task had been to oversee the 1870–1871 repairs to the Old Capitol. Twenty years afterwards, in his last public service, he pre-

sided over the decay of the same building. Though he warned of the dangers and called repeatedly on the legislators to repair the building, they refused. By the time Stone left office in 1896, the Old Capitol was on the verge of collapse. John Marshall Stone died on March 26, 1900, one month after the legislators authorized the construction of the New Capitol.

new leaks." The exterior of the building had not been painted for almost twenty years, and the floors in the house and senate chambers and in the committee rooms had needed replacement for years.[41]

On August 12, 1890, 134 delegates from Mississippi's seventy-five counties gathered in the chamber of the house of representatives at the rapidly decaying Old Capitol. They had been elected to write a new constitution for the state of Mississippi. A number of disparate groups with varied aims had coalesced to produce the convention. Many conservatives were opposed to the Constitution of 1868 because it was a creature of the hated Republican Radicals of Reconstruction. Small farmers from the hill counties wanted to increase their influence in state politics by reapportioning the legislature. Others wanted stronger regulation of railroads, or prohibition, or an end to leasing convicts to private contractors, or any number of other pet interests.

Whatever their feelings on other issues, however, by 1890 almost all Mississippi whites had come to favor the removal of blacks from politics. Perceptions of "black domination" during Reconstruction were strong. While black voters had largely been controlled by white conservatives since 1876, the threat always existed that the Republicans, nationally dominant in the late nineteenth century, would revive a "southern strategy" based on black voters, thereby effectively renewing Reconstruction. So the primary reason for the new constitution was to end voting and office holding by blacks and to do so in ways that would not obviously conflict with the Fourteenth and Fifteenth Amendments to the United States Constitution.

The delegates met for eighty-one days, and they produced a constitution that satisfied nobody completely on the issues of reapportionment, regulation, and reform. But they accomplished effectively the task of disenfranchising blacks through poll taxes, literacy tests, and long registration and residency requirements.

The convention met in a building that was, in the words of the keeper of the capitol, "in a dreadful state of decay," with cracking walls, falling plaster, leaking roof, and other ailments too numerous to list. Working amidst such crumbling surroundings, the delegates could hardly avoid addressing the obvious delapidation of the old building.

Soon after the convention assembled, the former Confederate general and current president of A & M College, Stephen D. Lee, called the Old Capitol unsafe and noted the certainty that a new capitol would soon have to be built. He asked for the appointment of a committee to investigate "the advisability of the state retaining the present penitentiary property as a location for the new capitol." The ground there was stable, he said, and the old penitentiary showed no signs of cracking or shifting. Convention president S.S. Calhoon appointed Lee to head a committee of five to study and report on the matter.[42]

Nichols's old penitentiary, on the nothern edge of town when it was built, now occupied a prime site in a growing downtown Jackson. The building had been burned by Sherman in May 1863, and after the war the legislature adopted the expedient of leasing convicts to private contractors. Even after the penitentiary was repaired during Reconstruction, it could not house all convicts, and the convict-lease continued. While Jacksonians complained of the penitentiary's presence in the middle of town, getting the land for a new capitol was no easy matter. Some people, including prison reformers, wanted to sell the land and use the money to end the convict-lease.

The *Clarion-Ledger* lent editorial support for a new capitol on the penitentiary site by declaring the Old Capitol "in senile decay . . . Too small, too old, and . . . disgraceful to the intelligence and manhood of the state."[43]

However, this first attempt to set aside the penitentiary site for a new capitol failed. One of the chief reforms expected from the delegates was the elimination of the brutal and corrupt practice of leasing convicts to private planters and contractors. Some reformers, led by delegate George G. Dillard of Noxubee County, advocated abolishing the convict-lease and establishing state prison farms. They wanted to generate the funds to buy prison farm lands by selling the valuable land in the center of Jackson on which the penitentiary stood.[44]

Lee's committee apparently considered that the constitutional convention would be willing to set aside the penitentiary site for a future new capitol. The delegates, however, refused to make such a commitment and left the disposition of the property to a future legislature. With that decision, Lee gave up on the penitentiary site. His committee recommended instead that the Old Capitol "be remodeled by making additions on the east and west sides and near the north and south ends, so as to thoroughly strengthen and brace the building." This could be done, the committee said, for no more than $100,000. "The entire matter," the committee concluded, should "be relegated to the legislature."[45]

In his message to the 1892 legislature, the first to convene under the new constitution, Governor Stone emphasized the sad state of the capitol and called for a joint committee to study the possibilities of general and permanent repairs. But the legislators appropriated only $5,000 for 1892 and $2,000 for 1893 for immediate repairs to the capitol and the grounds, and they named the governor, the secretary of state, and the auditor a committee to direct the repairs. In 1894, Governor Stone reported that the "small amount heretofore appropriated" had proved wholly inadequate for any "general improvements," and had been used entirely for repairs to save the building "from further damage and decay." The governor also warned of "the vast accumulation of worthless printed matter in some of the upper rooms, which, from its great weight, renders them unsafe and dangerous."[46]

Finally moved to action not only by the delapidation and the decay but by the positively unsafe conditions of the building, the legislators in 1896 empowered Governor Anselm J. McLaurin, Lieutenant Governor J.H. Jones, and Speaker of the House James F. McCool to hire architects who would make a thorough examination of the building and report to the legislature. Within weeks, the architects had done their work and filed their reports. The news was grim.[47]

L. M. Weathers of Memphis started his inspection with an examination of the foundation; then he worked his way around the building with a plumb line; finally, he made a detailed inspection of the timbers supporting the roof. He found nothing good. Sixty years before, William Nichols had created a foundation for the walls by throwing the rubble stone and brick from John Lawrence's false start into a trench. The inferior mortar used to cement the foundation never set, and even if it had, Weathers pointed out, the foundation was too small to support the weight of the walls.

The entire building was shifting south and west. The base of the south wall was a foot lower than the wall on the north, and nowhere were the walls in plumb. The south wall leaned out seven to nine inches; the front wall leaned to the west three to four inches; the rear wall leaned west four inches. The great weight of the roof had caused the inner walls to sink farther than the outer walls. Cracks in both the inner and outer walls abounded. Joseph Willis had tied the building together with iron rods capped with nine-inch iron washers. The enormous strain placed on these by the shifting building was gradually pulling the washers through the brick walls. The stone walls of the first story could "be crushed between the fingers." The ceilings over the house and senate

James Strother Madison

One of the most popular men to occupy this chair as Speaker of house of representatives, Madison was a cotton planter from Brooksville and a member of the progressive Farmers' Alliance political party. He was the first Speaker to be elected unanimously, and was presented an engraved tilting pitcher by the six black members of the House at the end of the 1890 session for his impartial rulings.

chambers were "in a dangerous condition" and "liable to fall at any time."

Weathers found that the roof trusses had "careened toward the south end of the building." The ends of many trusses had rotted away, as had the wall plate on which the trusses rested, and the unrotted trusses had settled and crushed the brick walls. The rotunda leaned southwestward more than six inches. Weathers concluded that "any money spent towards repairing the building would be virtually thrown away."

Another architect, William D. Hull, examined the building and reported the same defects as those found by Weathers. Hull's report conveyed a sense of real danger. Except for Willis's iron rods, he said, the south wall would almost certainly collapse. The roof, Hull noted, was "in worse condition than any public building I have ever inspected." To save the senate dome from collapse, wooden pilings had been erected through the offices of the governor and the secretary of state, probably in 1880, for support. But the roof trusses had rotted and split between the pilings, and the dome was yet in danger of falling. Hull then turned his attention to the house chamber where "a roof that will weigh seventy tons" was supported by trusses "which have rotted entirely off at the ends." "There can be no disguising the fact," Hull warned, "that real danger hangs over the heads of both halls of the Legislature." Somewhat anti-climactically, he reported that "the roof over the front portico is moving with the columns west." Like Weathers, Hull concluded that attempts to renovate and restore the building would be false economy.

A senate resolution calling for immediate adjournment until the secretary could locate a safe place to meet was offered and defeated by a narrow margin. Before the 1896 session ended, however, the senators passed a resolution allowing the governor, secretary of state, and attorney general to confer before the next session. If they deemed the capitol unsafe, they could select suitable offices for state government and a site for the next legislative session. The bill was tabled and died in the house.[48]

Two events occurred immediately as a result of the dismal reports of 1896. Over the years, the office rooms on the third floor had been abandoned. When the state library was moved into the old chancery court room on the ground floor in 1858, the old library on the third floor became a depository for seldom-used books and old papers. Gradually over the years, the clutter spread, and by the 1890s, the entire third floor had become a dumping ground for old state records. By 1896, the weight of these documents posed a serious threat to a building already on the verge of structural collapse. Secretary of State J.L. Power cleaned out the third floor in early 1896. He burned several tons of old papers that had accumulated over the previous fifty years. Several wagonloads of valuable documents were sent for storage to the penitentiary. Second, and perhaps more important, the governor and the legislators made plans to deal with the problem in an 1897 special session.[49]

The Drive for a New Capitol

Before adjourning their 1896 session, the legislators had appointed a committee composed of Governor McLaurin, Secretary of State J.L. Power, and Attorney General Wiley N. Nash to collect bids for a new capitol "costing not less than $550,000 nor more than one million dollars." The three officials were ordered to advertise for plans and bids and to "collate all plans and information . . . that would be useful to the Legislature in letting a contract for the erection of a new State House."[50]

On May 12, 1896, the committee issued specifications "for the information and guidance of competing architects," and they polled the legislators by mail to gain some impression of the preferred site. Apparently, most favored the Old Capitol location, for the specifications were written to produce a larger edition of the Old Capitol to be located on the same site. The new capitol would be three-sided like the old, with the front facing west down Capitol Street and with additional entrances on the north and south ends. The committee called for a building almost twice as large as the old. The old capitol was 200 feet long and 78 feet deep and occupied 15,600 square feet of ground space. Plans called for the new building to be 280 feet long and 110 feet deep and to occupy 30,800 square feet. Unlike the Old Capitol, the new building would have a basement for storage and for housing the heating plant. Otherwise, the building would be three stories in height, with a rotunda and a dome. The layout of offices, house and senate chambers, and hallways would be strikingly similar to the Old Capitol.[51]

Eighteen plans were submitted, and on July 16, 1896, with fourteen architects on hand to explain their designs, the committee members began to examine the proposals. Plans came from architects in Memphis, Atlanta, Lexington and Louisville, Kentucky, Grand Rapids, Michigan,

The House of Representatives in session in the late 1890s.

New Orleans, Fort Worth, San Antonio, and Chattanooga. While the mandate from the legislature did not include selecting a single plan, the competing architects requested that only one be selected by the committee. The members deliberated until Christmas Eve before finally approving the plan submitted by Weathers and Weathers of Memphis. The design called for a building 355 feet long, 110 to 170 feet deep, with a dome that rose to 160 feet. Cost was put at $750,000. On April 17, 1897, Governor McLaurin issued his call for a special session to meet on April 27. In his opening message, the governor recommended the Weatherses' plan and no other.[52]

A bill was immediately introduced in the house calling for the creation of a capitol commission to direct the construction of a new capitol. Disagreements erupted between the house and the senate almost at once. The house bill called for tearing down the Old Capitol and constructing the new building on the same site. The senate preferred instead to abandon the Old Capitol and to build the new capitol on the site of the penitentiary. The senate also rejected the Weatherses' design that had been presented by the governor as the committee's only choice. Instead, the senate wanted a plan by James Riley Gordon of San Antonio that had not been submitted to the committee.[53]

Upon examining the house bill, the senate presented sixteen amendments to the house. The house accepted those that dealt with minor details but voted overwhelmingly not to accept those that were aimed at constructing the new capitol on the penitentiary site. The house also by a large margin refused to write Gordon's design into the bill as

the senate desired. A conference committee was immediately formed. The house conferees gave way on Gordon's design, and the senate receded from its insistence on the penitentiary site. On May 20, both houses were in agreement. The building would be built on the site of the Old Capitol, and the design would be the Gordon plan, not the Weathers plan that had been recommended by the governor and his committee members. The bill was sent to the governor for his signature.[54]

The senators yielded to the house only because the immediate construction of a new capitol was imperative and urgent. The majority of senators favored the penitentiary site, calling the Old Capitol site too small and too unstable to support a building one-third larger than the Old Capitol. While most senators favored the Gordon design, some did not. Even as they yielded to compromise, some senators asked that their reasons be recorded. Freshman Senator D.A. McIntosh, representing Simpson, Covington, Marion and Pearl River counties, wanted it on the record that he had voted for the bill only as "a last resort and on account of the pressing needs for a building," for, he concluded, "I believe the legislature has made a great mistake in selecting both the site and the plan."[55]

Governor McLaurin was not pleased with the bill; he had doubts about its constitutionality. But he had little time to study it. All other business had been transacted, and the legislature was ready to adjourn. Feeling that five days was not enough time to study the bill, the governor asked the lawmakers to adjourn the session until the beginning of the next regular session in January 1897. Thus, he would have an additional seven months

Construction begins on the New Capitol. On the left is a portion of the penitentiary built by William Nichols in 1840.

to study the bill. The legislature refused, and on May 25, 1897, five days after receiving the bill, Governor McLaurin returned the bill with his veto.[56]

McLaurin's veto message was extremely long, but it contained only two principal objections. The legislators had reserved for themselves the right to elect the three members of the "State House Commission," the agency that would award the contracts for the new capitol and supervise the contractors. McLaurin pointed out, however, that the Constitution of 1890 gave the lawmakers only the right to elect their own officers, United States senators, presidential electors, and the state librarian. Thus, McLaurin argued, the act might be unconstitutional.[57]

But McLaurin objected most strenuously to James Riley Gordon's design and to the legislature's decision to write the design into the law. With the specifications embedded in the law, the governor argued, not even the architects could change them. The governor noted pointedly that his committee had never seen the plans. Further-

more, he charged, even a cursory examination of Gordon's specifications revealed that they had been drawn for a Texas courthouse, not for a Mississippi state house. The architect had used a pencil and eraser to change the specifications enough to make them appear to be suitable for a state house. But he had failed to correct them all. The governor pointed out that "in specifying for electric work . . . the specifications are left exactly as they were for a court- house." Thus, McLaurin rather sarcastically continued, the plans have "electric lights for a district court-room, commissioner's court-room and grand jury room; but none for the Senate Chamber, House of Representatives, nor Supreme Court room." The governor made no mention of dissatisfaction with the Old Capitol site. Construction would be funded by a $750,000 issue of forty-year bonds, the governor noted. In principal and interest the building would cost the people of Mississippi $1,950,000. "The people of this state cannot afford to spend this sum of money upon a doubtful experiment," he concluded.[58]

The capitol committee of the house rendered a report attempting to refute the governor's charges. The position of state house commissioner, the report argued, was not an office as defined by legal precedent, and Gordon's specifications were not a part of the bill, but the commissioners were only directed to use them as a guide for construction. Nonetheless, the bill was dead. When the house attempted to override the veto, supporters failed even to hold a simple majority; McLaurin's veto was sustained by a vote of fifty-nine to fifty-three.[59]

After the failure to agree in 1897, both Governor McLaurin and the legislators backed away from the issue. In his farewell message to the legislators in 1900, McLaurin failed even to mention a new capitol. Nonetheless, after the legislative debacle of 1897, popular and political sentiment quickly solidified in favor of a new capitol. In mid-1899, the editor of the Jackson *Evening News* predicted that the upcoming legislative session in 1900 was virtually certain to authorize a new capitol. "All opposition to the proposition to build a new state house," he wrote,

had evaporated. Everybody, he argued, could easily see the delapidation of the "Old Rookery," which, he said, could "collapse at any time."[60]

When the legislators gathered in January 1900, newly elected Governor Andrew H. Longino spoke to them sternly. Building a new capitol, the governor said, was the most important subject before the legislature. During his 1899 statewide campaign, he had found the people united in favor of a new capitol and of granting "a liberal appropriation" to build it. The people demanded, he warned, "that the legislature and incoming administration shall come together on this subject, lay aside all minor differences of detail and give to the people a Capitol building."[61]

The legislature acted promptly and decisively. By February 21, the legislators had passed and the governor had approved "an act to create a State House Commission, to secure drawings, plans and specifications for, and to authorize and provide for the building and erection of a State House." Oversight for construction was put in the hands of the "State House Commission," of which the governor was to be ex officio president. The thorny old questions of cost and location were easily resolved. The new capitol was not to cost more than $1,000,000, and it was to be located on the penitentiary site. The convicts would be moved to state prison farms, and the penitentiary building was ordered demolished. The governor was authorized to issue $1,000,000 in bonds to cover the costs of constructing and furnishing the new capitol.[62]

No doubt agreement was easier now than earlier because the state's economy had improved. The 1890s in Mississippi had been years of national depression and of low cotton prices. By 1900, the nation's economy was improving and so was Mississippi's. The state also received a windfall during the construction of the new capitol. Because of favorable court decisions in the Mississippi and United States Supreme Courts, the Yazoo and Mississippi Valley and the Gulf and Ship Island Railroads were forced to pay almost $1,000,000 in back taxes to the state of Mississippi. Although bonds were authorized to pay for the building, it was never necessary to issue them. These railroad payments allowed the state to avoid debt and to pay for the new capitol out of current revenues.[63]

Construction began on January 1, 1901. Governor Longino and other state officers moved into the New Capitol on September 26, 1903; three months later, in January 1904, the legislators gathered in the new building where they heard Longino's farewell. After praising the New Capitol, Longino suggested that the legislators consider selling some of the valuable real estate that the state owned in Jackson. The Old Capitol grounds headed his list.[64]

Lying in State

Gen. William Barksdale of Columbus was the only slain Confederate soldier given the honor of lying in state at the Old Capitol.

A former U.S. Congressman, Barksdale was killed at the Battle of Gettysburg in July 1863. His remains were moved to Jackson after the war. *The Daily Clarion* of Jackson reported the January 10, 1867, Masonic funeral service:

"Pursuant to the programme announced yesterday morning, the funeral of General Wm. Barksdale took place yesterday evening. The religious and Masonic ceremonies at the Capital Rotunda and at the grave, were impressive and appropriate. In respect to the deceased, the High Court adjourned over until this morning, and we noticed that all the stores in the city were closed while the procession was passing. Col. Walter, officiating as Master of Masonic ceremonies, took occasion to pay a brief, but eloquent tribute to the deceased."

Thirty years later, another statesman was similarly honored:

The brief announcement in Saturday's *Clarion-Ledger* that Senator J. Z. George was no more, cast a shadow of gloom over the city of Jackson and sent sorrow to thousands of homes in every portion of the State . . . Governor McLaurin telegraphed his sympathy and in behalf of the State asked that the remains be permitted to lie in state at [the State House in] Jackson before being taken to Carrollton. . . . [The committee of arrangements] entered at once upon their duties and by the arrival of the funeral train had everything in readiness. Several of their lady friends were pressed into service and in a remarkably short while the dingy old rotunda had been transformed into a very inviting place. The banisters on the second floor were profusely draped in mourning with streamers of black and white which hung in graceful folds, and around and about the rotunda were placed and effectively arranged banks of flowers, ferns, palms and other pot plants, evergreens, etc. The bright new flag that waived far overhead was placed at half-mast, carriages were secured, and everything else done that was possible on so short notice . . . There are very few people in Jackson, white or black, who did not visit the capitol during the twenty-four hours the body of Senator George laid there in state, and it was from no idle curiosity that they went—it was to show their appreciation of a great man, a profound lawyer, a distinguished citizen, a wise counsellor, a statesman of the highest order, a public servant of whom it may be truly said, "well done thou good and faithful." At 12 o'clock today religious services were held at the capitol, the sermon being preached by Dr. W. B. Murrah, president of Millsaps College, while John

Hunter invoked divine blessing. Miss Gaston presided at the organ while Mrs. Hayne rendered a beautiful solo "Nearer my God to Thee" and "Jesus Lover of my Soul." The services were appropriate to the occasion, and the tributes paid to the deceased were highly complimentary. The casket being sealed all that is mortal of Senator George was borne to the hearse and to the depot at 1 o'clock, being accompanied by the same escort as on yesterday, except that the Gem Band Trumpeters headed the procession, and a still larger contingent of citizens bringing up the rear.

—*Daily Clarion-Ledger*
August 16, 1897

The Confederate Monument

In the generation following the defeat of the Confederacy, memories of the South's defeat were transformed into a tragic but heroic myth by large and influential southern patriotic organizations like the United Confederate Veterans, the United Daughters of the Confederacy, and the United Sons of Confederate Veterans.

On June 16, 1886, a small group of Mississippi women met in the senate chamber of the Old Capitol and formed the Confederate Monument Association to erect a monument to the Confederate dead of Mississippi. For five years they worked at raising money and in 1888 persuaded the legislature to set aside the south Capitol Green for the site and appropriate $10,000 for the monument.

Dedication day, June 3, 1891, was the birthday of Jefferson Davis—scarcely eighteen months after the Confederate president's death. Twenty thousand people came to see the parade of Confederate veterans that preceded the unveiling of the monument by Jefferson Davis Hayes, the Confederate president's grandson.

The laying of the cornerstone of the Confederate monument, June 3, 1888.

NOTES

[1] Rowland, *Encyclopedia*, vol. 1, 938; vol. 2, 385.

[2] *House Journal*, (October), 1865, 11, 23–24.

[3] The most complete sources for Reconstruction from 1865–67 are James W. Garner, *Reconstruction in Mississippi* (New York: The Macmillan Company, 1901), chapters 3 and 4, and William C. Harris, *Presidential Reconstruction in Mississippi*, (Baton Rouge: Louisiana State University Press, 1967).

[4] *Laws*, 1865, 258–259.

[5] RG 9, Confederate Records, Roll no. 85, MDAH.

[6] *Laws* (November), 1865, 197–198; *House Journal* (November), 1865, 23–24.

[7] RG 27, Governors Correspondence, vol. 65, letter from Herod to Humphreys, Feburary 23, 1866.

[8] *Ibid.*

[9] *Ibid.*

[10] RG 29, Auditor, Container 82, Series G, vol. 212, State architect's estimates and specifications, January 12, 1866-December 9, 1867.

[11] *Senate Journal*, 1866, 12–13.

[12] *Ibid.*, 136–137.

[13] *Laws*, 1867, 393; RG 29, Auditor, Container 82, series G, vol. 212, State architect's estimates and specifications, January 12, 1866-December 9, 1867; RG 27, Governors Correspondence, vol. 68, letter from Herod to Humphreys, June 5, 1867.

[14] The most complete sources for Congressional Reconstruction in Mississippi, 1867–1876, are Garner, chapters 5–11 and William C. Harris, *The Day of the Carpetbagger: Republican Reconstruction in Mississippi* (Baton Rouge: Louisiana State University Press, 1979).

[15] Harris, *Day of the Carpetbagger*, 148–150.

[16] Harris, *Day of the Carpetbagger*, 139–148; Garner, 202.

[17] Harris, *Day of the Carpetbagger*, 146.

[18] Harris, *Day of the Carpetbagger*, 204.

[19] An excellent biography of Alcorn is Lillian A. Pereyra, *James Lusk Alcorn: Persistent Whig* (Baton Rouge: Louisiana State University Press, 1966).

[20] Sansing and Waller, 59; *Journal of the Proceedings of the Constitutional Convention of 1868* (Jackson: E. Stafford, Printer, 1871), 50–51, 144–145, 646–647, 670–671; *Senate Journal*, 1870, 290, 365, 379, 383, 451, 463.

[21] *Laws*, 1870, 610–611; *Senate Journal*, 1871, Appendix, 129, 143–145; *The Weekly Mississippi Pilot*, October 8, 1870.

[22] *Senate Journal*, 1871, Appendix, 120–131; McCain, 45, 49–53, 82.

[23] "Specifications of the Work and Material Required to Repair the State Capitol," *Senate Journal*, 1871, Appendix, 149–154.

[24] *Ibid.*

[25] *Ibid.*

[26] *Ibid.*

[27] *Ibid.*

[28] *Ibid.*

[29] *Ibid.*

[30] "Report of the Committee on Public Buildings," *Senate Journal*, 1871, Appendix, 129–132, 136–138; "Report of J. Willis, State Architect, of the Progress on the State Capitol," ibid., 173–176.

[31] Report by Willis, *Senate Journal*, 1871, Appendix, 173–176.

[32] *Ibid.*

[33] *Ibid.*

[34] McLemore, vol. 1, 601.

[35] Edward King, *The Southern States of North America: A Record of Journeys in Louisiana, Texas, The Indian Territory, Missouri, Arkansas, Mississippi, Alabama, Georgia, Florida, South Carolina, North Carolina, Kentucky, Tennessee, Virginia, West Virginia, and Maryland* (London: Blackie and Son, 1875), 314; "In Sunny Mississippi," *Harper's New Monthly Magazine* (May, 1895), 831–832.

[36] *Biennial Reports, State Librarian and Keeper of the Capitol*, 1876–1880.

[37] *Senate Journal*, 1880, 419.

[38] *Laws*, 1880, 13; *Senate Journal*, 1882, 36.

[39] Reports, State Librarian and Keeper of the Capitol, 1880–81, 1882–83, MDAH.

[40] Report, State Librarian and Keeper of the Capitol, 1884–85.

[41] Report, State Librarian and Keeper of the Capitol, 1886–87.

[42] Proceedings of the Constitutional Convention of 1890, 127, 130.

[43] Jackson *Clarion-Ledger*, September 1, 1890.

[44] *Ibid.*, 123.

[45] *Ibid.*, 186–187.

[46] *Senate Journal*, 1892, 48–49; 1894, 28; *Laws*, 1892, 19.

[47] The reports are printed verbatim in *Senate Journal*, 1896, 300–311.

[48] *Senate Journal*, 1896, 617.

[49] *Biennial Report of the Secretary of State, 1898–1899*, xii–xiii; *First Annual Report of the Director of the Department of Archives and History of the State of Mississippi*, March 14, 1902-October 1, 1902, MDAH.

[50] *Senate Journal*, 1897, 20.

[51] *Ibid.*, 20–22; *House Journal*, 1897, 196.

[52] *Senate Journal*, 1897, 16, 18–19; *House Journal*, 1897, 197.

[53] *House Journal*, 1897, 135–143, 204.

[54] *Ibid.*, 135–173, *passim.*

[55] *Senate Journal*, 1897, 133, 138–140.

[56] *House Journal*, 194, 198.

[57] *Ibid.*, 199.

[58] *Ibid.*, 203–205.

[59] *Ibid.*, 231–236.

[60] Jackson *Evening News*, July 4, 1899.

[61] *Senate Journal*, 1900, 86–87.

⁶²*Laws*, 1900, 55–68.
⁶³Rowland, *Mississippi, Heart of the South*, 283.
⁶⁴Rowland, *Encyclopedia*, 356–359; *Senate Journal*, 1904, 34–35.

ILLUSTRATION NOTES

p. 84   Stereographs by E. von Seutter, MDAH.

p. 86   Engraving. *Biographical and Historical Memories of Mississippi* (Chicago: The Goodspeed Publishing Co., 1891) 2 vols.

p. 87   Engraving: "The Ruins of Jackson, Mississippi from a sketch by D. H. Huyett," *Frank Leslie's Illustrated Newspaper,* October 7, 1865. MDAH.

p. 89   T. S. Hardee, State Engineer, 1872. "Hardee's Geographical, Historical, and Statistical Official Map of Mississippi."

p. 90   Engraving by D. Verdeil. Germany, 1870. MDAH.

p. 93   Photogravure. "Cotton and its Capital, Jackson, Mississippi." *Harper's New Monthly Magazine,* May, 1895.

p. 94   Line drawings by Bill Burris, 1990. Eley Associates Architects.

p. 94, 95   Photograph. MDAH.

p. 97   MSHM collections.

p. 98, 99   Stereographs by E. von Seutter. MDAH.

p. 103   Photograph. MDAH.

p. 106   Photograph by Tom Rankin. Collection of Mrs. Robert Ragan.

p. 106   Engraving. *Biographical and Historical Memoirs of Mississippi* (Chicago: The Goodspeed Publishing Co., 1891) 2 vols.

p. 106   MSHM collections.

p. 108, 109   Photographs. MDAH.

p. 110   Photograph. MDAH.

p. 111   Photograph. MDAH.

p. 112   Engraving (detail). "The Seceding Mississippi Delegation in Congress." *Harper's Weekly*, February 2, 1861.

p. 113   Engraving. Memorial Addresses on the Life and Character of James Z. George. . . . (Washington: Government Printing Office, 1898).

p. 114   Photograph. MDAH.

p. 114   Engraving. *Biographical and Historical Memoirs of Mississippi* (Chicago: The Goodspeed Publishing Co., 1891) 2 vols.

p. 114   Photograph by Patorno and Coovert. Manship Collection, MDAH.

From Decay to Reconstruction 1903–1959

State officers completed their move to the New Capitol during the fall of 1903, and legislators gathered there in January 1904 for their first session in the building. Except for periodic calls for the destruction of the Old Capitol and the sale of its grounds, the old building sat neglected and forgotten—a down-and-out derelict, an embarrassment to the "progressive" and expanding New South city of Jackson. Within a decade after the government moved out, the building had deteriorated almost beyond salvation. On the brink of collapse, its roof caving in, the Old Capitol was saved in 1916 when the legislature authorized its reconstruction. After a complete rebuilding of the inside, in 1917 the Old Capitol became a state office building that housed an expanding state government—its role until 1959.

Abandonment, 1904–1916

Since its beginnings in 1822, Jackson had languished, its economy supported only by state government and by business from the surrounding agricultural countryside. As long as commerce depended on river transportation, Jacksonians lived in the shadow of Vicksburg. But in the fifty years following the Civil War, steam locomotives supplanted steamboats, and inland towns began to eclipse river towns. In the early years of the twentieth century, thriving on its location as a major rail hub, Meridian overshadowed Vicksburg as Mississippi's premier city. At Jackson's fiftieth anniversary in 1872, the capital city, with scarcely 4,000 people, was only one-third the size of Vicksburg. At Jackson's seventy-fifth anniversary in 1897, the capital's population had grown to more than 7,000. But Vicksburg and the boom town of Meridian both numbered more than 14,000.

The first two decades of the twentieth century produced for Jackson a critical period of growth. In 1875 Jackson's businesses and residences extended in a narrow strip down Capitol Street to just beyond the railroad. But most Jacksonians worked and lived in a rectangle bounded on the north by High Street, on the south by Court Street, on the west by West Street, and on the east by State Street. Two miles of open country separated downtown Jackson from the state insane asylum (presently the site of the University Medical Center). Thirty-five years later, in 1910, North State Street was built up for that whole distance, and development had proceeded south to what is now Highway 80 and west to Livingston Park. Because government expanded and the town developed as a rail hub and a centrally located service center for statewide businesses, Jackson tripled in size during the first decade of the twentieth century—from 7,816 people in 1900 to 21,262 in 1910.

Politicians, no doubt recognizing the increased desirability and value of state-owned lands in downtown Jackson, began to consider selling state properties. The Old Capitol and the Governor's Mansion, both delapidated and seemingly obsolete, occupied strategic locations in the heart of the downtown business section.

Ironically, the first serious suggestion to sell

the Old Capitol property came from one of Mississippi's most history- minded chief executives, Governor A. H. Longino—the last governor to be inaugurated in the Old Capitol and the first to occupy the New Capitol. When leaving office in 1904, Longino recommended that the Old Capitol be demolished and the grounds sold.[1]

Within days, incoming Governor James K. Vardaman made the same recommendation. While he did not mention the Old Capitol in his 1904 inaugural, Vardaman recommended to both the 1906 and 1908 sessions of the legislature that the Old Capitol be torn down and the property sold, together with the land behind it that was used by the state fair. The recommendation, said Vardaman, seemed almost a sacrilege, but "decay and disintegration have done . . . their destructive work; the end has come." Despite his Delta background, Vardaman had run in 1903 as a candidate of the little people. He campaigned against the "interests" and the "Jackson Ring"; he was a critic

"The violent hand of an aggressive commercialism" as described by Bishop Galloway, threatened the Old Capitol from both State Street (right) *and Capitol Street* (below). *Even the fence* (far right) *gave way to advertising space.*

of the "aristocracy." In his inaugural, Vardaman, like his "aristocratic" predecessor Longino, recommended selling the Governor's Mansion, though for different reasons. To Vardaman, the mansion was a "relic of royalty" with "the odor of . . . effete aristocracy."[2]

Legislators made efforts in 1904, 1906, and 1908 to carry out Vardaman's wishes. In 1904 a bill was introduced in the senate to sell the Old Capitol and grounds; it failed in committee. In 1906 a bill was introduced in the house to remove the Confederate monument from the south grounds of the Old Capitol to the grounds of the New Capitol and to sell the Old Capitol. The bill passed committee but died without action on the house floor. Two bills came before the 1908 senate—one to sell the Old Capitol and another to restore it as a "Memorial Hall." Neither bill received final action by the senate. Meanwhile, a special senate committee investigated the validity of the state's title to the Old Capitol grounds. The members found the state's title valid but recommended against sale of the property. A final effort was made in the 1914 house. It failed in committee.[3]

The obvious ambivalence displayed by the legislators no doubt reflected the mixed emotions of their constituents. Nobody wanted to see the

building crumble completely, but few wanted to spend the large sums required to restore it. Thus, the 1906 legislators made an interim arrangement—they leased the building to the "Mississippi Industrial Exposition Company for the purpose of holding a State Fair." The lease was for six years but could be cancelled if the legislature chose to sell or otherwise dispose of the building and grounds. The state fair paid only ten dollars annually but was responsible for keeping the roof and windows in repair, for removing "all sheds, booths, signs and other obstructions between the building and State Street," and for protecting and preserving "all books, records, and archives" in the building. Apparently, the front of the Old Capitol had become a local billboard; shortly before the legislators leased the building, they had ordered the Capitol Commission to "keep all sign boards from in front of the building."[4]

The Old Capitol was evidently used by the state fair company from 1906 until the lease expired in 1912. Ticket booths were located on the north grounds, and during fair week, always in late October or early November, the old building was festooned with banners and flags. Some of the rooms were used for exhibits, and band concerts and other entertainments were held on the grounds. But after the state fair abandoned the building, it fell to ruin. By 1916, portions of the roof had collapsed, carrying down the ceilings in the house and senate chambers.[5]

After the legislature left, the Old Capitol became a messy and untended repository for old state records. Before construction could begin on the New Capitol, the old penitentiary had to be razed. The old records and books that had been moved to the penitentiary in 1896 were moved back and stacked in the halls.

Apparently, the legislators who gathered in 1902 for their last session in the old building were impressed by the clutter, for at that session they created the Mississippi Department of Archives and History and charged the new agency with collecting, preserving, and caring for the old records. The creation of such an agency had been recommended in 1901 by the Mississippi Historical Commission headed by ex-Confederate General Stephen D. Lee. In a report the commissioners pointed out "the unassorted materials relating to the early history of the state, now in the corridor of the old Capitol," and suggested that this material be turned over to a state archives. Even before the Department of Archives and History was established by law, the State House Commission granted two rooms in the uncompleted New Capitol to house the new agency.[6]

Dunbar Rowland, a thirty-seven-year-old lawyer from Coffeeville in Yalobusha County, was chosen by the Board of Trustees on March 14, 1902, to head the new agency. Until the New Capitol was finished, Rowland's department was assigned the two front rooms just outside the house chamber on the second floor of the Old Capitol. After a ten-day trip to Coffeeville to arrange his personal affairs, Rowland returned to Jackson and went to work on March 24, 1902.[7]

After working for six months, Rowland submitted his first report on the records that had traveled with Mississippi's itinerant government during the Civil War, that had lain mouldering in piles on the third floor of the Old Capitol for three decades after the war, that in 1896 had been unceremoniously dumped from third floor windows into open wagons below for transport to the penitentiary where they had remained untended for four years before being returned to the corridors of the Old Capitol. Not surprisingly, Rowland found them in a deplorable condition. At the penitentiary, the records had been packed without regard to organization in fifty boxes. When Rowland began to examine the boxes, he found papers from the offices of the governor, secretary of state, auditor, and attorney general all indiscriminately mixed.[8]

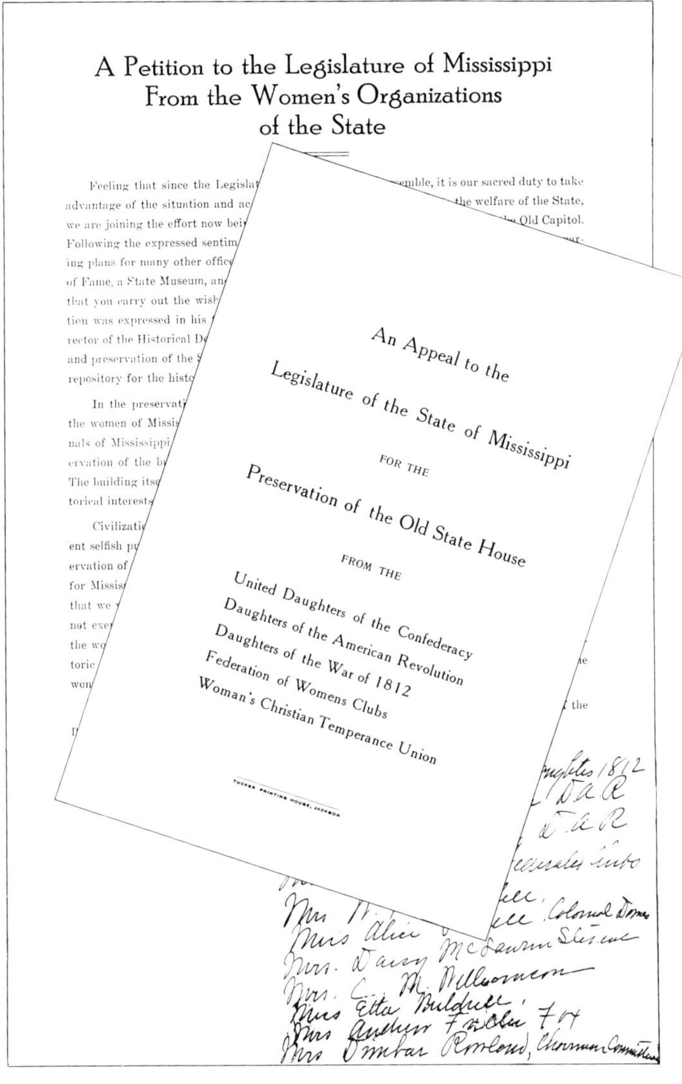

A Petition to the Legislature of Mississippi
From the Women's Organizations
of the State

An Appeal to the
Legislature of the State of Mississippi

FOR THE

Preservation of the Old State House

FROM THE

United Daughters of the Confederacy
Daughters of the American Revolution
Daughters of the War of 1812
Federation of Womens Clubs
Woman's Christian Temperance Union

newspapers, Rowland replied that they were still stored in the Old Capitol. Rowland, however, had made considerable progress in organizing the mess, for he promised to have the particular file brought over to the New Capitol so that the man could read the old newspapers there.[9]

As he worked to organize and preserve the oldest records, newer ones accumulated. On November 19, 1906, Rowland wrote to Governor James K. Vardaman that piles of old office records had been left behind by state officials when they vacated the Old Capitol three years earlier. These old office files were strewn about in open rooms where they could be picked over by any passersby or, worse still, carted away to destruction. They should be removed and secured immediately, Rowland warned the governor. Evidently, too, the state fair company failed to fulfill its agreement in the lease to safeguard the records that had been left in the building and to maintain the roof and windows in good repair. Rowland advised the governor that the clause in the lease requiring the fair company to "arrange and care for the records in the Old Capitol was "a dead letter."[10]

Efforts to preserve and restore the Old Capitol began almost as soon as the building was vacated in 1903. The campaign was inspired and led by Dunbar Rowland and his wife, Eron O. Rowland, who worked as his assistant. Both Rowlands were extremely active in the most powerful patriotic organizations of the day—United Confederate Veterans and Sons of Confederate Veterans, Daughters of the American Revolution, Women's Christian Temperance Union, Federation of Women's Clubs, and perhaps the most active and influential of all, the United Daughters of the Confederacy. Rowland, who had been a lawyer and part-time newsman before taking over the Department of Archives and History, also had numerous contacts among attorneys and editors.

Even as he moved his new department out of the old building in October 1903, Rowland envi-

Rowland's Department of Archives and History was the last state agency to leave the Old Capitol in 1903. On October 5, he moved his office into the New Capitol. Although he continued his work of organizing and preserving the archives, Rowland apparently had limited room in his new offices, and he had to leave many of the old records behind in the Old Capitol. In 1904 when a citizen of Natchez asked to see some old

sioned that he would someday move an enlarged
Department of Archives and History back into a
renovated Old Capitol—a befitting and permanent
home for his archives, his museum, and his hall of
fame portrait gallery of notable Mississippians.

The patriotic organizations lobbied and peti-
tioned the legislature continually from 1906 to
1916 for the preservation of the Old Capitol.
Their efforts, according to Rowland, almost certainly prevented the demolition of the building and
sale of the grounds. From 1904 to 1912, although
the legislators could not agree to sell the Old
Capitol, neither could they agree to restore it.
While early bills to restore the Old Capitol had
never gotten out of committee, a 1912 bill passed
the senate and the house public works committee
only to be killed in a voice vote on the house floor.
In that effort, Mrs. Rowland was especially active,
writing long newspaper articles and gathering petitions from women's clubs.[11]

By 1914 the pressure that would eventually
prove decisive began to appear. Mississippi's centennial was approaching in 1917, and a fitting
tribute would be the restoration of the Old Capitol. More important, however, was the fact that
only ten years after its completion, the New Capitol could no longer house all the departments of
government. A decade of progressive reform had
expanded old state agencies and created several
new ones. The Department of Agriculture had
expanded into committee rooms that had to be
relinquished during legislative sessions; the Board
of Health rented space in a downtown building for
$1,200 a year; the adjutant general paid $600
annually for rented space. As early as 1908,
Rowland complained that his department had outgrown its space.[12]

Although he had remained silent on the matter at his inauguration in 1912, Governor Earl
Brewer, in his opening message to the 1914 session
of the legislature, announced in favor of restoring
the Old Capitol. After much thought and discus-

The State Fair at the Old Capitol

For many years, the Old Capitol served as the
gateway to the fairgrounds. The fence surrounding
the state house defined the front perimeters of the
fair and provided an entrance gate for controlled
access.

As early as 1840 the legislature approved a state
agricultural convention to be held in Jackson and
from the beginning the grounds east of the Old
Capitol were used for the state fair. In 1871 the
lands were officially appropriated by the state as
fairgrounds and have been used for that purpose.

After the Old Capitol was abandoned in 1903,
the state fair moved inside the building. A description of the first "industrial exposition" held in the
Old Capitol appeared in *The Daily Clarion-Ledger*
of December 13, 1904:

". . . Every inch of available room has been used. Every nook and cranny of the ancient building has been filled with some fine product from Mississippi soil. The various rooms and apartments are crowded to overflowing, and yet the effect is artistic throughout. . . .

"The huge pyramid of cotton and the varied products of the soil in the main rotunda is a thing of beauty. . . .

"The display made by the Southern Railway and Mobile and Ohio roads . . . is located on the first floor in the quarters formerly occupied by the state library.

". . . The quarters occupied by the piney woods products are the rooms formerly occupied by the governor's office."

The 1871 fair program announced that a streetcar line would be completed from the Edwards House to the State Capitol in time for the fair.

sion and after having the building inspected by an architect, the governor explained his conclusion that "the most practical thing to do is to remodel it" so as "to render it serviceable for many purposes." An architectural examination, he told the lawmakers, indicated that the building was structurally more sound than most people had suspected. Shoring up the foundation and the walls in three places—at the northeast and southeast corners and inside the center of the front wall—would make the outer walls sound. Replacing the roof and floors, replastering the inside walls and patching the stucco on the outer walls would complete the job. By using convict labor, Governor Brewer argued, the rehabilitation could be done for $75,000, a cheap price for saving an historic structure and giving the state badly needed office space. Even better, he said, the renovation could be paid for by excess funds that were being generated by the Department of Agriculture. In fact, the governor noted, the idea had been given to him by Commissioner of Agriculture H. E. Blakeslee, who was seeking more office space for his department.[13]

But Governor Brewer was then involved in a bitter personal and political feud with Lieutenant Governor Theodore G. Bilbo, whose "redneck" constituents dominated the legislature, and thus the governor's plan remained only a suggestion.

Astute observers foresaw that the movement to restore the Old Capitol was likely to crest in the 1916 legislature. Sentiment played a role, but events were more critical. A new governor and a new legislature would be coming to town in 1916. The Great War in Europe had begun in 1914, and cotton prices had shot up, bringing Mississippians relative prosperity; government continued to expand, and the need for new office space continued to grow. The Old Capitol also had reached a crisis, for by 1914 the roof had collapsed in several places.

Mrs. Dunbar Rowland and the patriotic so-

cieties in 1915 gathered their forces and planned an intense campaign aimed at the 1916 legislature. Mrs. Virginia Redditt Price of Carrollton was president of the Mississippi Division of the United Daughters of the Confederacy, and she, in turn, appointed Mrs. Rowland to act as chairman of the Old Capitol Committee. Mrs. Rowland prepared letters to legislators and petitions for the local chapters to circulate. The petitions would later be submitted to the legislature.[14]

Mrs. Rowland also prepared a booklet dedicated to the 1916 legislature. In it she summarized past efforts to preserve the Old Capitol, surveyed the present reasons for doing so, and wrote a twenty-five-page history of the Old Capitol. Earlier restoration efforts had emphasized the building's great historical value, and earlier bills had specified that the building would be used purely for historical purposes—a museum, library, and memorial to the Confederacy. Governor Brewer's 1914 message was the first to use the more practical argument of added office space for crowded state agencies. Now Mrs. Rowland also took up that argument. Like Brewer, she suggested that the restoration be paid for out of Department of Agriculture profits. She even suggested that the north grounds of the Old Capitol could be divided into lots and sold.[15]

In 1916, Mrs. Price made at least two trips to Jackson to talk to legislators and to testify before legislative committees. She complained after her first visit that she got little help from the Jackson chapter of United Daughters of the Confederacy. Her second visit became a subject of controversy when she was accused by some members, including Mrs. Rowland, of using the campaign as a self-serving effort to become matron of Beauvoir, Jefferson Davis's last home. Mrs. Price hotly denied the charge.[16]

If the legislators felt political heat from these patriotic societies with dedicated and influential members in every community, they also faced pres-

sure from two governors. At the beginning of the
1916 session, outgoing Governor Brewer renewed
his 1914 recommendation that the building be
restored as a state office building. Incoming Governor Theodore G. Bilbo asked in his inaugural that
the legislators "combine utility with sentiment"
and authorize the renovation of the building for
state offices.[17]

Nonetheless, many legislators still opposed
the project. Most of the opponents believed either
that the building had deteriorated beyond repair or
that any money spent on the old structure would
be wasted in an unsatisfactory repair effort. Most
feared that the initial appropriation would be only
the beginning of never-ending requests amounting
to hundreds of thousands of dollars. Moreover, an
argument gained force in the 1916 legislature that
Mississippi's rural people cared little about restoring the Old Capitol. Mrs. Rowland attempted to
counter that charge with a handbill sent to all
legislators.[18]

The energetic efforts of the United Daughters
of the Confederacy notwithstanding, the bills authorizing the restoration and making
appropriations had to be pressed by influential
legislators. Representative Alfred Holt Stone of
Washington County took up the task of shepherd-
ing the necessary Old Capitol bills through the
1916 legislature. Stone, a lawyer and Delta planter
from Greenville, had a deep sense of civic responsibility and a serious interest in history. He was an
expert on the history of blacks in the South, and at
the time he dedicated his efforts to saving the Old
Capitol, he had already published a book called
Studies in the American Race Problem.[19]

When Stone took up his task, the outcome
was by no means certain. Early in the session,
Stone introduced a resolution in the house of
representatives to investigate the restoration of the
Old Capitol as a state office building. It failed.
Then two bills were introduced to tear down the
Old Capitol. Both failed. Apparently, the legis-

*Former High Court of Errors
and Appeals, 1915*

lators were again afflicted with the same
ambivalence that they had experienced for a decade. But Stone continued to work quietly among
his colleagues, and almost six weeks after the
failure of his original resolution, Stone secured
passage of a resolution employing Theodore C.
Link of St. Louis, the architect of the New Capitol,
to inspect the Old Capitol and report to the
legislature. Link agreed to a fee of $100, hardly
enough to pay his train fare from St. Louis.[20]

Link's report may have turned the legislative
tide. In the company of Representative Stone, Link

spent several days examining the structure, and
Governor Bilbo introduced him to the legislature
to make his report. Link's recommendations were
succinct: preservation was feasible; the building
could be made "perfectly safe"; the work "must be
done without . . . delay"; the exterior appearance
of the building should remain unchanged. But,
Link warned, to get 24,000 square feet for ap-
proximately sixty offices would require the loss of
the house and senate chambers and arranging the
two upper floors much like the ground floor. Link
comforted the legislators on cost—the Old Capitol
would provide a good state office building at far
less cost than an addition to the New Capitol and
at only half the cost of a new office building of the
same size. By using convict labor and producing
some materials at the penitentiary, Link estimated
that the job could be done for $125,000.[21]

Link rendered his report on March 17, 1916.
Within two weeks both the house and senate had
passed bills by overwhelming margins authorizing
the renovation and appropriating the necessary
$125,000. On April 8, Governor Bilbo signed the
bills.[22]

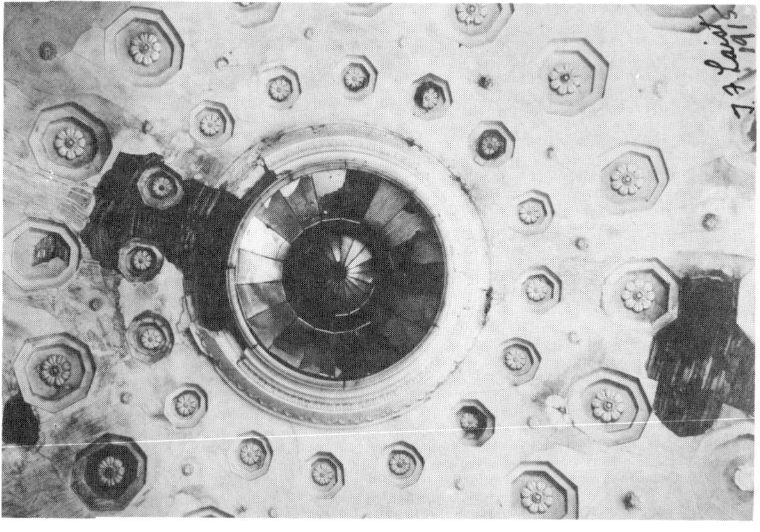

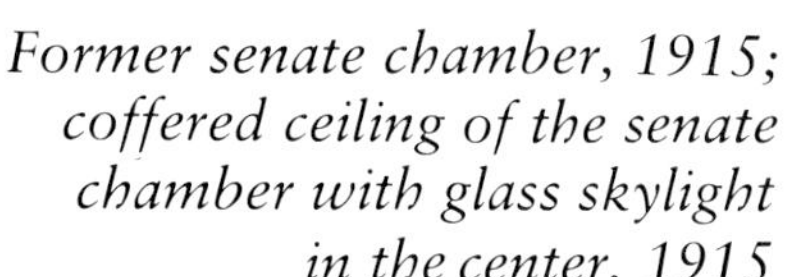

Former senate chamber, 1915;
coffered ceiling of the senate
chamber with glass skylight
in the center, 1915

Renovation, 1916–1917

The law called for preserving the Old Capitol's exterior, but for reconstructing the interior to provide "suitable rooms for offices of the state" and "repositories for a portion of our state records." The act ordered the employment of an architect to plan and oversee the reconstruction and ordered the penitentiary to furnish the brick and "convicts and teams to do all such labor as they can properly perform." The lawmakers appropriated $125,000 for the renovation to be raised by a bond issue. Fearful that they might have begun throwing money down a bottomless pit, the legislators provided explicitly that in no event would the cost exceed "the said sum of $125,000 appropriated by this act" excluding the bricks and labor furnished by the penitentiary.[23]

The law charged the Capitol Commission with administering the renovation. The commission was ordered to hire an architect to plan and supervise the renovation, and the commissioners, at their discretion, could employ a contractor to perform the work. The Capitol Commission had been created in 1904 to succeed the State House Commission, the agency that had directed the construction of the New Capitol. The Capitol Commission consisted of the governor as ex officio president, the secretary of state, insurance commissioner, and state revenue agent. The commission's permanent responsibility was to care for all state property located in Jackson.[24]

In 1916 the Capitol Commission consisted of Governor Bilbo, Secretary of State Joseph W. Power, Insurance Commissioner T. M. Henry, and State Revenue Agent Stokes V. Robertson. In addition to supervising the renovation, the commissioners, of course, all had many other heavy duties. Thus, to keep the records for the Old Capitol project, the commissioners hired a full-time assistant secretary: A. S. Coody, a druggist and former mayor of Lucedale, who was an avid Vardaman and Bilbo supporter. As architect, they hired Theodore C. Link, the designer of the New Capitol whose evaluation of the Old Capitol had convinced the legislators to proceed with the project.[25]

Link's inspection of the building had convinced him that the outer walls were sound. Most of the settling, he concluded, had occurred in the early history of the building, and the walls had not shifted in the last twenty-five years. The walls had, however, suffered damage from bearing the great weight of the roof and the floors. If he could somehow free the walls from having to support these burdens, he reasoned, they would stand indefinitely. Link's plan was simple. He would tear out the interior of the building and erect a skeleton of steel beams and girders inside the walls of the building. Upright steel columns would rest on concrete foundations, cross girders would support the floors, and steel trusses would support the roof. The outer walls would be tied to this steel framework. In such a design the load of the roof and the floors would be transferred to the steel frame. Thus relieved, the outer walls would cease to crack and crumble.[26]

Link's mandate to transform the decaying old building into a modern state office building made faithful preservation of the building's interior impossible. Economics and utility combined to produce a renovation rather than a restoration. Link's scheme made it impossible to preserve the house and senate chambers; and, because of the locations of the steel columns, many changes would be required in the interior layout. He planned also to introduce modern conveniences—steam heat (a boiler house was to be built behind the building), electric lights, and an elevator. Nonetheless, Link appreciated the beauty of the building and planned to preserve its most striking interior features—the main entrance, the speaker's rostrum and the columns behind it, the rotunda, and the dome.[27]

Capitol Street, 1925

Soon after the legislation was approved, a team of convicts arrived on the Old Capitol grounds and began to build a camp to house sixty convict workers. They fenced the grounds to prevent escapes, built cooking shacks, and erected quarters for the guards. The building still contained much furniture and very large quantities of old records. Under the supervision of Dunbar Rowland, the records were boxed and moved to the basement of the New Capitol. The old furniture, which had been left behind in 1903, was stored in a temporary building on the capitol grounds. Some of it was refurbished and used by the agencies that occupied the Old Capitol in 1917.[28]

Then, during the summer of 1916, the demolition of the interior began. This work was delicate and hazardous, for almost all of the interior had to be stripped out without disturbing the weak outer walls. An unskilled, inexperienced superintendent could cause the collapse of the entire building. On the recommendation of architect Link, the commissioners hired William C. Musick of St. Louis to supervise both the demolition of the interior and the erection of the steel framework. The work was done by convicts. All interior walls except those in the corridor on the ground floor and the ones immediately north and south of the rotunda were removed. The only original items saved and put back into the renovated building were the doors and door frames from the ground floor. The steel framework, prefabricated by the American Bridge Company of Pittsburgh, arrived in September, and the convicts began to put it in place.[29]

The convicts, none of whom were experienced steel workers, erected sixty-six steel columns, set on concrete foundations, from north to south in four rows twelve feet apart. Then they tied them together with "I" beams at each floor level. The outer walls were tied to this steel skeleton with three hundred anchor rods. On the ground and third floors five-inch reinforced concrete floors were laid on these beams. The second floor was constructed of wood laid on wooden joists. Forty-four rooms were partitioned "corresponding to the location of the [steel] columns," but only the rooms on each floor immediately adjacent to the rotunda retained their original configurations.[30]

128

As specified in the law, and as promised by Link, the exterior of the building remained largely unchanged. A flagpole was substituted for the carved cypress magnolia bloom at the top of the dome. At the rear of the building, the door leading to the rear stairs on the house side was replaced by a window because the stairs were torn out. The rear door on the senate side remained as an entrance into the Department of Agriculture's offices on the ground floor. A new door was cut in the center of the rear bay to give access to new stairs and an elevator was placed there.[31]

The first floor corridor and rotunda were restored to represent closely the original. The original doors and door frames, removed earlier, were repaired and put back in by one of the convicts who was an expert cabinetmaker. The second-floor balcony around the rotunda was restored, but an entirely new balcony, made of steel and concrete, was constructed around the rotunda at the third-floor level. The speaker's rostrum and the columns behind it were restored on the north wall of the building, but the third floor was extended entirely through the house and senate chambers to the end walls. That space on both floors was partitioned into offices. The spiral stairways just inside the front entrance were removed, and on the second and third floors that area was converted into offices. The rear bay on all three levels was now occupied by stair halls, a stairway, and an elevator.[32]

Rowland v. Bilbo

In the spring of 1917, as the workmen began to finish the interior of the building, a bitter political fight erupted. The contestants were Governor Theodore G. Bilbo and Archives and History Director Dunbar Rowland. At stake was the allocation of space in the Old Capitol to Rowland's department. His agency had led the campaign to preserve the Old Capitol, and he believed that his department should occupy the entire second floor of the renovated building. Bilbo thought otherwise.

No doubt the two men's antithetical origins, political views, constituencies, and values aggravated their antipathy. Bilbo presented himself as a common man, a champion of the little people, and he cultivated an outrageous, sometimes clownish image. He gleefully goaded his enemies; he was shrewd and smart but not deeply educated. At times, his behavior was calculatedly boorish. Rowland fancied himself an aristocrat; he was somewhat pompous and stuffy; he was self-conciously "cultured" and traditional and ambitious; he thought of himself as cosmopolitan and urbane—a member of the American intellectual elite. He was an energetic and prolific scholar. These two state officials fought for eighteen months, frequently through proxies. Yet as different as they seemed, both men were stubborn, combative, and energetic. Their fight spanned one lawsuit that went to the Mississippi Supreme Court and two sessions of the legislature.

Until early 1917 Rowland assumed that he had been assured the second floor when the renovation was complete. The second- floor plans had been drawn to suit his department, and three of the four members of the Capitol Commission—Secretary of State Power, Insurance Commissioner Henry, and State Revenue Agent Robertson—favored moving Rowland's department to the second floor. Yet in February 1917, Rowland smelled a rat. He sensed that Robertson was deserting to Governor Bilbo's position. The governor wanted the Department of Education, headed by his appointee Willard F. Bond, to have the second floor of the Old Capitol. Rowland wrote a long letter to Robertson hoping to convince the wavering commissioner to continue his support.[33]

But Robertson deserted, and Bilbo had the ally that he needed. With Robertson's support, Bilbo ordered Link to adapt the plans of the second floor to the needs of the Department of Education. Rowland correctly concluded that Bilbo wanted to give the entire second floor to the Department of Education and to deny any space in the Old Capitol to Archives and History. With the encouragement of the other two capitol commissioners, Secretary of State Power (who also would desert Rowland) and Insurance Commissioner Henry, Rowland found an anti-Bilbo ally in Attorney General Ross Collins. In a letter to Collins, Rowland asked the attorney general if the legislators in their 1916 bill had intended to provide space in the building for Archives and History. Collins answered unequivocally, "Yes." When Rowland discovered that the second floor was being constructed according to different plans, he formally requested that Collins "take the necessary legal action to stop the unauthorized work now going on."[34]

Collins filed suit against Bilbo, Robertson, Link, and the contractor, Standard Construction Company, in Hinds County Chancery Court. He sought a temporary injunction to stop work on the Old Capitol. Collins claimed that Link's original plans, approved by the Capitol Commission, had allocated the entire second floor to the Department of Archives and History. But, he alleged, on orders from Bilbo, Robertson, and Link, the contractor was not following the approved plans for the second floor. Collins also claimed that the legislature's clear intent in restoring the building was to provide a place for Rowland's archives and museum. Bilbo, Robertson, and Link denied that the 1916 law authorizing the renovation had specified or even implied that Archives and History would be housed in the building. The defendants also claimed that Standard Construction Company's contract was awarded on plans and specifications different from those claimed by the plaintiff. Nevertheless, the court granted a temporary injunction until a final hearing could be held.[35]

Dunbar Rowland

On April 20, 1917, the Capitol Commission ordered work to cease, but the stoppage lasted only ten days. In the final hearing before the Chancery Court, the judge dismissed the injunction. Collins appealed the dismissal. At the final hearing, Secretary of State Power had abandoned his former allies and asked that the complaint be dismissed.[36]

Collins's appeal was not heard by the Mississippi Supreme Court until March 1918, almost a year after the dismissal. Meanwhile, by the fall of 1917 work on the Old Capitol had been completed, and the agencies designated by the Capitol Commission had begun to move in. The supreme court upheld the right of the Capitol Commission under the 1916 law to approve plans and make

Theodore Bilbo

contracts for the renovation. One justice admitted that it was common knowledge that the legislature intended for Rowland's department to occupy the building. But, the court said, the case was now moot. How could the court issue an injunction stopping work on a building that had already been finished?

Long before the supreme court decision was handed down, Rowland had carried his fight to the legislature. Despite his rather minor official position, Rowland could mobilize powerful political pressure. As always, he depended primarily on the women of the United Daughters of the Confederacy. But Bilbo also could mount considerable political pressure. In 1916, upon the resignation of W. H. "Corn Club" Smith, Bilbo had appointed

Willard F. Bond state superintendent of education. Support for public education in the early twentieth century was especially strong among rural Mississippians, and Bond soon became a very popular education spokesman. Bilbo and Bond could call upon local superintendents and teachers for political clout.

Bilbo called a special session of the legislature to meet on September 25, 1917. Rowland had spent the summer readying his campaign. If the Capitol Commission would not allow him to occupy the second floor, perhaps the legislature would. He mailed out printed cards to all legislators asking if they favored the removal of Archives and History to the Old Capitol. When Rowland submitted the printing bill for the polling cards, Bilbo refused to approve it, saying that it was not official business. By the end of June 1917, Rowland had received ninety- six favorable replies, but he needed twenty-five more pledges before he could be assured of having a two-thirds majority, enough to override a Bilbo veto. By the end of July, Rowland claimed to have ten more votes than needed to override a gubernatorial veto.[37]

A concurrent resolution giving Rowland the second floor of the Old Capitol passed the house of representatives easily by a vote of eighty-seven to twenty-seven. But a fight occurred in the senate. The senate invited both Rowland and Bond to present their cases to the senators. Rowland's resolution failed in the senate on two very close votes. First, an amendment to allocate eight rooms on the second floor to the Department of Education passed by a vote of sixteen to fourteen. Then the resolution to move Rowland to the Old Capitol failed seventeen to thirteen. Nineteen senators failed to vote.[38]

Rowland immediately went to work preparing for round three. The week following his failure in the senate, Rowland publicly charged Bilbo, Power, and Robertson with "thwarting the people's wishes" and announced that he would carry the

Travels of the Jefferson Davis Statue

A life-sized statue of Jefferson Davis stands in the library of the Old Capitol Restoration. Davis has occupied that place only since 1961. The statue was originally carved as the centerpiece of the Confederate Monument on south Capitol Green. The Davis statue was placed in the vault in the base of the monument in 1891. After 1903, when the New Capitol was completed, Davis presided over Old Capitol grounds that were abandoned except during the week of state fair. Vandals reaching through the iron gate broke all the fingers from Davis's extended right hand. In an attempt to put the statue out of the vandals' reach, Davis was placed ten feet above the ground on the front of the monument.

In 1922, five years after the Old Capitol had been renovated as the state office building, the legislature appropriated $2,500 to repair the hand, to build a pedestal for the statue, and to move the statue into the center of the Old Capitol rotunda. State authorities ordered a new hand to be sculpted by the Wieblen Marble and Granite Company of New Orleans and to be attached to the right arm. Columbus Marble Works carved a granite pedestal and moved the statue into the Old Capitol rotunda. For the next 37 years Davis presided over office workers passing through the corridors or sipping their cold drinks bought from the concession stand in the rotunda. There Davis stood until the restoration of the Old Capitol was completed in 1961, when the statue was installed in the rear ellipse forty-eight feet from the previous position in the rotunda.

matter directly to the people in an initiative campaign. In 1916 the Mississippi Constitution had been amended to allow the people, on petition of 7,500 qualified voters, to propose laws and to vote on them in general elections. Rowland planned to use this new provision to get the second floor of the Old Capitol.[39]

In a letter to his friend A. L. Bondurant, a professor at the University of Mississippi, Rowland revealed his real plan. The Department of Education was "being used as a barricade behind which the opposition . . . is conducting its campaign," he said. Rowland disclosed that he had already gone before the Capitol Commission with Bond and "agreed to release five rooms" for the use of the Department of Education. Later, however, "at the instigation of Bilbo," Bond increased his demand to ten rooms. Rowland also divulged that he would not file the petitions "until next June or July," presumably in time to be voted on by the people in the fall elections of 1918. Meanwhile, he noted, "the influence of the petitions at the coming [1918] session of the Legislature will be very great."[40]

On November 1 Rowland wrote the editors of Mississippi's largest papers and the Memphis *Commercial Appeal*, the Mobile *Register*, and the New Orleans *Times-Picayune* asking that the enclosed news release announcing his initiative campaign be used "in its entirety." He suggested that the papers might "make editorial mention" of his campaign. He also mailed a form letter to all other newspapers in Mississippi. By mid-November Rowland had put four hundred petitions into circulation. His primary agents for circulating the petitions were attorneys, local chapters of the United Daughters of the Confederacy, Daughters of the American Revolution, and the Sons of Confederate Veterans. Rowland asked that the petitions be notarized and returned to him by January 1. He agreed to pay those who circulated the petitions two cents per name.[41]

Although he failed to meet his goal of 7,500 signatures by January 1, Rowland made remarkable progress. He devoted almost all of his time from November 1917 through February 1918 to the petition campaign. He wrote scores of letters. By mid-December he had over 4,000 signatures; by early January almost 6,000; by the end of March over 8,000—500 more than necessary to get the issue on the ballot in November 1918.[42]

When the legislators gathered in January for their 1918 session, work on the Old Capitol had already been completed, the building had been dedicated, and the occupants had moved in. Perhaps Bilbo wanted to present the 1918 legislature with a *fait accompli*, thus undercutting Rowland's certain campaign to get legislation granting him the second floor. Landscaping and work on the outside walks was still going on when the first state agencies, the health and the banking departments, moved into the building in early October

1917. The renovated building was dedicated on Friday, October 26, 1917. Neither Rowland nor any major officer of the patriotic organizations had a role in the ceremonies. Governor Bilbo, Senator L. C. Franklin, and Speaker of the House Martin S. Conner all spoke. They praised the building, each other, the legislature, the women of Mississippi. Kate Markham Power, sister of Secretary of State Power, spoke for the women of Mississippi and their part in preserving the Old Capitol. No mention was made of Dunbar Rowland nor of the Mississippi Department of Archives and History.[43]

Evidently at the request of the legislative leaders, Rowland and Bond negotiated a compromise, wrote it out, and signed it on March 7, 1918. Rowland would concede six rooms in the south wing of the second floor to the Department of Education. The two would submit their agreement to the legislature in the form of a concurrent resolution. If, however, the legislature failed to pass the compromise resolution and if Rowland exercised his petitions and submitted the matter to the voters in the fall election, Bond agreed not to oppose Rowland's initiative. If Rowland won, Bond would comply in carrying out the arrangement.[44]

On that basis the bill granting Rowland's department space on the second floor of the renovated building passed the senate by a vote of twenty-three to fifteen and easily passed the house by a vote of seventy-seven to eighteen. But the house had passed the bill in the last five days of the session, so when the bill went to Governor Bilbo, he exercised his constitutional prerogative and refused to sign it. Almost two years later at the beginning of the 1920 session, just before he handed over the governorship to Lee Russell, Bilbo vetoed the bill. Bilbo explained that Rowland's department had ample space in the New Capitol in rooms that had been specially designed for his needs. The Old Capitol, Bilbo said, was "filled to overflowing by the great active service departments of the state," departments that were, he wrote with a hint of sarcasm, "serving the people."[45]

Thus, as the new occupants moved into the historic Old Capitol, Dunbar Rowland and the Department of Archives and History remained behind in the New Capitol.

State Office Building, 1917–1959

The Old Capitol entered a third incarnation, a prosaic and largely uneventful career as a state office building. The major executive officers of the state—the governor, the secretary of state, the treasurer, the auditor, the attorney general—all remained in the New Capitol. So did the supreme court and the state library. During the last months of 1917, other state agencies moved to the Old Capitol.

Nine agencies received space in the building. The ground floor went to the Department of Agriculture and the Board of Health. The second floor was occupied by the Department of Education, and the third floor housed a number of smaller departments: adjutant general, insurance, banking, geological, and highway.[46]

Link's plan of renovation proved solid, for the structural problems that had always plagued the Old Capitol all but disappeared. During the 1920s, a new roof was laid, and the water and steam pipes under the ground floor rusted and had to be replaced. Otherwise, nothing but routine maintenance was required. As usual, the legislature proved niggardly, and by 1930, the secretary of state was pleading with legislative committees to inspect both capitols to see for themselves the need for more maintenance funds. According to the secretary of state, funds were needed to replace pipes and toilets, to repair sidewalks, and to repaint doors and windows.[47]

The Great Depression of the 1930s struck Mississippi's agricultural economy especially hard, and by 1932, state government was practically bankrupt. Franklin D. Roosevelt's New Deal, in efforts to prime the nation's economic pump, poured more federal money into the states than ever before. In 1934 the Federal Emergency Relief Administration matched a $200,000 state appropriation for repairing all state buildings. The legislators allocated $5,500 for materials necessary to repair and repaint both capitols. The appropriation was contingent upon payment of $25,000 labor costs by the Civil Works Administration, a New Deal unemployment relief agency. The Old Capitol received a thorough facelift. The building was repainted and redecorated inside and out.[48]

The greatest problem facing those who worked in the Old Capitol was space. Within a decade after the 1917 renovation, some agency heads found it necessary to commandeer corridors to house their growing office forces. Storage space was especially scarce. In 1935, the secretary of state reported that "every available nook and corner" had been converted to storage space. Even the vestibules and entrances were used for "makeshift" offices. Twenty years after the Old Capitol had solved the state's office space problem, three government agencies were again renting space in downtown Jackson.[49]

In May 1937, a fire broke out on the third floor, damaging the building and burning a number of files. When the Capitol Commission ordered an investigation, the cause was found to be "defective and overloaded" wiring. The Old Capitol's electrical system was being overwhelmed by the packed building.[50]

In 1934 the legislature dedicated the north grounds of the Old Capitol as a "perpetual memorial to the veterans of World War I." In 1938, the legislators appropriated $150,000 to build a "War Memorial Building" on the site. The building was intended to fill a dual purpose—to serve as a

Old Capitol, c. 1930, housing the State Board of Health

memorial to Mississippi's veterans and war dead and to provide offices. The Public Works Administration, a New Deal agency, agreed to match the state appropriation. The War Memorial Building was finished by July 1940, and the offices of various veterans organizations moved in.[51]

Yet the new building did little to relieve the overcrowding at both capitols; only one state agency got quarters there. The Department of Archives and History occupied the north wing of the War Memorial Building on February 10, 1941, four years after Director Dunbar Rowland's death in 1937, and almost a quarter century after his

stubborn struggle with Bilbo over the second floor of the Old Capitol. Even with new quarters, however, the department's museum remained in the corridors on the first floor of the New Capitol.[52]

The Great Depression and the New Deal in the 1930s followed immediately by the Second World War produced an unprecedented growth in state government. Obviously, state government had far outgrown both capitols long before the war ended in 1945. The war years turned prewar depression into prosperity—economic growth that continued in the postwar decade. In the era of wartime shortages, state agencies had to make do.

First floor corridors used as additional office space for the Board of Health

Even before the war ended, however, state officials began to plan a mammoth building that could house all state agencies under one roof.

In August and October 1945 the Building Commission bought a large tract of land directly west of the New Capitol from Isidore Dreyfus and the Southern Bell Telephone Company. Governor Thomas L. Bailey urged the legislature in 1946 to appropriate $3,000,000 to construct a large state office building on the property.[53]

The Building Commission planned a fifteen-story, 300,000- square-foot building that could house twenty-eight state agencies and relieve the state from paying $60,000 annually for Jackson office space. Although the $3,000,000 requested by Governor Bailey was appropriated in 1946, even the lowest bid for the building exceeded that amount, and the 1948 legislature was forced to appropriate an additional $900,000. Work on the building started in 1948, and on March 16, 1950, the new structure was dedicated as the Woolfolk State Office Building, named for popular Tunica County legislator E. T. Woolfolk.[54]

An exodus from the Old Capitol followed

136

completion of the Woolfolk Building. The Board
of Health, one of the original tenants in 1917,
inherited the entire Old Capitol—a building that
since its 1917 renovation had begun to show the
wear and tear of constant, overcrowded use. In
1948 the agency heads housed in the Old Capitol,
led by Board of Health Director Dr. Felix J.
Underwood, had addressed a letter to Secretary of
State Heber Ladner pointing out the poor condition of the building and grounds. In response,
the building received repairs and some renovation
in 1949–50, but by 1954 structural problems
began to reappear on the north and south walls.
The southeast wall was repaired, but in 1955
Secretary of State Ladner wrote to Governor Hugh
L. White pointing out the "hazardous" condition
of the north wall.[55]

Even as the Board of Health inherited the Old
Capitol in 1950, state officials assumed that in the
near future a building would be specially constructed for that agency. Informal talks had
already begun about the possibility of transforming the Old Capitol into a state museum.[56]

*A second balcony, on third floor, was added in
1916 to improve traffic circulation among offices.
It was removed in the 1959–60 restoration.*

NOTES

[1] *Senate Journal*, 1904, 34–35. Longino also recommended selling the Governor's Mansion and building a new house for the governors away from the center of the business district. He proposed using some of the property occupied by the state school for the deaf on North State Street.

[2] *Senate Journal*, 1904, 125; 1906, 25; 1908, 42–43.

[3] *Senate Journal*, 1904, 582; 1908, 766–768; *House Journal*, 1906, 410; 1914, 1541, 1679.

[4] *Laws*, 1906, 153–154, 279.

[5] *Report of the State Capitol Commission on the Repair and Restoration of the Old State Capitol* (Jackson, 1918), 16, MDAH; Theodore Laist, "Two Early Mississippi Valley State Capitols," *The Western Architect* (May 1926), 56.

[6] *Laws*, 1902, 43–45; "Report of the Mississippi Historical Commission," *Publications of the Mississippi Historical Society*, V (1902), 32, 34, 123.

[7] *First Annual Report of the Director of the Department of Archives and History of the State of Mississippi* (Jackson, 1902), 7–8, 13–14.

[8] *Ibid.*, 15–18.

[9] Letter, July 7, 1904, RG 31, Department of Archives and History, vol. 3.

[10] Letter, Rowland to Vardaman, November 19, 1906, RG 31, Department of Archives and History, vol. 4.

[11] *Senate Journal*, 1912, 274; *House Journal*, 1912, 1151; Memphis *Commercial Appeal*, January 28, 1912; *The Official and Statistical Register of the State of Mississippi*, 1917, 407; *Tenth Annual Report of the Director of the Department of Archives and History of the State of Mississippi*, 1912, 54.

[12] *Senate Journal*, 1914, 24–29; *Seventh Annual Report of the Director of the Department of Archives and History of the State of Mississippi* (Nashville, 1909), 14.

Capitol Street, c. 1942

[13] *Senate Journal*, 1914, 24–29.

[14] Letter, undated, Mrs. Alice Talbert Turner to Mrs. Rowland; letters, Mrs. Price to Mrs. Rowland, July 19, October 5, 1915, Mrs. Dunbar Rowland Papers, Box 4, MDAH.

[15] Mrs. Dunbar Rowland, *The History of Mississippi's Old Capitol and the Movement for its Preservation* (n.p., n.d.), MDAH

[16] Letters, Mrs. Price to Mrs. Rowland, February 1, March 3, 1916, *ibid.*, Box 3.

[17] *Senate Journal*, 1916, 75–76, 112–113.

[18] A. S. Coody, "Repair of and Changes in the Old Capitol," *The Journal of Mississippi History*, XI (April 1949), 91–92; undated handbill, Mrs. Dunbar Rowland subject file, MDAH.

[19] Alfred Holt Stone subject file, MDAH.

[20] Coody, "Repair of . . . the Old Capitol," 93–94.

[21] *Senate Journal*, 1916, 1621–1624; Coody, "Repair of . . . the Old Capitol," 94.

[22] Coody, "Repair of . . . the Old Capitol," 95; Laws, 1916, 68, 157–159.

[23] *Laws*, 1916, 68, 157–158.

[24] Hemingway's Code, 1917, 1963 (*Laws*, 1904).

[25] *Report of the State Capitol Commission on the Repair and Restoration of the Old State Capitol* (Jackson, 1918), copy in MDAH.

[26] *Ibid.*, 15–16.

[27] *Ibid.*, 16.

[28] Coody, 96–97; *Report of the Capitol Commission*, 8.

[29] *Report of the Capitol Commission*, 8–9; Coody, 96, 99, 101.

[30] *Report of the Capitol Commission*, 9.

[31] Coody, 98; *Report of the Capitol Commission*, 9–10.

[32] Coody, 99; *Report of the Capitol Commission*, 9–10.

[33] Letter, Rowland to Robertson, February 19, 1917, RG 31, Department of Archives and History, vol. 7, MDAH.

[34] *Clarion-Ledger*, April 22, 1917; letter, Rowland to Collins, May 29, 1917, RG 31, Department of Archives and History, vol. 7, MDAH.

[35] 118 *Mississippi Reports* 469.

[36] *Ibid.*

[37] Form letter, Rowland to all legislators, June 13, 1917 and letter, Rowland to Capt. J. S. McNeily, July 25, 1917, RG 31, Department of Archives and History, vol. 7, MDAH; form letter, Rowland to all legislators, June 28, 1917, Dunbar Rowland Papers, box 15 and poll card, box 5.

³⁸ *Clarion-Ledger*, October 6, 26, 1917; *Senate Journal*, 1917, 120, 138.

³⁹ *Clarion-Ledger*, October 9, 1917; Handbill, "The Initiative Invoked in Mississippi First Time, Let the People Rule," November 3, 1917, in Rowland Subject file, MDAH.

⁴⁰ Letter, Rowland to Bondurant, November 19, 1917, RG 31, Department of Archives and History, vol. 7, MDAH.

⁴¹ *Ibid*; form letter to editors, November 1, 1917, Rowland subject file, MDAH; letter, Rowland to editor, *Commercial Appeal*, November 1, 1917 (duplicates to New Orleans *Times-Picayune*, Mobile *Register*, Meridian *Dispatch*, and Vicksburg *Herald*), RG 31, Department of Archives and History, vol.7, MDAH; various petition letters, Dunbar Rowland Papers, Boxes 4,5,6,7,8, MDAH.

⁴² Letter, Rowland to Firman Smith, December 20, 1917; letter, Rowland to N. B. Forrest, January 10, 1918; letter, Rowland to George C. Harris, April 1, 1918, RG 31, Department of Archives and History, vols. 7(Smith letter) and 8, MDAH.

⁴³ Jackson *Daily News*, October 9, 28, 1917; *Clarion Ledger*, October 26, 1917.

⁴⁴ "Agreement between the Mississippi Department of Education, through Superintendent W. F. Bond, and the Mississippi Department of Archives and History, through Director Dunbar Rowland, concerning the rooms and apartments for the use of said departments, on the second floor of the Old Capitol," RG 31, Department of Archives and History, vol. 8, MDAH.

⁴⁵ *Senate Journal*, 1918, 1020; 1920, 73; *House Journal*, 1918, 1609.

⁴⁶ *Senate Journal*, 1920, 73; Old Capitol subject file, MDAH.

⁴⁷ *Biennial Reports of the Secretary of State, 1923–1925*, 7; 1927- 1929, 7; 1929–1931; 23; 1931–33, 15–16.

⁴⁸ *Ibid*., 1933–1935, 18–19; Old Capitol subject file, MDAH; *Laws*, 1934, 46–47.

⁴⁹ *Biennial Reports of the Secretary of State, 1925–1917*, 7; 1933- 1935, 18; 1937–1939, 11.

⁵⁰ *Ibid*., 1935–1937, 19.

⁵¹ *Laws*, 1934, 570; 1938, 54, 407–410; War Memorial Building subject file, MDAH.

⁵² *Biennial Report of the Mississippi Department of Archives and History, 1943–1945*, 8; Old Capital Subject file, MDAH.

⁵³ *Laws*, 1946, 466–467; *Senate Journal*, 1946, 36.

⁵⁴ Woolfolk Building subject file, MDAH.

⁵⁵ Letter, Underwood to Ladner, October 4, 1948; letter, Ladner to White, January 17, 1955.

⁵⁶ *Biennial Report of the Mississippi Department of Archives and History, 1947–1949*, 24.

ILLUSTRATION NOTES

p. 118   Photograph by Harry Hiatt. MDAH.

p. 119   Postcard. Collection of Forrest Cooper.

p. 119   Photograph by E. von Seutter. MDAH.

p. 121   Broadsides. MSHM Collections.

p. 122   Illustration. *Southern Scribe*. October 23, 1909. MSHM.

p. 123   Postcards. Collection of Forrest Cooper.

p. 123   *Mississippi State Fair Catalog* (Jackson: 1910). MDAH.

p. 123   MSHM collections.

p. 125   Photograph by T. F. Laist, 1915. MDAH.

p. 126   Photographs by T. F. Laist, 1915. MDAH.

p. 128   Photograph by Harry Hiatt. Collection of Gil Ford.

p. 130   Engraving. *History of Mississippi, Heart of the South* by Dunbar Rowland (Chicago-Jackson: S. J. Clarke, 1925) 4 vols.

p. 131   Photograph. MDAH.

p. 132   Photograph. MDAH.

p. 135   Photograph by Harry Hiatt. MDAH.

p. 136   Photograph. Historic American Buildings Survey. Library of Congress.

p. 137   Photograph. Historic American Buildings Survey. Library of Congress.

p. 138   Photograph by Emmett King. MDAH.

p. 140   Photograph by Frank Noone. MDAH.

The Old Capitol's facade was extensively dismantled during the 1959 restoration.

Restoration

The Old Capitol had been saved from destruction in 1916 but at a great architectural loss. Political leaders, to justify their expenditures, transformed the Old Capitol into a state office building. As a result, most of the original interior was ripped out in a renovation that was designed to make the building economically useful. By 1950, however, time had again passed the historic building by—most state agencies had moved to the modern, massive Woolfolk skyscraper—and the state Board of Health, already maneuvering for a new modern building, inherited the fading structure.

The fortuitous appearance of strong political figures, led by Governor J.P. Coleman and including Secretary of State Heber Ladner, Speaker of the House Walter Sillers, and State Tax Collector William Winter, once again saved the old building. This time, however, their aim was not utility; it was instead to educate Mississippians about their heritage and to restore the old state house to its original beauty.

Getting Started

From its beginnings under Dunbar Rowland in 1902, the Mississippi Department of Archives and History had been responsible for the state archives and historical library, the museum collection, and a collection of portraits of notable Mississippians called the "Hall of Fame." When Rowland moved to the New Capitol in the fall of 1903, all three collections went with him.

On the ground floor of the New Capitol, Rowland's department was allocated ample space—two large semi-circular rooms, one under the senate chamber and another at the opposite end of the building under the house chamber. He put the Hall of Fame portraits and museum display cases in the room on the east end and the library, archives, and reading room on the west end. Rowland occupied two offices on the north side of the building. As the years went by, the Hall of Fame portraits and museum cases spread into the first floor corridor.[1]

Rowland's collection of artifacts was hardly a museum in the modern sense. Nineteenth-century Americans viewed museums as "cabinets of curiosities"—haphazard collections of the odd and the bizarre. Throughout Rowland's tenure from 1902 to 1937, the museum received less attention than the archives and the library, for which genealogists and Civil War veterans and their widows provided a vocal and influential patronage. Patriotic societies like the United Daughters of the Confederacy and the Daughters of the American Revolution frequently searched genealogical records to confirm membership qualifications; Confederate veterans and their widows sent research requests hoping to establish their eligibility for state pensions. The museum had a less visible and less organized patronage.

Rowland's museum collection grew over the years mainly through donations. Contemporary museum practice called for little interpretation. Items were labelled and displayed without regard to thematic or chronological unity, and, like most

The original museum display cases filled the first floor hallways of the New Capitol.

nineteenth- and early twentieth-century museums, Rowland's collection was wildly eclectic. Displayed in the same case with a "red rose gathered from the site of Fort Maurepas," the first settlement in French Louisiana, were various items from World War I, including "German shoe strings" and "exploded French shells" and an international artifact—a "knife made by a French soldier from a German bomb and an Austrian shell." "Leaves from the grave of Robert E. Lee" were displayed in a case along with a copy of the Koran. Included also were crates of fossils and bones, a "Mississippi" rifle carried by a Mississippi soldier at the Battle of Buena Vista in the Mexican War, a spur taken from the foot of Mexican General Santa Ana, and a dagger and flintlock pistol from Turkey. A "block from the tree under which Washington first took command of the American Army" rested near a collection of articles from American Samoa. A meteorite that fell in Jackson in October 1913 was displayed with a piece of granite removed from Stone Mountain, Georgia, while sculptors carved the figure of General Lee.[2]

While Rowland acquired some valuable archaeological specimens, the most popular acquisitions had little to do with Mississippi history—the grotesque little Egyptian mummy lying in her small glass-topped, red velvet-covered coffin, attired in a satin Victorian dress; a pair of size-24 shoes worn by a black man from North Carolina in World War I; a Polynesian headdress. Few Mississippi children from 1923 to 1959 escaped a trip to the New Capitol to see the "mummy."[3]

In 1941, the archives, library, and Hall of Fame moved to the north wing of the War Memorial Building. The museum remained behind in the New Capitol. The museum collection had been secondary among Rowland's priorities, and after Dr. William D. McCain became director of the Department of Archives and History in 1938, the museum remained dormant. A staff of three people, pressed with administrative and research demands, hardly had time for the museum.[4]

Even as the archives, library, and Hall of Fame occupied the War Memorial Building and the museum collection languished unattended in display cases on the ground floor of the New Capitol, a few people insisted that someday the Old Capitol would be restored and would provide a place for Archives and History, the Hall of Fame, and a first-class state historical museum. Dunbar Rowland had spoken often of a "Hall of History" or a "Memorial Hall" of Mississippi history housed in a restored Old Capitol. His two successors, William D. McCain (1938–1955) and Charlotte Capers (1955–1969) included similar recommendations in their biennial reports.[5]

As early as 1945, McCain and the trustees of the archives had discussed the possibility of gaining space in the Old Capitol, but nothing came of it. The building was already crowded with state offices. As most of the agencies housed in the Old Capitol were packing up to move to the new Woolfolk Building in 1949, McCain saw an opportunity for Archives and History to lay claim to some space in the Old Capitol. In late 1949 he spoke with Dr. Felix Underwood, the director of the Health Department, about sharing the building.[6]

McCain and Secretary of State Heber Ladner

William D. McCain

had formulated a plan to get the legislature to refurbish the abandoned Jackson Charity Hospital on North State as a new home for the Health Department. If Dr. Underwood could be convinced to move his department there, Archives and History could inherit the Old Capitol. When McCain approached Dr. Underwood with the idea, he met with stubborn and determined opposition.[7]

Under Dr. Underwood, the health agency had been pioneering programs in rural public health and had expanded from a base of two divisions when it entered the renovated Old Capitol in 1917 to a statewide agency with scores of employees and fourteen programs by 1950. The Health Department had not only spread into the corridors of the Old Capitol and into several outbuildings but was renting downtown office space as well.[8]

Beginning in 1950, the Health Department was the sole tenant in the Old Capitol. The first floor offices were occupied chiefly by Vital Statistics. In the northwest corner was the library, and the office across the hall in the northeast corner was occupied by Dr. Underwood. In the rotunda, the statue of Jefferson Davis, which had been moved from the Confederate monument in 1922, overlooked benches and a small concession stand. On the second floor were the divisions of Public Health Nursing, Health Education, Communicable Diseases, Venereal Diseases, Mental Health, School Health, and Maternal and Child Care. The third floor housed Field Services, County Health, Sanitary Engineering, and Environmental Health.[9]

Immediately to the rear of the north wing was a two-story frame building, built in 1921, housing the laboratory. Another outbuilding, directly to the rear of the bay, straddled the bluff. It housed offices and a print shop. A small ramshackle barn below the bluff housed sheep and rabbits that were used in the laboratory.[10]

In layout and design, the Old Capitol hardly suited the needs of the Health Department. The building lacked air conditioning, and the heating was antiquated. It also showed fifteen years of neglect. On the inside, cracked plaster was falling and paint was peeling. The exterior was marred by cracked and dingy stucco on the walls and flaking paint on the columns. Yet, despite its delapidated appearance, Link's 1917 steel framework held the walls rigid, and the building was structurally sound.[11]

In the early 1950s, those who contemplated the restoration of the Old Capitol and the creation of a state historical museum faced a number of interdependent obstacles. Like a parlayed bet, each successive accomplishment depended upon the success of previous steps. Powerful political leaders had to put their will and their clout behind the restoration. New quarters to house the Health Department had to be built. Finally, money had to be found at a time when the state had higher priorities—especially the equalization of white and black schools and the creation of the Minimum Foundation Program, which would require much larger state support for local school districts.

Unlike in the years before 1916, when Mrs. Rowland and her legions of patriotic ladies launched an intensive campaign to renovate the Old Capitol, in the mid-1950s no organized group lobbied the legislature to restore the building. Likewise, no unified calls for its destruction were heard. As early as 1948, some legislators talked informally about moving the University of Mississippi School of Law to Jackson and housing it in the Old Capitol. Others raised the possibility of demolishing the Old Capitol and erecting a new office building on the site. In the early 1950s, other priorities—education, economic growth, and the aftermath of the 1954 Brown school desegregation decision— caused the fate of the Old Capitol to be viewed with considerable indifference.[12]

Nonetheless, a group of legislators, led by thirty-one-year- old Representative William Winter, from Grenada County, introduced a bill in the house in 1954 directing the State Building Commission to construct a building for the Health Department in north Jackson near the Medical Center and to "repair, restore, and renovate the Old Capitol building." The bill was approved in the Committee on Public Buildings and Grounds, but when it came before the full house, the bill was resubmitted by a vote of seventy-four to sixty to the Appropriations Committee and was thereby killed.[13]

Despite the failure of the 1954 effort, the legislators clearly were not prepared to demolish the old building, and they wanted it refurbished and made more presentable. A special session in 1955 called the Old Capitol the "most important single historic landmark in the entire state" and authorized the Building Commission to refurbish the exterior "to the end that the appearance of the building may be more in keeping with the esteem in which it is held by the citizens of the state." The

The State Board of Health erected auxiliary buildings behind the Old Capitol to provide additional office space.

legislature passed a similar resolution in the 1956 session. If the legislators were still unwilling to pass a large appropriation to restore the Old Capitol completely, they clearly wanted to save the building and improve its appearance.[14]

Into this atmosphere of indecision came a new governor with a great love of Mississippi history and with decisive and unambiguous opinions about the Old Capitol. In 1955, James P. Coleman was a forty-one-year-old lawyer from Ackerman who had already fulfilled several careers. Elected district attorney at age twenty-five, he moved up to circuit judge in 1946 at age thirty-two. Four years later, he was appointed to the Mississippi Supreme Court, and a year after that, he became attorney general. Coleman was elected after his first race for the governorship, thus breaking a traditional pattern in Mississippi politics. He defeated former governor Fielding L. Wright, three-time aspirant Paul B. Johnson, Jr., and Ross Barnett, who had already run for the governorship twice.

In 1958, as plans for the Old Capitol restoration were being discussed, Governor Coleman told the legislators that Mississippi had a "noble history," but that state leaders had been "quite indifferent to the material preservation and development of . . . important symbols of a respected past." The Old Capitol, he added, "should be only the beginning" of a program to build historical parks celebrating specific events in Mississippi's past.[15]

Other powerful state leaders as well had deep

interests in state history and a dedication to saving the Old Capitol. Speaker of the House Walter Sillers, a political figure perhaps more powerful than the governor, supported the project. He also served as a member of the Building Commission and of the Board of Trustees of the Department of Archives and History. Sillers's father had served in the old building as a legislator in 1886–1887. The speaker's wife, Lena Roberts Sillers, and his sister, Florence Sillers Ogden, were powerful leaders in the women's patriotic societies.

Secretary of State Heber Ladner held a master's degree in history from Duke University, where his thesis dealt with the history of Mississippi politics in the era of Vardaman and Bilbo. William Winter, a young reform-minded legislator, left the legislature in 1956 to become state tax collector. He was elected to the Department of Archives and History Board of Trustees in 1957 and played a key role in both the restoration and the creation of the State Historical Museum.

Also playing roles were two historians, both members of the Archives and History Board of Trustees: Richard A. McLemore, president of Mississippi College, and John K. Bettersworth, chairman of the Department of History at Mississippi State University. They had substantial influence in state government as well as expert knowledge of Mississippi history.

Governor Coleman personally set in motion and led the restoration of the Old Capitol and the creation of the State Historical Museum. The governor was ex officio chairman of the State Building Commission—the agency that directed the construction, renovation, and repair of all state buildings. The commission was vested with wide, unusually discretionary powers. The 1944 act that created the commission and defined its duties did not require specific and separate appropriations for each building project, and while the commission was required to submit regular reports to the legislature, the commission had "full power to

James Plemon Coleman

erect buildings, make repairs, additions, or improvements, and buy materials, supplies, and equipment, for any of the institutions or departments of the state." The "intent and purpose" of the act, said the law, was "to clothe the commission with large discretionary powers and authority in the expending or allocation of any funds appropriated for expenditure under this act, in order that the commission may act in the interest of economy and sound business judgment."[16]

In the original 1944 bill, membership on the Building Commission had been specified—the governor as ex officio chairman, the chairmen of the Senate Finance Committee and the House Appropriations Committee, and a senator and representative appointed respectively by the lieutenant governor and the speaker of the house. The 1956 legislature amended that portion of the act. The governor remained as ex officio chairman, but now he could appoint all eight other members of the commission, who would serve "at the will and pleasure of the governor."[17]

Coleman's appointments to the Building Commission were shrewd. Although the 1956 amendment required that appointees need only be "qualified electors," the governor appointed Speaker Walter Sillers, Lieutenant Governor Carroll Gartin, and six legislators. All of the legislators were staunch Coleman supporters. From the senate he chose finance committeemen William F. Turman of DeSoto County and John Clark Love of Attala County, as well as freshman senator Charles N. Field of Webster County. From the house he picked Joel Blass of Stone County, a member of the Ways and Means Committee, Delos Burks of Pearl River County, and Bennett Smith, a neighbor from Ackerman. Senator Turman died in September 1957 and was replaced on the commission by Dees Stribling, a freshman senator from Neshoba County.[18]

Following the intent of the law, the legislature made large appropriations to the Building Commission and did not earmark the funds for specific projects. Consequently, no appropriations were ever made by the legislature for either the construction of the Underwood Board of Health Building or for the restoration of the Old Capitol. Yet the Building Commission had ample funds to carry out both projects.

The legislature appropriated $4 million in 1956 and another $4 million in 1958 to the Building Commission for discretionary construction, renovation, and repair projects. In addition, the 1956 legislature authorized the bond commission to issue up to $10 million in bonds for building projects. Projects amounting to $7

million were specified in the bill, but $3 million was left to the discretion of the Building Commission.[19]

The money for the Old Capitol restoration came from the $3 million discretionary bond authorization of 1956 (Senate Bill 1930) and from the $4 million discretionary appropriation of 1958 (House Bill 1107). Bonds from Senate Bill 1930 furnished $1 million, and $617,948 was allocated from House Bill 1107.[20]

The Building Commission first took up the restoration of the Old Capitol on May 14, 1956. Governor Coleman appointed a subcommittee of Lieutenant Governor Carroll Gartin, Senator Charles Field, and Senator W.F. Turman to investigate the matter. Similarly, he instructed the commission's attorney, James T. Kendall, to "prepare and present a full brief on the legal authority of the Commission to remodel and restore both the exterior and interior of the Old Capitol and to provide other facilities for housing the State Board of Health, such brief to include the question of what funds are available for such purposes."[21]

The only explicit authority for renovating the Old Capitol was contained in a 1956 concurrent resolution authorizing the Building Commission to renovate the exterior of the building. Governor Coleman wanted to make certain that the commission had legal authority to proceed and the right to spend money allocated to the commission for a complete restoration. Kendall's brief and the subcommittee report both gave the commission "a green light."[22]

Six months elapsed. On November 19, 1956, Governor Coleman announced to the commission that he intended to appoint a subcommittee to oversee the restoration of the Old Capitol. After the subcommittee was organized, the next step would be to recommend to the commission the employment of an architect. Governor Coleman named Senator John Clark Love chairman of the subcommittee on the Old Capitol. At the next full meeting of the Building Commission, on January 15, 1957, the governor added Speaker Sillers and Representative Joel Blass to the subcommittee.[23]

At the same meeting, the Building Commission authorized the restoration and employed the firm of Overstreet, Ware and Ware as architects for the restoration. Simultaneously, the subcommittee on the new health building reported that the architect's plans for that building had been accepted and approved. They expected that the Board of Health would be able to vacate the Old Capitol and move to new quarters in the last months of 1958. Thus, work on the Old Capitol could begin in late 1958 or early 1959.[24]

On March 25, 1957, an agreement was signed between the Building Commission and Overstreet, Ware and Ware. The architects would receive eight percent of the cost of the work and would furnish plans for approval by the commission, supervise the work of the contractors, and furnish preliminary estimates. No mention was made in the agreement about the historic restoration beyond the statement that the Building Commission intended to "remodel and restore the Old Capitol Building." The agreement specified that funds for the work would be provided by bonds authorized by "Senate Bill 1930, Regular Session of 1956."[25]

Planning the Restoration and Museum

On a winter day in 1957, Charlotte Capers and Charles Hudspeth, an employee of Overstreet, Ware and Ware, drove to Sanatorium, forty miles south of Jackson. They were following a lead to find a cache of forty-year-old documents dealing with the Old Capitol. Overstreet, Ware and Ware had just been notified that it would get the contract for restoring the building. Immediately, N.W.

Overstreet told Hudspeth to get over to the Mississippi Department of Archives and History and try to locate historical documents on the old building. Hudspeth found Charlotte Capers, the department's director, already at work searching for the same documents.[26]

A. S. Coody, the secretary of the Capitol Commission in 1917–18, had written in 1949 that all of the old documents used by the commission in the 1916–17 renovation had been stored in the vault at the tuberculosis sanatorium.[27]

Capers and Hudspeth found the dark and stuffy vault filled with musty documents and evil-smelling alcohol vats. Despite the unpleasant atmosphere, they located two boxes of papers and ordered them sent to the secretary of state's office in the New Capitol so that Hudspeth could look through them. Later, Governor Coleman wrote Dr. Clyde A. Watkins, superintendent of the sanatorium, and requested that all records not concerned with that institution be sent to Jackson. Watkins sent a single box.[28]

Hudspeth's employer, Overstreet, Ware and Ware, was one of Jackson's most prestigious architectural firms. Overstreet, a long-time Jackson architect, had only recently formed a partnership with Joe and John Ware, two younger architects who had been born in Nova Scotia and reared in Memphis and Gulfport. Joe Ware had been educated at Georgia Tech and Harvard; John, at the University of Illinois. In 1957, when John Ware was appointed project architect for the restoration, he was in his mid-forties. Before he could begin his plans to restore the Old Capitol, he had to do considerable historical research.[29]

Charlotte Capers, director of the Department of Archives and History, was also searching for historical information on the Old Capitol. Born in Columbia, Tennessee, she had come to Jackson at age five when her father, Rev. Walter B. Capers, became rector of St. Andrews Episcopal Church. After graduating in English from the University of

Mississippi in 1934, she became in 1938 secretary to William D. McCain, the newly appointed director of Archives and History. She took over as acting director during World War II and the Korean War, when McCain was called into active military service. In 1955, just before the Old Capitol restoration, McCain accepted the presidency of Mississippi Southern College, and the Board of Trustees named Capers director of Archives and History. The first five years of her fourteen- year tenure were almost completely absorbed with the restoration of the Old Capitol and the creation of the State Historical Museum.

The Building Commission had authority for the restoration. That commission, with the governor as chairman, was not in continuous session. Nevertheless, the full commission exercised control over all major decisions—hiring architects, approving plans, opening bids, hiring the contractor, and even approving the purchase of furnishings and artifacts for the museum. Daily administration for the Building Commission was carried on by a permanent staff headed by secretary-auditor E.J. Yelverton.

The Department of Archives and History was charged by Governor Coleman with planning and creating a state historical museum to be housed in the restored Old Capitol. The role of the Department's Board of Trustees in planning the museum was roughly analogous to that of the Building Commission's role in the restoration. As director of Archives and History, Charlotte Capers was responsible for carrying her board's policies into effect and creating a museum.

This division of responsibilities—with the Building Commission and its architect, John Ware, taking charge of the restoration and the trustees of Archives and History and Director Charlotte Capers planning the museum—seemed neat, clear, and logical. In practice, however, the relationships proved less than precise. Charlotte Capers had a direct stake in John Ware's restoration plans, since

The long-time friendship between Charlotte Capers and Governor Coleman was a key ingredient in assuring the high quality of the Old Capitol restoration.

the historic building itself would be the museum's primary exhibit. Governor Coleman recognized that interrelationsip clearly in an early letter to Overstreet, Ware and Ware. After stressing the necessity for speed in order "to utilize the available appropriation" and after reemphasizing that the commission did not want "a patchwork cover-up but a real restoration," Governor Coleman emphasized that the purpose of the restoration was to house the state historical museum. "As to plans for

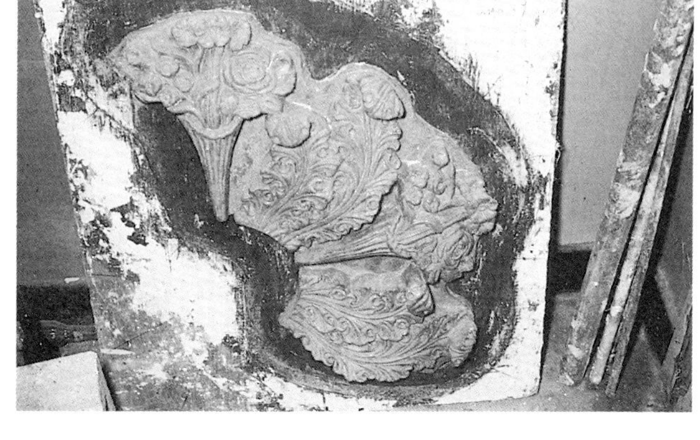

a museum and historical activities," he wrote, "we want you to consult fully with the Department of Archives and History and follow their plans and formulae in this regard."[30]

While Charlotte Capers had a large and direct stake in the restoration, she had no mandate from the Building Commission for the restoration and no formal authority over the architect. She did, however, have powerful informal influence. She and Governor Coleman had been schoolmates at Ole Miss; she was a personal friend of Secretary of State Ladner and of Speaker Sillers as well as his wife and sister. The Archives and History Board of Trustees included Speaker Sillers and State Tax Collector William Winter.

While Overstreet, Ware and Ware was a well-known and highly capable firm, it had little experience in historical restoration, a somewhat rare architectural specialty in Mississippi at that time. In 1957, as restoration planning was just beginning, everyone involved assumed that the firm was facing almost pure restoration, not adaptive use. Charlotte Capers believed that she had agreement from the Building Commission to bring in a restoration architect to consult with Overstreet, Ware and Ware. Capers's investigation revealed that the most experienced restoration architect in the area

was Richard Koch of New Orleans. Even before the written agreement between the Building Commission and the Overstreet firm was signed, Capers wrote Koch. The governor, she said, had asked her to recommend a restoration architect to consult with Overstreet. Coleman and the Building Commission, she said, were "determined to restore the building to its original form." Governor Coleman instructed Capers "to continue the negotiations with Mr. Richard Koch of New Orleans with reference to his services as a consultant, until such time as he will submit a fairly definite figure for his work." In April, Capers invited Koch

Interior scenes during reconstruction.

to Jackson under the impression that he would be employed by the commission. By the time Koch's plane arrived, Capers had been informed that Koch would not be hired. A similar episode occurred later with Lucian Dent, a restoration architect from Memphis. The issue came up again in 1958, when an attempt was made to hire a restoration architect from Nashville, and again in 1959, when the Building Commission authorized Governor Coleman and Secretary Yelverton to investigate hiring a restoration architect. Nothing came of these efforts either. Capers concluded that the Building Commission would not hire out- of-state architects.[31]

Although the search for historical documents that could shed light on the original building and the changes that had occurred over the years produced some valuable sources for the restoration, Nichols's original plans were never found. Nonetheless, helpful documents abounded. The building had been examined by several architects during the nineteenth century, and some of these records were available. Most useful of all was a large ledger book called the "Proceedings of the Commissioners of Public Buildings." The book contained daily entries of contracts, specifications, materials, payments, and minutes—all arising from the construction of the Old Capitol from 1836 to 1842. Overstreet, Ware and Ware had the complete volume transcribed, producing a thick typescript bound in a looseleaf notebook.[32]

The laws and house and senate journals furnished other hints about the original design and changes. The Capitol Commission's records and the architect's reports from the 1916–17 renovation furnished information on the building before it had been rebuilt. Photographs from before 1917 revealed especially the design of the house and senate chambers. Photographs from the 1930s showed the largely unchanged rotunda and ground floor corridor. After Overstreet, Ware and Ware advertised for the public to furnish information or pictures, it received additional material.[33]

In March 1957, Cecil Pearson, an employee of the Overstreet firm, set up a small office in the south wing of the second floor. He spent the next six months in the building, making measurements and drawings, examining the structure thoroughly, trying to dig out hints about its original design.[34]

On March 6, 1958, one year after Pearson set up shop in the Old Capitol, John Ware had gathered enough information and made sufficient progress to present a report to the Building Commission including tentative outline plans and

Charlotte Capers

create a modern and nationally recognized historical museum in a building designed as a historical restoration. At best, the two aims were somewhat incompatible. More difficult still, the museum was to be housed in a building on which work had not yet begun.[36]

Capers faced daunting tasks. She had to develop policies and rationale for a state historical museum; she had to develop an exhibit plan; she had to match her rationale and her exhibits plan to John Ware's restoration plans.

She began by educating herself and by establishing contacts with the museum world. Both Capers and the Archives and History Board of Trustees were dedicated to creating an exemplary historical museum. Mississippi's image then was at a low ebb. The state's angry and defiant reaction to the Brown desegregation decision attracted unpleasant national attention. Therefore, Capers and the department's board wanted a museum that would portray Mississippi's heritage in a positive way. Capers and the board concluded that they must seek advice and consultation from national experts and museum authorities, even though this was not always a popular practice, as Capers had found in her search for a restoration consultant.[37]

During 1957 and 1958, Capers wrote hundreds of letters seeking advice and help, and she joined professional museum associations and attended their meetings. She established contacts and corresponded regularly with Colonial Williamsburg, the National Trust for Historic Preservation, and the National Park Service. Gradually, these broad and numerous contacts began to narrow and to focus. By the beginning of 1958, she had established a close professional relationship with Dr. Arnold B. Grobman, director of the Florida State Historical Museum and president of the Southeastern Museums Conference. For exhibit expertise Capers turned increasingly to Ralph H. Lewis, chief of the National Park Service's museums branch. From Grobman, Capers

specifications. The commission responded by making its first partial payment to Overstreet, Ware and Ware. Three months later, on June 4, Ware presented a full report, though it was still tentative in some details; and on November 11, 1958, Ware presented the final plans.[35]

Charlotte Capers's job in planning the state historical museum would have been relished by few administrators. She labored under every handicap. She had no museum experience, no museum staff, and no budget. During a time of rapidly changing museum practice, she was attempting to could get expert advice on museum policies, space allocation, budget, and staffing. From the National Park Service, she could get expert help in designing exhibits.

By February 1958, John Ware had finished drawing the preliminary plans for the restoration, and Capers was able to invite Grobman to come to Jackson to review the plans. Ware's plans called for the museum to occupy the south wing of the ground floor and the committee rooms of the second floor. Museum offices and work space would occupy the north wing of the ground floor. Capers wanted a shop where work could be done on exhibits, but Ware said a shop could not be provided in the building, and he did not plan one outside.[38]

Grobman agreed to come to Jackson, and on April 24, 1958, he spent the day with Capers and Ware reviewing the plans and inspecting the building. Grobman agreed to furnish a complete report making recommendations on the issues of pure restoration vs. adaptive use, allocation of space, and museum staff. His report arrived in Jackson at the end of May.

On the issue of restoration or adaptation, Grobman struck a sensible compromise that was adopted almost unchanged. He recommended against any attempt to restore the entire building. Even if it were technically and historically possible, Grobman said, such an attempt would be a "luxury" far beyond the resources of the "wealthiest state in the nation" and would "not at all satisfy the needs of Mississippi for a historical museum." Instead, he recommended careful restoration only in specific areas—the building's exterior, the office of the governor, the house and senate chambers, the rotunda, and other "public space."[39]

Grobman suggested that exhibits and administrative offices be limited to the first and second floors, with the third floor reserved for the storage of collections not on public display. Although some patriotic societies were already lobbying for space in the restored building, Grobman insisted that the museum should not offer them any space. Even by reserving the third floor for storage, the museum would still have a greater percentage of its space devoted to exhibits than most museums, and, thus, would be short of room for offices and other work areas. Instead, he suggested, one room in the public area should be reserved for changing exhibits, and local societies should be encouraged to set up their own temporary displays. Finally, he recommended hanging the Hall of Fame portraits throughout the building, but since those paintings would take up most available wall space, he suggested that the portraits of Mississippi governors be retained in the New Capitol.[40]

Grobman recommended that a museum staff of seven be hired. The staff should be headed by a curator, who would report to the director of Archives and History. An artist and a museum assistant would help with the creation and design of exhibits. A full-time docent or guide should be included on the staff, and a secretary to the curator would double as a records specialist to maintain the documents attendant upon a large collection of historical materials. Two janitors would fill out the staff.[41]

The National Park Service, Branch of Museums, had few peers in creating historical exhibits. National Park Service historians from the Vicksburg National Military Park and from the Natchez Trace Parkway were very active in the Mississippi Historical Society, and Charlotte Capers was secretary-treasurer of that organization. She also knew of park service restoration work done at Mount Locust on the Natchez Trace. One of Capers's first pleas for help was addressed to Frederick L. Rath, former director of the National Trust for Historic Preservation. "All I know about museums," Capers wrote, "is that we do not want one like the one we have had." Could Rath, Capers asked, recommend any museum consultants, especially in the areas of layout and equipment? Rath replied that Ralph Lewis's "Park Service boys . . . are among the best in the business." Rath raised the possibility that museum specialists might be hired temporarily while they were on vacation leave from the park service.[42]

Capers filed the information, but she did not forget it. In early 1957, Archives and History was far from ready to lay out and design exhibits. Before museum planning could proceed, a set of governing policies had to be written and accepted. Two thorny issues had to be resolved—the theme and purpose of the museum and the display of donated items. Rowland's collection contained many items that had no connection with Mississippi's history. Most of these items were donations. In short, for reasons of good will or on personal whim, Rowland had accepted and displayed everything. Clearly, written policies governing exhibits and donations were essential.

Capers, with advice from board member R.A. McLemore, prepared a set of policies and submitted them to the board of trustees. On December 6, 1957, the board approved the policies. The museum, the board declared, would be a division of the Department of Archives and History. The museum staff would be headed by a curator who, in turn, would be hired by and report to the director of the department. The board also declared that "the scope of the State Historical Museum shall be the field of Mississippi history, from earliest times to the present," and that the museum's purpose was to educate the public in Mississippi history. Two key policies settled the previous problems of eclecticism. The museum would accept "only items directly related to events, eras, or persons in Mississippi history," and the museum would "accept nothing with the stipulation that it must be displayed." With these issues settled, Capers awaited the architect's final plans before she began to plan the exhibits.[43]

Two years later, in January 1959, John Ware's

An art glass window was installed behind the rostrum of the house chamber, 1916–1959.

plans had been completed, the Health Department employees in the Old Capitol were packing up to move to their newly completed quarters near the medical center, and work was about to begin on the restoration. Schedules called for completion of the work eighteen months later, in September 1960. If the historical museum were to be ready on time, an exhibit plan had to be put together and approved. Otherwise, there would not be time enough to construct the exhibits.

Capers wrote to the Museums Branch of the National Park Service in Washington on January 28, 1959, asking if the park service could make available museum consultants "on a reimbursable basis." Ralph H. Lewis, chief of the Museums Branch, responded that their Eastern Exhibit Planning Team, composed of a museum specialist and a designer, was "nearly caught up with their current assignments" and perhaps could be made available. Although the men had worked mainly with natural history and archeology, Lewis wrote, they both had a "real knack" for creating exhibits. It would take the men four to five weeks to develop an exhibit plan for twenty-five exhibits, Lewis estimated. The costs for salary, travel, and per diem, he told Capers, would total no more than $2,500.[44]

Capers replied immediately to Lewis. She would be delighted to get the two specialists, and she could find the necessary $2,500. (The Mississippi Historical Society granted the funds.) But she wanted the park service team to come with no illusions. "We are on a very tight schedule," she emphasized, and "we do not have a museum at all, in any real sense of the word." Nor, she warned, was "the subject matter well defined and ready for translation into exhibits." On the other hand, she and her small staff were familiar with Mississippi history, and the library and archives of the department furnished a rich mine of useful materials. Finally, she asked, what information and materials should she and her staff gather in anticipation of the team's arrival?[45]

Lewis replied that the team could work in Jackson from May 4 to May 30 and that Capers and her staff should gather information on the major artifacts to be used, compile a narrative sequence of events they wanted to depict, identify the primary audiences for the museum, and provide architectural drawings of the museum space. Also, he emphasized that "specialists familiar with the subject matter should be on hand at all times while the team is at work." Finally, Lewis assured Capers, "Our planners feel that you are presenting an interesting and worthwhile problem to them."[46]

On the morning of May 4, Myron Sutton, museum specialist for the National Park Service, arrived in Jackson and immediately went to work in the basement of the War Memorial Building gathering ideas, references, and artifacts, preparing for the arrival a week later of his teammate, Exhibits Construction Specialist Edward Bierly. Capers and staff members Patti Carr Black and Carl Ray devoted all of their time to the work. Over the next four weeks, in a crash effort, working long days and into the nights, seven days a week, these five people hammered out an exhibits plan of permanent exhibits, relating the history of Mississippi from prehistory through the Constitution of 1890. For each of the thirty exhibits, Sutton and Bierly left with Capers a color sketch and a detailed outline, including the location of each exhibit in the museum, the size and type of display case needed, a detailed list of the artifacts and artwork needed, and suggested labels. In addition, they left a cost estimate and miscellaneous recommendations on placing the Hall of Fame portraits and for collecting, displaying, and caring for artifacts.[47]

The $2,500 paid to Sutton and Bierly was well spent. With no prior knowledge of Mississippi history, using John K. Bettersworth's high school Mississippi history text as a guide and the Archives and History staff as assistants, Sutton and Bierly in four weeks had created the plan for permanent exhibits at the future State Historical Museum. Charlotte Capers praised their efforts mightily. To Lewis, their supervisor, she wrote that the two museum specialists were "energetic, intelligent, and conscientious." They had, she predicted, "laid down guidelines toward . . . one of the outstanding history museums in the South."[48]

Restoring the Building

More than two years after Governor Coleman first presented to the Building Commission the idea of restoring the Old Capitol, in June 1958, the commission approved John Ware's layout of rooms and Arnold Grobman's plan of selective restoration. The governor's office, house and senate chambers, and the rotunda would be "faithfully" restored except that modern seats would be placed in the house so that meetings could be held there. The remainder of the building would be restored for museum space.[49]

On November 11, 1958, the commission met to approve John Ware's final plans. After the meeting, the commission advertised for bids on the restoration and, exactly one month later, awarded the contract to the low bidder, Robert C. Crouch and Company of Memphis. The Crouch Company's bid was $1,498,000.[50]

The commission's actions were timed to coincide with the approaching completion of the Underwood Board of Health Building. Work had begun on the health building in July 1957; in early 1959, it was ready, and the health department employees packed up their offices and moved into their new quarters two miles up North State Street. The contractors began work on the Old Capitol in mid-February 1959.[51]

Architects who had examined the Old Capitol over the decades since 1839 had all come to a similar conclusion—that William Nichols's foundation was inadequate to support the weight of such a large building and to ensure the stability of the walls. For 120 years, nothing had been done to strengthen the old foundation. Not only did the original foundation allow the walls to lean and crack, but the rubble brick from which it was made was porous, so that ground water running down the slope from north to south seeped into the foundation and up into the soft brick walls. As usual, the chief problems lay in the north and south walls. At last, however, the architects and engineers who planned the restoration determined to go to the source of the problem and to set new foundations under those walls. Therefore, when Clarence Waddle, the supervisor assigned to the job by Crouch Construction Company, arrived on the site, he faced the initial task of taking down the walls to replace the foundations on both ends of the building. Overstreet was so concerned about the possible collapse of the rear wall during the demolition of the north and south walls that he bought a large insurance policy from Lloyd's of London to cover that possibility.[52]

The fifteen-inch-thick end walls were taken down entirely, and the old brick was stacked around the grounds. Then new foundations were put in on both ends of the building. Concrete pilings with large bell-shaped bottoms were set in place and concrete plates laid across them. Under the front and rear walls Nichols's 120-year-old foundation remained in place. However, in an attempt to waterproof the old foundation under those walls, the contractor drove "sheet pilings" (plates of sheet steel) about eighteen inches out from both the front and rear walls and poured concrete between the pilings and Nichols's foundation.[53]

Nichols's original front and rear walls were not taken down. The stucco covering was removed and the soft, sandy original brick was exposed. Workmen patched the cracks and replaced spots where the old brick had crumbled with good brick that had been removed from the end walls. The original mortar on the front and rear walls was so weak that it had to be scraped out to a depth of three-quarters of an inch and replaced with new mortar, a process called "tuck-pointing." Some of the original brick was so soft that superintendent Waddle concluded that much of it had never been baked in a kiln—that it had simply been laid on the ground and dried in the open air. Deer tracks discovered on some of the old bricks lent evidence to Waddle's theory. It seems more likely, however, that the bricks had been laid out on the ground for some time before being baked.[54]

The first major alteration in the original plans came up soon after work began. In addition to the areas selected for restoration inside the building, the exterior, perhaps the least changed part of the

The dismantled north end of the Old Capitol with the old brick stacked along State Street.

building over its 120-year life, was to be carefully restored to its original appearance. When first built, the outer walls were brick covered with stucco and scored to resemble the stones in classical buildings. Because of this stucco, Ware's plans called for discarding all the old brick from the end walls and instead using new brick, since the exterior brick would be plastered with stucco anyway.[55]

As the end walls were taken down to reveal the 1917 steel framework, the old brick was stacked around the grounds, where it could be easily pilfered by passersby who wanted a brick from the Old Capitol as a memento. Charlotte Capers, whose War Memorial Building office overlooked the rail line behind the Old Capitol, glanced up one morning to see a carload of the old bricks being shipped out. A Memphis resident had bought them to build his new home. She immediately called Gene Yelverton, secretary of the Building Commission, to protest. He explained that the contractor was entitled to dispose of the debris around the construction site, and the bricks were not needed. Nonetheless, the sale of the bricks was stopped, and in speeches and in newspaper articles Capers pled with the public to stop taking souvenir bricks.[56]

Old brick was fashionable in the late 1950s,

and after the stucco was removed from the front and rear walls, Jacksonians remarked on the beauty of the old brick walls. Although stuccoed brick on Greek Revival buildings was common at the time the Old Capitol was built and antebellum travel accounts showed that the building had a stuccoed exterior, neither Capers nor the architects found conclusive evidence that Nichols stuccoed the building when he constructed it. Possibly the stucco had been added at a later time. While Capers suspected that Nichols had stuccoed the building originally, she reasoned that nothing would be lost in the restoration by leaving the brick exposed. If necessary, stucco could be applied later.

Capers, with Governor Coleman's agreement, recommended to the Building Commission on March 16, 1959, that the end walls be faced with old brick and that the building not be stuccoed. In fact, facing the building with original old brick rather than with stucco-covered new brick would allow the use of more of the original materials. And clearly, the public preferred the look of the old brick. The commission approved and ordered John Ware to prepare a change order for the contractor. The change order added $17,277 to the contract.[57]

The end walls were rebuilt with new brick and faced with old brick that matched the original brick of the front and rear walls. To protect the old brick from the elements, all the exterior brick walls were covered with a clear silicone water-proofing solution.[58]

The roof, a perennial problem second only to that of the foundation, was entirely replaced. New steel trusses were installed to support the roof. Then treated wood decking was laid, and over that a new metal roof was placed. Initially, some questions were raised about the necessity of replacing the copper on the dome, but an inspection by William Winter, Heber Ladner, and the architects led to the conclusion that any attempt to repair the old covering would be "false economy."[59]

Nichols's original stonework on the exterior of the ground floor had to be entirely replaced. Indiana limestone replaced the original soft and rotting Hinds County limestone from near Mississippi Springs. Superintendent Waddle set up a drafting table in the building and had the required stones measured and drawn. They were then ordered precut from Indiana and shipped to the site. A small crane hoisted the stones into place. In tight spots that could not be reached by the crane, Waddle rigged small hand winches with electric motors for the workers to lift the stones into position.[60]

Perhaps even more tedious and delicate than restoring the exterior was work on the interior of the building. The steel framework put in by Link in the 1916–17 renovation would remain in place, but the house and senate chambers had been lost when Link extended the third floor through both chambers and cut them up into offices. To restore the house and senate chambers, workers had to cut out all of the steelwork from the second-floor level to the roof on both ends of the building. The remaining steel framework prohibited restoring Nichols's exact floorplan; so did the plans to use the building for a museum.[61]

Nevertheless, insofar as possible, the additions and changes of 1916–17 were torn out. Out went the partitions; the space for the spiral staircases was restored by taking out the offices in the entryway. The stairway in the rear bay was torn out, and the door that had been cut in the center of the rear bay was closed up. The ground floor corridor and rotunda, left intact by Link, remained unchanged except for the removal of Link's third-floor balcony around the rotunda. The doors and back stairs on the north and south wings that had been taken out by Link were restored. Researchers apparently failed to discover the changes made by architect Joseph Willis in 1870–71, especially those in the house chamber and front

The design, materials, and craftsmanship of the rotunda dome, shown in this 1930s photograph, have remained intact and unchanged since the building was completed in 1840.

portico, but based on the available historical evidence in 1957 and 1958, with the exceptions of office arrangement, furnishings, carpets and drapes, flooring materials, and modern necessities like heating, air conditioning, and lighting, the building was "faithfully" restored.

Perhaps most difficult of all was the detail work on the interior—plastering and repairing or fabricating columns, capitals, and decorative work. Plastering was contracted to Don P. Whalen of Memphis. His crew began by tearing out all of the old plaster and lathing. In some places, they discovered plaster more than three inches thick, especially in places where plaster had been used to correct errors in construction—corners that were not square or cornices that failed to meet. New laths were installed and the errors corrected with furring. After the building was replastered, only in one place was there an error of as much as three-sixteenths of an inch.[62]

Only in the rotunda was the plaster sound enough to be patched rather than replaced. Even there, however, two men worked for eight days on high scaffolding to patch the plaster and ornamentation. The domed senate ceiling, which originally had octagonal coffers and a circular skylight, was completely redesigned. The skylight was eliminated, and large new circular coffers were molded with layers of hemp to give strength, then raised to the ceiling with a portable jack.[63]

For ornamental and restoration plaster work, Whalen hired Stefano Giuliano. Giuliano, using some of the surviving ornamental work as guides, made molds to produce new column capitals and ornaments such as medallions, rosettes, and friezes. "If restoration had been delayed any longer," he said, "most of the ornamental work would have been destroyed, leaving nothing as a guide."[64]

New columns and pilasters had to be made to replace those that had been torn out and disposed of in 1916. Forty columns had been sold to Governor Bilbo in 1917, including sixteen from the senate. The Bilbo family returned them, but only two were considered sound enough to use. New columns were fashioned by Jackson millwork firm Scanlon and Taylor, and the capitals were molded by Giuliano.[65]

The seemingly clear, but, in fact, ambiguous division of roles in the restoration produced some disagreements between architect John Ware and Charlotte Capers. Capers recognized that Ware was ultimately responsible to the Building Commission, the final authority for the job. Although she knew that she had no direct authority over the architect and that her primary duty was to create the museum, Capers nevertheless had a mandate from the Board of Trustees to advise and consult on the restoration. Governor Coleman, the Building Commission, and the Board of Trustees of Archives and History all agreed that the restoration should be as pure as possible. The restored building would be the centerpiece for Capers's state historical museum, thus making the entire building, in a sense, a grand museum exhibit.

Disagreements almost always concerned the "purity" of the restoration or the use of national vs. local talent. Except in construction and engineering matters, the two had many differences of opinion. Capers wanted many of the existing columns to be used, especially those that remained in the old house chamber and the senate columns contributed by the Bilbo family. Ware declared that they were rotten and insisted on well-made replicas. Capers went to great effort in finding national experts who could offer advice on paint patterns and colors used in Greek Revival buildings. Ware preferred to work with a local decorator. Ware suggested hanging a chandelier in the rotunda; Capers suggested that they check with Greek Revival specialists first.[66]

In these disputes with Ware, Capers sometimes enlisted support from powerful friends like Governor Coleman and Speaker Sillers. On the matter of colors and the chandelier, she sent copies of her letter to John Ware to Governor Coleman, Secretary of State Ladner, Speaker Sillers, and William Winter. Sillers promptly wrote a letter to Ware supporting Capers's position, returning to Capers a copy with the note: "I am greatly pleased that you sent me a copy of your letter to John Ware and I have hastened to let him know how I feel about it." Capers also had free access to the governor, and she frequently consulted with him in person and by telephone.[67]

Capers lost the battles of the columns and the colors; she won the battle of the chandelier. And yet to come, just as the restoration was being completed in August 1960, was the conflict over the stained glass window.

During the 1916–17 renovation, architect Theodore Link had installed a stained glass window on the north end of the building behind the speaker's rostrum. Capers suggested on two grounds that the stained glass be removed. First, she said, stained glass was not typical of Greek Revival buildings, and second, the window was clearly not original to the building. Capers offered evidence to support her arguments. She handed Ware the official report showing that the window had been purchased in 1916, and she provided testimony from experts that the window was inappropriate for a Greek Revival building. Nonetheless, Ware remained adamant. In frustration she pled to Speaker Sillers that the matter be brought before the Building Commission. "I have mentioned this [matter] to John Ware several times," she wrote, "but got nowhere."[68]

Before Sillers could act, the Executive Committee of the Archives and History Board of Trustees called Ware to a meeting. Capers presented her evidence, which included the report showing purchase in 1916, photographs taken in 1915 in which the window is not present, a statement from A.S. Coody, secretary for the 1916–17 renovation saying that Link installed the

Old Capitol, restored, c. 1961

window, and statements from experts saying that the window clearly did not suit a Greek Revival restoration. Ware refused to accept the evidence but nevertheless yielded and agreed to remove the window.[69]

Creating the Museum

In her biennial report of 1959, Charlotte Capers assured the legislature and the general public that the "planning of the Mississippi Historical Museum has not been haphazard," and that it "represents the best thinking in the museum profession in America." When Capers wrote those words, planning was virtually complete. Edward Bierly and Myron Sutton had just finished their designs and specifications for thirty permanent exhibits. Except for Sutton's and Bierly's bills, which were paid by the Mississippi Historical Society, all the planning up to mid-1959 had been paid for out of regular Archives and History funds.

Old Capitol Restoration dedication ceremony, June 3, 1961.

Now the plans had to be approved, and money to hire staff and create the exhibits had to be found.[70]

As the contractors dismantled the north and south walls of the old building to start the restoration, Capers began her efforts to stimulate public interest in the museum. In March 1959 she published the first issue of the *Mississippi History Newsletter*. "Scaffolding was up around Mississippi's venerable Old Capitol," she informed her readers, and the building would soon be "restored to its original architecture and used as a state historical museum." Over the next three years Capers visited key legislators to enlist their support and made countless speeches to civic clubs

and patriotic societies. Some large costs, such as furnishings for the restored areas and the offices, would be borne by the Building Commission. Yet costs for constructing the exhibits, building the exhibit cases, and hiring a museum staff had to come from the Archives and History budget. For the years 1956–58, the department received $87,820, and for the 1958–60 budget period, a slight increase to $95,165. Capers emphasized to the Budget Commission that this small increase would only allow the department "to operate *as we are now operating*." She asked for no museum funds. Staff was equally meager. In 1956, Capers had a staff of seven; one of these was a janitor and three were clerical workers. In 1958, a clerk was added, increasing the staff to eight. None was a museum specialist.[71]

As usual, when Capers began preparing her staff and budget requests for the 1960–62 biennium, the budget that would include money for museum staff and for creating the exhibits, she sought advice on salaries and estimates on exhibit costs from other museum directors in nearby states. With their advice, her request included eight additional full-time employees and one half-time. Two of these positions were janitorial and two were professional—museum curator and an archivist-editor. The others were clerical. When she submitted the budget to the Commission of Budget and Accounting on August 24, 1959, she noted that she was asking for "a sizeable increase" from $95,165 in the previous biennium to $246,492, but that $53,000 of the increase was for "museum exhibits and cases" and was, therefore, "a non-recurring item." Even with that disclaimer, however, Capers was asking for more than a 100 percent budget increase.[72]

A rumor reached Capers in September that her request would be cut by $12,000, and she wrote her friend Speaker Sillers asking for help. The request, she said, was "an honest estimate," and a cut would "cripple us in staffing our museum." The department received $248,075 for the 1960–62 biennium and a new museum staff of five, headed by a museum curator.[73]

The first curator of the State Historical Museum went to work in April 1960. Dr. Robert S. "Stu" Neitzel was by training and temperament a field archaeologist. However, his latest experience had been in designing, building, and administering a museum at the Etowah archaeological area near Cartersville, Georgia. Born, reared, and educated in Nebraska, Neitzel had worked in the South since 1938, principally as an archaeologist in Louisiana and in Georgia.[74]

Neitzel's first job was to move the collection from the New Capitol. Restoration work was still going on in the Old Capitol, so in June 1960, Neitzel set up shop in the old health department laboratory building in the rear of the Old Capitol. There, he spent the summer classifying, cataloging, cleaning, and preserving artifacts so that the items would be ready when the exhibits arrived from the contractor.[75]

The artwork and exhibit cases for the permanent museum exhibits and the furnishing and decorating of the restored areas of the building—the governor's office, the house and senate chambers—had earlier been contracted to outside professionals. Earl Hart Miller, a Dallas interior designer then living at Natchez, who had designed the interiors and furnishings for a number of the restored mansions in that city and who was recommended by Mrs. Walter Sillers, was hired by the Building Commission to select the carpets, draperies, and colors in the house and senate chambers. He would also design and furnish the governor's office, which would be restored to the 1850s, the period in which Miller specialized.[76]

Miller worked with Renna Johnston, an interior designer with Overstreet, Ware and Ware. Like Miller, Johnston had connections both with Natchez and Texas. After completing high school in Natchez, Johnston had studied fine arts at Texas Women's University. Miller took complete charge of designing and furnishing the governor's office, but in the remainder of the building, the furniture, draperies, and carpets were selected jointly by Miller and Johnston. Johnston selected all of the interior colors and paints.[77]

None of the original furnishings had survived, so, with little evidence of how the rooms had been furnished and decorated, Miller faced the prospect of restoring period rooms. Since the house chamber would be fitted out with modern theater seats and the senate would contain no furniture, Miller had only to select drapes, carpets, and colors for those rooms. The governor's office posed his largest problem. Although a search was made for

The diorama depicting DeSoto crossing the Mississippi River was one of 32 exhibits installed in the new museum in 1961.

original pieces of furniture, none were found, so Miller went on the antique market to find period pieces. He bought many items from the antique dealers along Royal Street in New Orleans and billed them to the Building Commission. Of necessity, the governor's office was not a restoration, but the recreation of an elegant office in 1850—almost certainly a more lavishly furnished and richly decorated office than any Mississippi governor who worked there would have recognized.[78]

The thirty permanent exhibits designed by Sutton and Bierly called for considerable artwork—panels of drawings and paintings with printed explanations, models, and three dioramas. Capers again went to the National Park Service for advice. What firms, she asked, were capable of doing this kind of artwork capably and on time? The park service furnished the names of three firms in Washington, D.C. All had done work for the park service in designing exhibits, and park

service officials assured Capers that any of them could do an excellent job on the museum exhibits for the state historical museum. They cautioned, however, that someone familiar with Mississippi history and with the exhibit plan would need to work closely with the artists.[79]

The contract for $38,753 went to Creative Arts Studio, one of the firms recommended by the National Park Service. Three specified dioramas were described in the original plan of exhibits— DeSoto's discovery of the Mississippi River, the signing of the Treaty of Doak's Stand in 1820, and Union boats running by the batteries at Vicksburg in 1863. Artists at Creative Arts felt that the latter design could be more dramatically depicted with a large back-lighted transparency behind modeled figures in the foreground. Capers accepted this substitution. The contract was signed on July 22, 1960, and the exhibits were to be completed by December 1, 1960.[80]

*The temporary exhibits
are designed to fit
unobtrusively into the
Old Capitol's historic
spaces. The permanent
exhibits occupy spaces
remodeled for that
purpose.*

The museum provides programs for school groups as well as adults.

The contract for the construction of exhibit cases was awarded to Westbrook Manufacturing Company of Jackson. Westbrook agreed to supply sixteen recessed wall cases, one hanging wall case, three lockable cases with doors, one small wall case, and the diorama cases for $12,996. They agreed to have all the cases installed by November 15, 1960.[81]

When Capers negotiated these contracts, the target date for opening the restoration and the museum was January 5, 1961, only four days short of the one hundredth anniversary of Mississippi's secession. Plans called for work on the restoration to be completed by mid-September 1960, leaving almost four months to get exhibits installed. By early fall, it was evident that neither the building nor the museum would be ready for a January 5 opening. In December 1960, the Building Commission still had not accepted the building from the contractor, and Capers announced that it was "unlikely" that the museum would be open before February or March.[82]

Capers went to Washington in November 1960 to look over the progress on the exhibits, and on January 25, she went back for a final inspection. Snowed in for three days, she used the time to make a "gruelling two-day check of all artifacts, artwork, captions, and texts," and she found only a few errors to be corrected. "On the whole," Capers reported, she was "delighted with the exhibits." By then, she was projecting a March opening for the museum.[83]

The first months of 1861 had witnessed some momentous events in Mississippi history—secession, the creation of the Confederacy, the beginning of the Civil War. The hundredth anniversary of these events in 1961 brought the celebration of the Civil War Centennial. That celebration added to the already mounting enthusiasm for the opening of the restoration and the museum.

The Old Capitol opened on March 21, 1961, although the building and the museum were still unfinished in some details. That date had been chosen to coincide with the formal opening of Mississippi's Civil War Centennial set to begin on March 28. On Tuesday, March 21, Archives and History staff member Patti Carr Black became the first to register at the new State Historical Museum in the restored Old Capitol. She was followed that day by one thousand others.[84]

One week later, on March 28, "Secession Day" featured a giant parade with three thousand members of the Mississippi Greys, all "colonels" commissioned and led by Govenor Ross Barnett and all in Confederate uniforms. The Mississippi Greys and thousands of other Mississippians then gathered in front of the restored Old Capitol to watch a play written by Mississippi College Professor Louis Dollarhide depicting the Secession Convention. Students from local colleges and employees of the State Highway Department played the hundred delegates. Afterwards, the crowds trooped through the Old Capitol.[85]

More than six thousand people came in the last ten days of March. Almost fifteen thousand came in April and another ten thousand in May. By the end of June, a little more than three months after the opening, more than forty thousand people had toured the building. Only one question marred the universal praise—Where was the "mummy"? Lacking any connection to Mississippi history, the "mummy" had been sent into storage.[86]

On June 3, 1961, all the principals—members of the Building Commission, Trustees of the Department of Archives and History, Charlotte Capers, and John Ware—gathered in the house chamber for the official dedication. By then, J.P. Coleman was no longer governor. That office had been assumed in January 1960 by Ross Barnett. Coleman was only a freshman representative for Choctaw County in the legislature. Nonetheless, Coleman, who, more than any other, was the

The Christmas tree in the rotunda is an annual tradition which began when the museum staff placed a small tree on the portico balcony in 1961.

moving force behind the Old Capitol restoration and the State Historical Museum, gave the principal address. The building, Coleman said, was "an emblem of the faith that was new and shining in 1839, 122 years ago, and which continues today." Appropriately too, Charlotte Capers presided.[87]

NOTES

[1] Interviews with Charlotte Capers, July 6, 1989, and W.D. McCain, July 31, 1989.

[2] Inventory of Museum Collection, c. 1929, State Historical Museum, Jackson, Mississippi.

[3] Capers interview.

[4] *Ibid.*; McCain interview.

[5] *Ibid.*; *Biennial Report of the Department of Archives and History, 1953–1955*, 31–32.

[6] *Minutes of the Board of Trustees of the Department of Archives and History*, October 19, 1945, October 14, 1949, January 13, 1950, RG 31, MF 51.

[7] McCain interview.

[8] *Biennial Report of the Mississippi State Board of Health,* 1953–1955, 6–17.

[9] Interview with Johnnie Wagner, Paul Rankin, and Dick Andrews, Board of Health employees who worked in the Old Capitol in the 1950s, July 12, 1989.

[10] *Ibid.* Sheep's blood was used as a medium for lab cultures. Rabbit brains were used to manufacture rabies vaccine.

[11] *Ibid.*

[12] Interview with William Winter, July 9, 1989.

[13] Old Capitol Subject File, MDAH; *House Journal,* 1954, 2, 58, 120, 186.

[14] *Laws,* 1954, 303–304; 1956, 723.

[15] *Senate Journal,* 1958, 9–10.

[16] *Laws,* 1944, 549–50.

[17] *Laws,* 1956, 509.

[18] *Biennial Report of the Building Commission, 1956–1957;* RG 43, Minutes of the Building Commission, September 12, 1957, MDAH. Before Governor Coleman's term ended in January 1960, there was more turnover of the commission. Burks, Field, and Smith went off after resigning to accept other appointments and were replaced by house members E.L. Boteler, Jr., of Grenada County and Vardaman Webb of Winston County and by senate member Hushel Moss of Smith County.

[19] *Laws,* 1956, 21–22, 344–349; 1958, 76–77.

[20] *Ibid.; Biennial Report of the Building Commission, 1956–57,* 21; *ibid.,* 1958–59, 14. The Underwood Board of Health Building was funded partially by bonds from Senate Bill 1930 and partially from a federal grant; Jackson *Daily News,* February 18, 1957; *Biennial Report of the Mississippi State Board of Health, 1957–59,* 16.

[21] Minutes of the Building Commission, May 14, 1956, RG 43 MDAH.

[22] *Laws,* 1956, 723; interview with former governor J.P. Coleman, August 1, 1989.

[23] *Ibid.,* November 19, 1956, and January 15, 1957.

[24] *Ibid.,* January 15, 1957.

[25] *Ibid.*

[26] Charlotte Capers's Journal, March 3, 1958, RG 31, vol. 74; interview with Charles Hudspeth, August 1, 1989.

[27] Coody, "Repair of . . . the Old Capitol," 103.

[28] Letter, Coleman to Watkins, March 5, 1958; letter, Watkins to Coleman, March 6, 1958; letter, Capers to Watkins, RG31, Department of Archives and History, vol. 74, MDAH.

[29] Interview with Joe Ware, August 2, 1989.

[30] Letter, Coleman to N.W. Overstreet, January 28, 1957, RG 31, Department of Archives and History, vol. 74.

[31] Letters, Capers to Koch, February 20, March 11, April 20, 1957; Capers interview; letter, Florence Sillers Ogden to Capers, March 10, 1958; letter, Capers to Ogden, March 14, 1958; Minutes of the State Building Commission, March 16, 1959.

[32] Interviews with Joe Ware, former partner in Overstreet, Ware and Ware, August 2, 1989; Charles Hudspeth; Cecil Pearson, former employee of Overstreet, Ware and Ware, August 7, 1989; Charlotte Capers.

[33] *Ibid.*

[34] Pearson interview.

[35] Minutes of the Building Commission.

[36] Capers interview.

[37] Capers interview.

[38] Letters, Capers to Grobman, March 20, April 11, 17, 25, 1958, RG 31, Department of Archives and History, vol. 74.

[39] *Report of Dr. Arnold B. Grobman,* State Historical Museum Subject File, MDAH.

[40] *Ibid.*

[41] *Ibid.*

[42] Capers interview; letter, Capers to Rath, January 31, 1957; letter, Rath to Capers, February 6, 1957, RG 31, Department of Archives and History, vol. 74.

[43] *Biennial Report of the Department of Archives and History, 1957–59,* 10; Minutes of the Board of Trustees, December 6, 1957, RG 31, Department of Archives and History, MF 51.

[44] Letter, Lewis to Capers, March 3, 1959, RG 31, Department of Archives and History, vol. 74.

[45] Letter, Capers to Lewis, March 11, 1959, RG 31, Department of Archives and History, vol. 74; Capers interview.

[46] Letter, Lewis to Capers, March 31, 1959, RG 31, Department of Archives and History, vol. 74.

[47] *Biennial Report of the Department of Archives and History, 1957–59,* 8–9; Capers interview; letters, Capers to Lewis, May 7, September 3, 1959, RG 31, Department of Archives and History, vol. 74; Exhibit Plan, Mississippi State Historical Museum, May 4–28, 1959, RG 31, vol. 741.

[48] Capers interview; letter, Capers to Lewis, June 19, 1959, RG 31, vol. 74.

[49] Minutes of the Building Commission, June 4, 1958, RG 43, State Building Commission, MDAH.

[50] *Ibid.,* November 11, December 11, 1958.

[51] Minutes of the Building Commission, January 15, 1957, RG 43, State Building Commission, MDAH; Jackson *State Times,* February 4, April 16, 1959; MDAH Newsletter, March 1959.

[52] Interview with Clarence Waddle, August 9, 1989.

[53] *Ibid.*

[54] *Ibid.*

[55] Capers interview.

[56] *Ibid.;* interview with Charlotte Capers by Patti Black on the Old Capitol Restoration, November 3, 1982.

[57] Capers interview with author; Capers interview with Black; Minutes of the Building Commission, March 16, May 20, 1959. Evidence has been found that the building was originally stuccoed. On October 28, 1838, the Commissioners of Public Buildings made a contract with Caleb Parker to plaster the exposed brick on the front and ends of the building to imitate the stone exterior of the ground floor.

[58] Waddle interview.

William Winter's Inauguration

Governor A. H. Longino in 1900 was the last governor to be sworn into office in the Old Capitol while the building served as the seat of government. Eighty years later the old building witnessed yet another governor's installation. In 1980 the New Capitol, then in its seventy-seventh year, was undergoing a renovation. William Winter, member of the Board of Trustees of the Department of Archives and History, student of Mississippi history, and newly elected governor, chose the Old Capitol as the site for his inauguration.

January 22, 1980, inauguration day, brought a cold rain that forced the ceremonies inside the building. Legislators, state officials, and Mississippi's congressional delegation gathered in the house chamber while other spectators crowded the

In a unique addition to the gubernatorial inaugurations, Mississippi leaders from the arts, academia, business, and politics participated in a pre-inaugural symposium conducted by William Winter in the house chamber.

Governor Winter, Eudora Welty, Leontyne Price, and Elise Winter.

Four former governors attended the ceremonies: William Waller, John Bell Williams, Paul Johnson, Jr., Ross Barnett.

rotunda and the first floor corridors to listen to the inauguration over the public address system.

Leontyne Price, Metropolitan Opera soprano, sang the national anthem and outgoing Governor Cliff Finch introduced the new governor. After taking the oath of office, William Winter spoke.

"Gathered as we are on this historic site, in a capitol building erected 140 years ago, I am conscious of the historic significance of this occasion, the uniqueness of this event, and the responsibility that it imposes.

". . . I have not come here today, however, to reminisce or to look back, but I do ask you to join with me at this particular time and place in history to establish the proper perspective for deciding where we want our state to go. This involves basically the selection of those values and standards that will enable us to preserve our political system and to transmit to another generation of Mississippians a culture and a quality of life worthy of preservation."

59 Waddle interview; letter, Ladner to Capers, July 8, 1958, RG31, Department of Archives and History, vol. 74.

60 Waddle interview.

61 Capers and Waddle interviews.

62 "Old Capitol Restored by Masters in Plaster," *Red Topics: The Magazine of Lathing and Plastering*, Issue 2, 1962, 5.

63 *Ibid.*

64 *Ibid.*

65 Capers interview; Waddle interview; Minutes of Building Commission, January 8, 1960.

66 Capers interview with Black; Capers interview with author; letter, Capers to Ware, August 4, 1958, RG 31, Department of Archives and History, vol. 74; Memorandum, Capers to Building Commission, January 30, 1959, *ibid.*

67 Letter, Capers to Ware, August 4, 1958; letter, Sellers to Ware, August 5, 1958, both in RG 31, Department of Archives and History, vol. 74; Capers interview with Black; Capers interview with author.

68 Capers interview with Black; Capers interview with author; letter, Capers to Sillers, August 2, 1960, RG 31, Department of Archives and History, vol. 74.

69 Capers interview with Black; Capers interview with author; Minutes of the Executive Committee of the Board of Trustees of the Department of Archives and History, August 5, 1960, RG 31, Department of Archives and History; letter, Capers to Sillers, August 5, 1960, RG 31, vol. 74.

70 *Biennial Report of the Department of Archives and History, 1957–59,* 9.

71 *Laws,* 1956, 8; 1958, 9; *Biennial Report of the Department of Archives and History, 1955–57,* 5; 1957–59, 5; letter, Capers to Frank Ellis, Secretary, Budget and Accounting, July 22, 1957, RG 31, Department of Archives and History, vol. 41.

72 Letter, Capers to Commission of Budget and Accounting, August 24, 1959; Archives and History budget request, 1960–62, RG 31, Department of Archives and History, vol. 41.

73 Letter, Capers to Sillers, September 22, 1959, RG 31, Department of Archives and History, vol. 41; Laws, 1960, 9; *Biennial Report of the Department of Archives and History, 1959–61,* 7–8.

74 MDAH Newsletter, May 1960; Jackson *Daily News*, May 7, 1960; *Biennial Report of the Department of Archives and History, 1959–61,* 7.

75 MDAH Newsletter, September 1960.

76 Capers interview; Minutes of the Building Commission, September 30, 1959.

77 *State Times*, June 21, 1959; interview by the author with Renna Johnston Clark, September 19, 1989.

78 *Ibid*; Minutes of the Building Commission, December 14, 1960, RG 43, MDAH.

79 Letters, Floyd A. Lafayette, Acting Chief, Museum Branch, National Park Service, to Capers, November 3, 1958; letter, Ralph H. Lewis, Chief, Museum Branch, National Park Service, to Capers, June 10, 1959, RG 31, Department of Archives and History, vol. 74.

80 Letter, Capers to Milton R. Tinsley, President, Creative Arts Studio, with contract attached, July 22, 1960, RG 31, Department of Archives and History, vol. 149.

81 Bid, June 7, 1960, and contract, July 7, 1960, from Westbrook Manufacturing Company, RG 31, Department of Archives and History, vol. 149.

82 MDAH Newsletter, December 1960.

83 MDAH Newsletter, November 1960; February 1961.

84 Jackson *Clarion-Ledger*, March 19, 22, 1961.

85 Jackson *Clarion-Ledger*, March 28, 29, 1961.

86 *Biennial Report of the Department of Archives and History, 1959–61,* 15; Capers interview with author.

87 Jackson *Clarion-Ledger*, June 4, 1961.

ILLUSTRATION NOTES

All photographs are from the collections of the Mississippi Department of Archives and History.

Epilogue

In January 1961, as the contractors put finishing touches on the interior and as Capers and Neitzel struggled to get the museum exhibits installed, the Building Commission negotiated one final contract. Then, on June 9, 1961, the state issued a check for the work to Jackson Wrecking and Building Supply Company with the curt administrative notation "demolition of buildings behind the Old Capitol building." The last reminder of the Old Capitol's recent past as an office building was gone.[1]

The restored Old Capitol opened its doors in 1961 at a time of great social and economic change in the state whose history the restoration and the new museum were designed to celebrate. Ghosts from Mississippi's racial past had arisen. Alongside newspaper stories about the opening of the museum were printed headlines of civil rights demonstrations and stories of adamant white opposition to the end of segregation. Much of the spirit behind Mississippi's celebration of the Civil War Centennial and the "Secession Day" activities that were coupled with the opening of the restoration and the museum no doubt could be traced to white resentment of a second Reconstruction by a federal government once again awakened to civil rights almost a century after the failure of the first.

Yet if the Old Capitol was still haunted by some ghosts from the past, the building nonetheless looked out on a changing downtown Jackson. Jackson's businesses before the Civil War had congregated along South State Street below the Old Capitol. By the early twentieth century Capitol Street from the Old Capitol to the Illinois Central depot contained the heart of Jackson's business district. Mercantile establishments, restaurants, hotels, banks, and law offices gave the business district a diverse economic and social tone. After 1961, however, the Old Capitol witnessed a rapidly changing downtown scene. Restaurants and mercantile establishments fled to the suburbs, and Capitol Street was increasingly inhabited only by lawyers, bankers, brokers, and government workers. A generation after the restoration, the Old Capitol looks down Capitol Street banked on both sides by tall office buildings and a few old nineteenth- and early twentieth-century brick buildings once filled with hardware, feed and seed, clothing and shoes but now gentrified in pastel colors to house law offices and stockbrokers.

Looking east from the bluff at the rear of the Old Capitol, one can still see old and familiar sights—the fairgrounds and the Pearl River bottoms. But one sees also the coliseum, Interstate 55 lined with auto dealers, business offices and motels built on old swamp land that is now protected by levees. An elevated interstate connector encroaches on south Capitol Green to dump commuters from I-55 into downtown Jackson. As surburbanites come down from the elevated highway and approach the intersection of South State and Pearl Streets, they pass within a few feet of the Charlotte Capers Archives and History Building, a square, stone, vault-like building on south Capitol Green behind the Confederate Monument.

Like the Old Capitol restoration that had been long sought to house Dunbar Rowland's museum collection, a permanent, specially

During excavation for the Archives and History building in 1970, the Old Capitol's original brick-lined cistern was unearthed. It was built in 1839 by E. Moody.

equipped home for the state archives and historical library had been a vision of both the Board of Trustees of the Department of Archives and History and of the Mississippi Historical Society. Neither the space in the New Capitol nor the space in the War Memorial Building had proved satisfactory, and after 1961, the Old Capitol, already housing the State Historical Museum, could not furnish adequate quarters for the archives and library.

In 1964, Dr. R.A. McLemore served simultaneously as president of the Board of Trustees of the Department of Archives and History and of the Mississippi Historical Society. The sesquicentennial of Mississippi's statehood would occur in 1967. Both the board of trustees and the Mississippi Historical Society formed sesquicentennial committees. These committees jointly called on state leaders to meet in the house chamber of the Old Capitol on August 31, 1965, to begin planning the state's observance of its 150th anniversary. At that meeting Governor Paul B. Johnson, Jr., pledged his support to a new building for Archives and History. Meanwhile, a subcommittee of the

board of trustees had recommended the south Capitol Green as the best available site.[2]

The 1966 legislature disappointingly failed to authorize the building, but a special session in January 1967 approved $1,120,000 for an Archives and History building. Construction began in 1969 and, like the Confederate Monument in 1891, the New Capitol in 1903, and the Old Capitol restoration in 1961, the archives building was dedicated on June 3, Jefferson Davis's birthday, in 1971.

Administrative changes also have come to the Old Capitol since 1961. Capers stepped down as Director of Archives and History in 1969 to become Director of Information and Education for the department. She was succeeded by R.A. McLemore who held the post until 1973, when Elbert Hilliard became director. In 1976 Patti Carr Black, the staff member who worked diligently to help Sutton and Bierly design the museum exhibits in 1959, became director of the State Historical Museum, where she began organizing the creation of new exhibits to replace the original ones.

Some aspects of Capitol Green remain permanent. The beauty, strength, and simplicity of Nichols's Greek Revival building still charm visitors. The presence of the old building in a downtown dominated by sterile steel and glass skyscrapers provides Mississippians with a comfortable sense of continuity. Some old and familiar problems also endure. On occasion, the roof still leaks and the soft brick walls still wick up water from the porous foundation.

A full generation into its third incarnation, the Old Capitol approaches its 150th anniversary with an air of both change and permanence. It sits, as always, at the head of Capitol Street presiding over downtown Jackson, still symbolizing government—Jackson's first reason for being. But, though it may look much as it did in 1840 when William Nichols finished it, over a 150-year life the building has reflected the shifting fortunes of Mississippi's history: it was built in a fluid frontier society, battered by the Civil War, rebuilt during Reconstruction, and almost abandoned in the early twentieth century, when the old structure was seen as a decaying relic marring the image of a new, progressive age. Saved by utilitarian needs in 1917, the building was renovated but at the cost of its faded and crumbling beauty. Finally, newly restored in 1961, the building still serves as a reminder of Mississippi's past in a New South capital city and in a state poised on the edge of further change.

NOTES

[1] Minutes of the Building Commission, January 11, 1961; letter, Yelverton to Jackson Wrecking and Building Supply Company, June 9, 1961, RG 31, vol. 41, MDAH.

[2] Two articles contain complete information on the planning and construction of the Archives and History Building. Charlotte Capers and R.A. McLemore, "The Archives and History Building, 1971," *The Journal of Mississippi History*, 33 (May, 1971), 87–101; Charlotte Capers, "The Archives and History Building," in John E. Gonzales, ed., *A Mississippi Reader* (Jackson: Mississippi Historical Society, 1980), 301–315.

Index